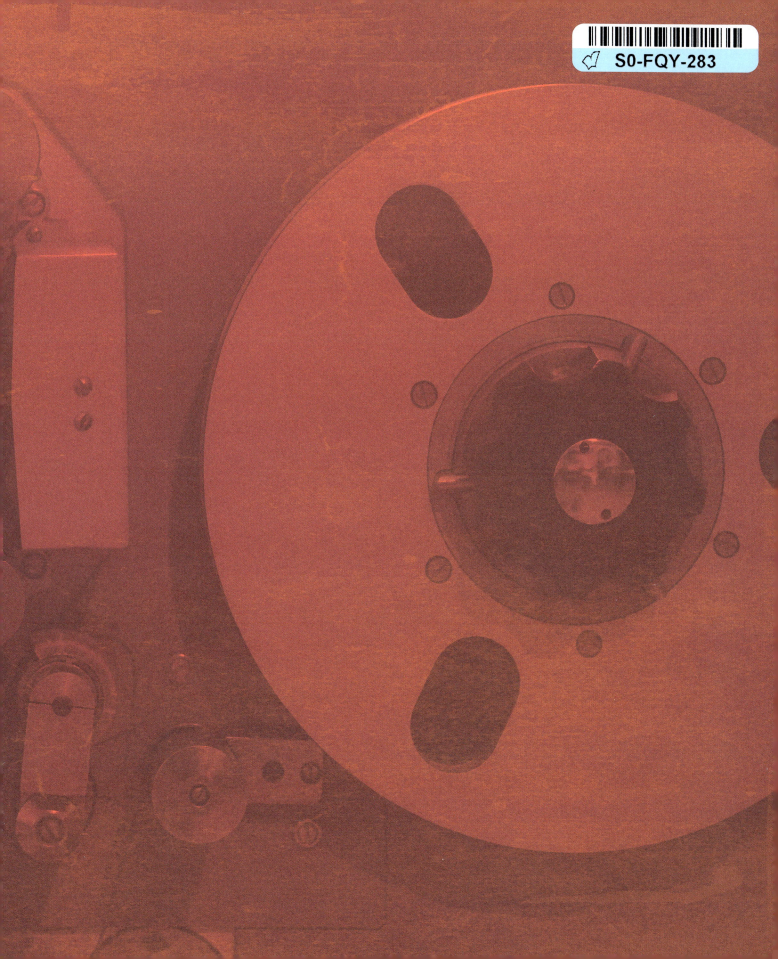

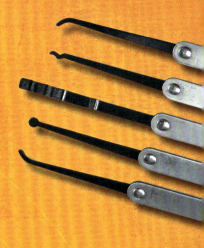

THE SECRETS OF
SPIES

weldon**owen**

THE SECRETS OF
SPIES

Heather Vescent • Adrian Gilbert • Rob Colson

weldon**owen**

Publisher Roger Shaw
Associate Publisher Mariah Bear
Senior Editor Ian Cannon
Art Director Allister Fein
Production Manager Binh Au
Managing Editor Lauren LePera

Weldon Owen International
1150 Brickyard Cove Road
Richmond, CA 94801
www.weldonowen.com

Designed and edited by Tall Tree Ltd

Weldon Owen would like to thank
Kris Hirschmann for editorial assistance,
and Francesca Hillier for the index.

Library of Congress Control Number on file
with the publisher.

ISBN 13: 978-1-68188-533-9

10 9 8 7 6 5 4 3 2 1
2024 2023 2022 2021 2020
Printed in Italy

CONTENTS

CONTENTS

INTRODUCTION

It seems that most of us are fascinated by spying. Library bookshelves are packed with spy titles, both fiction and non-fiction, and espionage is a constant staple of film and TV programs. Spying's enduring appeal lies in its air of mystery and illicit nature; we are irrevocably drawn to unraveling a forbidden secret. Another attraction is the vicarious pleasure we enjoy from idealizing the spy as a hero. They become a lone individual taking on the might of the state, armed only with intelligence and cunning—a false move could mean capture, interrogation, and even death.

In this book, we hope to reveal some of the secrets of spying, and how and why spies go about their clandestine business. Taking the classic dictionary definition, a spy is a person employed by a government or other organization to secretly obtain information from a competitor or enemy. From the word "spy" we have the term "espionage," the practice of spying. Throughout the long history of espionage, there have been many types of spy, performing different functions according to the demands of their masters. It is perhaps worth describing some of the key roles adopted by spies so that we better understand the development of espionage in the pages that follow.

At the top of the espionage hierarchy are the case officers or handlers, who find, recruit, and direct the people doing the actual spying. Typically, they will operate from one of their country's overseas embassies, which provide them with a convenient base—and diplomatic protection if they are caught. On the downside, their public profile makes them well known to the opposition, who will attempt to track their every move and so limit their effectiveness. By contrast, "illegals" are case officers who operate entirely undercover, and if they are good and sufficiently lucky they will remain undetected to develop their agents to the highest level. One of the most capable illegals was Soviet case officer Oscar Deutsch, who recruited and trained the Cambridge spies in the 1930s.

The case officer will recruit people working in key strategic areas such as the military, armaments industries, and any high-technology operation where secrecy is important. These individuals—prepared to betray state secrets—are assiduously cultivated and become highly prized assets. But the crown jewel of spy recruitment is the double agent—a spy from one intelligence service who is prepared to secretly work for an enemy intelligence service. CIA agents Aldrich Ames and John Walker, Jr., both worked for the KGB, providing (among other things) invaluable information about US intelligence operations directed at the Soviet Union.

In the modern era, spies in the field are backed by a small army of auxiliaries who provide logistical and administrative support. Among these desk-bound operatives is a new and increasingly important type of intelligence officer—the analyst. The volume of information that flows into an intelligence organization has become an exponentially growing flood that needs teams of analysts to control and make sense of it all.

Also working behind the scenes are the cryptographers, encoding written messages to make them unintelligible to all but the intended recipient. They are countered by the codebreakers who, having intercepted the message, attempt to find out what it means. Over many centuries, enormous intellectual effort has been directed at the making and breaking of codes. For those who have cracked a code, the information it provides can be priceless, as demonstrated by the Allied decipherment of the German Enigma codes during World War II.

If spying is primarily concerned with the gathering of secret information, then it is mirrored by the counterintelligence of security services that work to deny the enemy this clandestine information—and to apprehend those conducting the spying. In the United States, while the CIA is deployed abroad to gain intelligence, the FBI tracks down enemy spies operating on home soil.

What makes people become spies? American intelligence uses the handy acronym MICE to assess motivation. Money: Sheer greed or financial difficulties bring a surprising number of people over to the enemy—Ames and Walker both actively offered their services to the KGB for hard cash. Ideology: A rather smaller number are motivated by belief in the superiority of the social or political systems of another, hostile country, but their commitment tends to be long-lasting, as was the case with idealistic American and British citizens prepared to spy for Soviet communism. Compromise: This usually involves some form of sexual coercion, where an individual is typically confronted with photographic evidence of their indiscretions, espionage against their own country being the price for silence. Ego: Certain individuals are susceptible to flattery and, with suitable encouragement, are prepared to become spies for the sheer enjoyment of seeming to be superior to those they are spying on.

The motivations for becoming a spy will vary according to time and circumstance, but we can be sure that espionage will continue as it has done for centuries. The end of the Cold War and the collapse of communism has not led to a more benign intelligence environment. Rather, intelligence targets have increased in number and become more diffuse and unpredictable.

Western intelligence agencies have had to extend their interests beyond superpower and state rivalries to confront new threats, including Islamist terrorism, organized crime, and industrial espionage on a mass scale. Rapid advances in surveillance technology and artificial intelligence also need to be taken into account. But the greatest espionage challenge—or opportunity, depending on your standpoint—has been the development of cyberspying. This is transforming espionage, and those that fail to understand its nature and react accordingly face potential disaster.

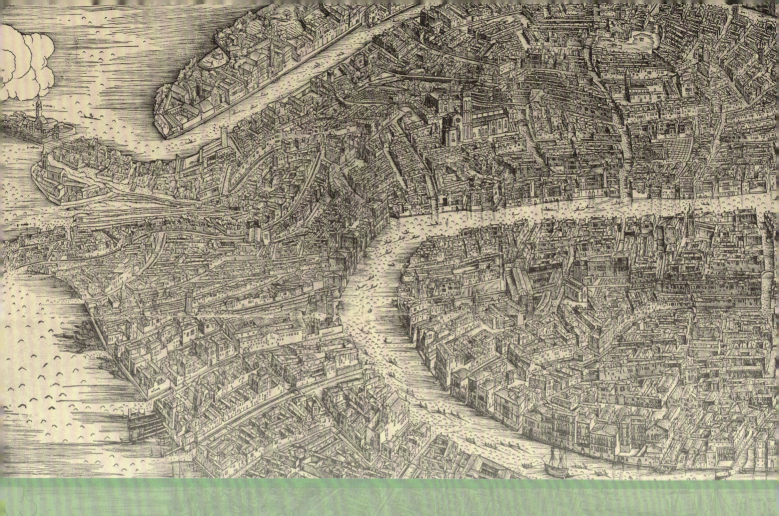

— CHAPTER 1 —

THE FIRST SPIES

Every ruler has always wanted to know what their adversary is thinking and doing, and what their own reaction should be. The traditional response to this problem was to seek divine inspiration. In Ancient Egypt and in the early civilizations of China and India, priests and oracles would perform elaborate rituals in an attempt to discover what the future might hold. In Greece and Rome, animal entrails were closely examined to help make key decisions. But some more clear-sighted leaders looked to their fellow humans for assistance in the form of spies or secret agents.

The Chinese manual on statecraft, *The Art of War*, was the first work to provide a framework for spycraft: gathering information while spreading disinformation; bribing or seducing officials; and even assassinating troublesome individuals. Over time, many of the intelligence techniques we know today came into being, not least the sending of coded messages and the counter-methods—developed by Arab scholars—of breaking these codes. Foremost among medieval spy pioneers was the city state of Venice, which, by the early 1500s, had developed an elaborate intelligence network spread across Europe and Asia.

ANCIENT EGYPT AND BIBLICAL TIMES

We can be fairly sure that spying dates back to the creation of the first city states nearly ten thousand years ago. The discovery of information about rivals—or even allies—could be vital for a state's survival and prosperity. However, it was only with the development of writing thousands of years later in the civilizations of the Near East that we find clear evidence of our ancestors' desire for covert knowledge.

EVIDENCE FROM CLAY TABLETS

Written on a clay tablet around 2000 BCE, the earliest intelligence report we know of describes a secret mission to spot fire beacons being lit in villages along the Euphrates River in Mesopotamia. However, it is only a fragmentary account. We do not know why the beacons were being lit or what happened subsequently. A better intelligence record is found several centuries later in the Amarna letters from Ancient Egypt, written on clay tablets between 1400 and 1300 BCE.

The letters are exchanges between the Pharaoh in Egypt and rulers of his vassal states in Canaan (roughly present-day Israel and Lebanon). The Pharaoh expresses concerns over the vassal rulers' loyalty. In one letter, it is clear that the Pharaoh had received a report from a spy about the behavior of Amurru, ruler of Aziru, who had been consorting with the ruler of Qidša, an enemy of Egypt. The Pharaoh threatens Amurru with decapitation if this continues.

> **"YOU ARE AT PEACE WITH THE RULER OF QIDŠA. THE TWO OF YOU TAKE FOOD AND STRONG DRINK TOGETHER. WHY DO YOU ACT SO? WHY ARE YOU AT PEACE WITH A RULER WHOM THE KING IS FIGHTING?"**
>
> The Pharaoh rebukes his vassal ruler, Amurru

Left: The Amarna letters are written on clay tablets in Akkadian cuneiform, the script of Ancient Mesopotamia. Akkadian was the language of diplomacy at the time. The tablets were discovered in Egypt in 1887.

Right: Judas identified Jesus to the authorities by kissing him on the cheek.

BIBLICAL SPIES

As depicted in the Bible, Canaan was the scene of another spying mission. Having escaped from Egypt, the Jewish tribes under Moses were looking for a place to set up a new home. According to the Bible story, God commanded Moses to "spy out the land of Canaan." Moses dutifully sent out twelve men on a covert reconnaissance mission. They returned saying Canaan was a "land flowing with milk and honey," but only two of the spies recommended that they march on to conquer Canaan. The others believed the Jews lacked the necessary strength to overcome the people of Canaan. Displeased by this intelligence assessment, the story tells that God punished the Jews by forcing them to wander in the wilderness for forty years.

According to The Book of Joshua, the Jews were finally led into Canaan by Joshua. As he advanced into Canaan, Joshua was confronted by the powerful fortress city of Jericho. He infiltrated spies into the city, and they brought

Left: The original Wall of Jericho was built around 8000 BCE—more than 6,000 years before the events related in the Bible.

back information that morale was poor, with the inhabitants fearful of the forces arraigned against them. The Jews were greatly encouraged by this report, and the fall of Jericho's city walls was the first step in Joshua's conquest of Canaan. However, as with the story of Moses, no archeological evidence has been found to corroborate the story.

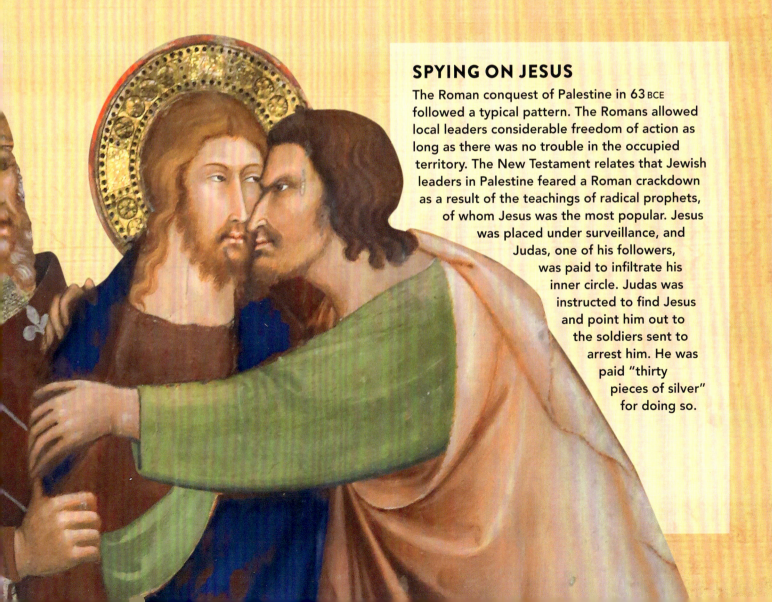

SPYING ON JESUS

The Roman conquest of Palestine in 63 BCE followed a typical pattern. The Romans allowed local leaders considerable freedom of action as long as there was no trouble in the occupied territory. The New Testament relates that Jewish leaders in Palestine feared a Roman crackdown as a result of the teachings of radical prophets, of whom Jesus was the most popular. Jesus was placed under surveillance, and Judas, one of his followers, was paid to infiltrate his inner circle. Judas was instructed to find Jesus and point him out to the soldiers sent to arrest him. He was paid "thirty pieces of silver" for doing so.

SPYING OUT
THE ART OF WAR

As in other classical civilizations, in ancient China, emperors, kings, and other leaders consulted oracles or made sacrifices to discover what decisions they should make. However, the manual *The Art of War* suggested a new approach, largely based on the acquisition of secret knowledge.

The Chinese general and military theorist Sun Tzu, who lived in the fifth century BCE, was traditionally credited with writing *The Art of War*, but it is now thought that it was a collaborative work written at a later date, most probably in the third century BCE.

THE ART OF SPYING

The book's title suggests that it is military treatise, but in fact *The Art of War* emphasizes the avoidance of battle if at all possible. It encourages the leader to deploy stratagems such as deceit and subterfuge to achieve his goals. Spies play a key role in this strategy, employing bribery and seduction to corrupt enemy officials and gain intelligence, all the while spreading disinformation. Spies are also expected to take direct action, including the assassination of important individuals. If these methods are successfully used, argues *The Art of War*, the enemy's army will collapse with little resistance.

Good assassins in ancient China were highly regarded and expected to go to great lengths to fulfill their mission. Perhaps the most extreme example of this involved Yao Li in the third century BCE. He was instructed by King Ho-lü to kill the exiled Prince Ch'ing Chi. To establish a cover story that he had been maltreated by Ho-lü and desired revenge, Yao Li cut off his own right hand and killed his wife and children. He arrived in Ch'ing Chi's court with a suitably horrific—and believable— cover story, and was able to gain access to his intended victim, whom he promptly killed.

Left: The mausoleum of Emperor Qin Shi Huang contained a Terracotta Army of over 8,000 men. Qin unified China in 221 BCE and is said to have used *The Art of War* as a strategic guide during his conquests.

"SECRET AGENTS STRIKE FEAR IN THE ENEMY'S GENERAL STAFF, SLAY THE ENEMY'S BELOVED GENERALS, AND CAUSE CHAOS IN THE ENEMY'S ESTIMATES AND STRATEGIES."

Chinese military strategist Jie Xuan

EAVESDROPPING AND SIGNALING

The Chinese were pioneers of early spy technology. This included a forerunner of the electric bugging device—an earthenware jar used by spies to eavesdrop on conversations of interest. The jar was wide at its middle but had a narrow mouth over which was stretched a leather membrane. The jar was partially buried in the ground and the spy placed his ear against the leather covering, which picked up nearby sounds. These eavesdropping spies were often blind, taking advantage of a heightened audial acuity.

Other techniques included the use of invisible inks, made from mixtures of water and alum or, at a stretch, from water left over from boiling rice. Pigeons were employed to carry messages, while kites were flown as part of a simple signaling system. Kites—known as *Zhiyuan* (paper birds)—were often used during sieges. The defenders would send up colored kites to inform spies stationed behind the besieging force, transmitting information such as the state of their provisions or requests for help.

THE ART OF WAR IN THE TWENTIETH CENTURY

Revolutionary leader Mao Zedong was influenced by *The Art of War* in his protracted guerrilla campaign to seize China for communism. Similarly, General Giáp and his fellow Vietnamese communists gave credit to the book for their victories in Vietnam. After translation into English in 1910, its influence extended to the United States. CIA chief Allen Dulles described it as the "first remarkable analysis of the ways of espionage," while in the US Army it has been endorsed by generals Douglas McArthur, Colin Powell, and Norman Schwarzkopf. Its fame has spread beyond the military, however, providing a template for management self-help books, legal and educational studies, and even works designed to improve readers' sporting abilities.

Above left: Vietnamese General Võ Nguyên Giáp, a former history teacher, was heavily influenced in his tactics by historical texts.

Above right: Pictured here in the 1940s, Mao Zedong consulted *The Art of War* to develop his tactics in the Chinese Civil War (1927–1949).

STATEHOOD AND SPYING IN ANCIENT INDIA

The Mauryan Empire, which reached its height in around 270 BCE under the reign of Ashoka, included most of modern-day India, Pakistan, and Bangladesh. It was during this time that the first parts of the great book the *Arthashastra* were written.

The *Arthashastra* was written at roughly the same time as the Chinese *The Art of War*. It is a more general manual of statecraft, but it too emphasizes the importance of spying, not only against possible enemies but to also gauge the loyalty of the ruler's own subjects. A particular feature of the *Arthashastra* is a plea for the monarch to develop a regular intelligence service rather than using spies on an *ad hoc* basis.

Spies were expected to master the sending of coded messages and the adoption of disguises. They were encouraged to take on the mantle of traveling people, who could mix with strangers without arousing suspicion. Among these were monks, merchants, doctors, peddlers, entertainers, dancers, and prostitutes. Women were considered especially useful in winkling out information through seduction from corrupt officials.

Assassination was a vital tool in state policy: "A single assassin can achieve with weapons, fire, or poison, more than a fully mobilized army." Given their importance, assassins were to be "recruited from the bravest in the land." As well as obvious, public assassinations, intended to deter potential malcontents, covert assassinations were also recommended for treacherous government officials.

Left: The *Arthashastra*'s supposed author, Chanakya, was an advisor to the founder of the Mauryan Empire, Chandragupta. The empire was later expanded by Chandragupta's grandson Ashoka, who built magnificent lion monuments.

"TO UNDERMINE AN ENEMY OLIGARCHY, MAKE THE CHIEFS OF THE RULING COUNCIL INFATUATED WITH WOMEN POSSESSED OF GREAT BEAUTY AND YOUTH."

Arthashastra

MAURYAN EMPIRE

Pataliputra, the capital city of the Mauryan Empire, was one of the largest cities in the world, with a population of more than 150,000 at the height of the empire.

FIVE KINDS OF SPY

The *Arthashastra* lists five main types of spy as of particular use to a nation's ruler in finding out his subjects' views and influencing them in his favor.

THE STUDENT
He would engage in fierce intellectual arguments with his fellows and report back on those students opposed to the regime, as well as discovering the general attitudes of the young.

THE HOLY MAN
He would gain credit from appearing to eat only grass and roadside vegetables (while eating well in secret) and gather around him credulous disciples. He would then make prophecies that supported the ruler.

THE FARMER
He would work among the peasants, who formed the vast bulk of the population, and report on their attitudes toward the government.

THE BUSINESSMAN
He would have established networks with other traders and merchants and gain good intelligence from these contacts.

THE RELIGIOUS LEADER
Sponsored by the state, he would establish religious sites in country areas (ashrams), drawing in the local people to be influenced by his pro-government teachings.

The *Arthashastra* proposes several methods to deal with officials, including sending a spy disguised as a doctor to convince the seditious official that he is suffering from a severe disease, before administering medicine that includes a fatal dose of poison.

The *Arthashastra* was consulted by Indian rulers until the twelfth century CE, when it seems to have disappeared from view. It was rediscovered by an Indian archivist in 1904. Since then, the book has been championed by many Indian politicians as an indispensable reference on the art of running the country.

SECRET SHADOWS: JAPAN'S NINJAS

In the Western world, Japanese ninjas are often seen as mystical figures with special powers to transcend normal physical limitations: able to walk on water, become invisible at will, and have control over the natural world. The reality was rather different, but ninjas did exist and they were formidable opponents—a combination of spy and special-forces soldier.

> **"CONCERNING NINJA, THEY WERE SAID TO BE FROM IGA AND KŌGA, AND WENT FREELY INTO ENEMY CASTLES IN SECRET. THEY OBSERVED HIDDEN THINGS, AND WERE TAKEN AS BEING FRIENDS."**
>
> From *Nochi Kagami*, an early Ninja history

HEREDITARY GUILDS

The word "ninja" comes from Chinese and roughly translates as "one who endures." Although ninja-like warriors had existed since the sixth century, it was only in the fifteenth century that the proper ninjas emerged. They came from the remote, mountainous Iga and Koga regions, and formed hereditary guilds that ensured their exclusive clan nature.

The aristocratic samurai warrior class favored individual combat as a form of public display. The ninjas took an opposite path, keeping in the background as they went about their secret activities. The samurai disdained the ninjas, but they were reliant on their skills.

NINJA TRAINING

Preparation began in childhood, with an emphasis on physical training, including long-distance running, swimming, climbing, silent walking, and martial arts. Within all these disciplines, the goal was to develop stealth. For example, the student was taught to make breathing tubes out of reeds and to scatter duckweed over the water to conceal underwater movement. As they matured, the ninjas undertook advanced studies in medicine, scouting, espionage (including the use of disguises), and, if necessary, assassination.

The prime role of the ninja was to gather intelligence, relying on good memories. Their existence was intended to be like that of a shadow. Ninjas would often disguise themselves as travelers— fortune tellers, peddlers, merchants, or monks—to avoid suspicion. They would engage with the local people to discover information about the enemy.

Above: Rokkaku Yoshikata was the head of the Rokkaku clan. He engaged in many battles over control of the Kyoto region.

CAPTURING SAWAYAMA CASTLE

Ninjas used deception to conduct sabotage missions. In 1558, the samurai overlord Rokkaku Yoshikata ordered the ninjas under his command to break into the besieged Sawayama Castle in the city of Hikone. One of the ninjas stole a lantern that bore the enemy's crest and used it to produce a series of replicas. A group of ninjas marched to the castle gates carrying the lanterns and were allowed in without question. Once inside, they set fire to the castle, allowing Yoshikata to capture it.

At the end of the sixteenth century, both Iga and Koga were overrun in the fighting that led to the unification of Japan under the Tokugawa shogunate. From then on, the ninja way of life declined, becoming a subject for folklore and legend.

NINJAS IN THE POPULAR IMAGINATION

In nineteenth-century Japan, popular literature celebrated the ninjas as a form of super warrior, with prints depicting black-clad men scaling castle walls armed with a variety of special weapons, most unknown to actual ninjas. The original ninja aspiration to be as invisible as possible was transformed into a fictional ideal that they could actually become invisible. After World War II, growing Western interest in Japanese martial arts brought ninja stories to global attention. Ninjas became comic-book heroes, featuring in animated films and games, and, in perhaps their ultimate humiliation, as denizens of the New York sewage system as the Teenage Mutant Ninja Turtles.

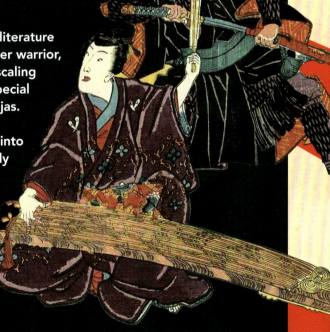

Above: Nineteenth-century artist Utagawa Kunisada portrayed the ninjas clad in black, performing daring assassinations.

ESPIONAGE IN ANCIENT GREECE

When planning major enterprises, the Ancient Greeks looked first to the gods for help. Oracles were consulted and animal entrails examined by seers to discover whether fate was for or against them. But the Greeks also valued the more basic information provided by their spies, and they took special pride in their skills in the art of deception. The most famous of these ploys was the legendary Trojan Horse.

GIFT HORSE

According to Homer's *The Odyssey*, Greek warrior Odysseus was determined to break the Greeks' ten-year siege of the city of Troy. His stratagem involved the construction of an enormous, hollow wooden horse, which was left in front of the Trojan city gates at night. The Trojans awoke to discover that the Greeks had disappeared, leaving just the horse. They dragged the horse inside the walls and joyfully celebrated their triumph.

During the next night, Odysseus and a band of Greek soldiers emerged from the horse, killed the sentries, and opened the gates. The main Greek army, which had silently returned under the cover of darkness, rushed into the open city and conquered Troy.

Right: The modern myth of the Trojan Horse is taken mostly from the retelling of the story by Roman poet Virgil (70–19 BCE), pictured here in a mosaic from the third century CE.

"DO NOT TRUST THE HORSE, TROJANS. WHATEVER IT IS, I FEAR THE GREEKS EVEN WHEN THEY BRING GIFTS."

From Virgil's *Aeneid*, a warning the Trojans failed to heed

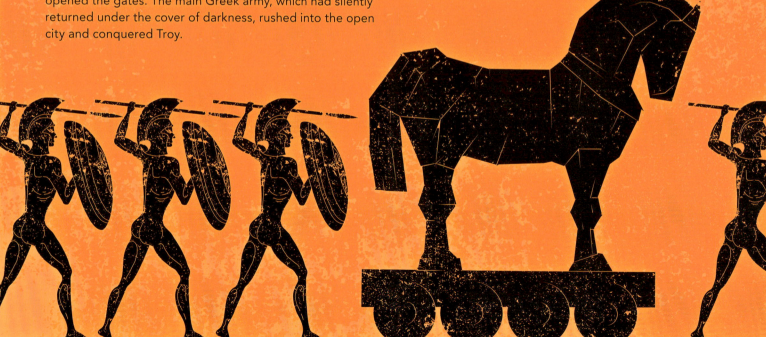

REPELLING THE PERSIANS

Homer's story of the Trojan Horse—with later additions by the Roman writer Virgil in the first century BCE—comes from the mists of history and myth, but the Persian invasion of Greece in 480 BCE provides a solidly documented account of Greek skill in deception. A large Persian fleet had forced the Greeks to abandon Athens and assemble their own smaller fleet, composed of ships from several city states, in the narrow straits by the island of Salamis. The Athenian commander Themistocles hoped that this confined stretch of water would nullify the Persians' numerical superiority in a battle.

A traitorous Greek slave named Sicinnus approached the Persian admiral, informing him that the non-Athenian Greek ships were preparing to flee. He asserted that, should this happen, the loyalty of Themistocles to the Greek cause would be uncertain. Unknown to the Persian admiral, however, Sicinnus was operating as a double-agent. He was a trusted slave of Themistocles, and his task was to encourage the Persians to attack the Greek positions.

Sicinnus was extremely plausible as a traitor and the Persians fell for his ruse, rowing their ships into the narrows in expectation of an easy victory. Aware that defeat would mean enslavement, the Greeks launched a ferocious counter-attack. The tightly packed Persian ships were now unable to maneuver effectively, and they were vulnerable to the underwater rams of the Greek triremes. After losing 300 vessels—roughly half their original fleet—the Persians fell back in disarray. Salamis was a turning point in the war and following a later land defeat, the Persians retreated back to Asia Minor for good.

Above: The invading Persians were led by their ambitious king, Xerxes I, pictured (left) approaching the gods on his tomb at Naqsh-e Rostam in modern-day Iran.

HIDDEN MESSAGES

The Greeks were pioneers in the sending of concealed messages, whether hidden inside another innocuous text or in clothing or footwear. Messages placed inside the sole of a traveler's sandal were popular, but they were an obvious hiding place and easily discovered. A more ingenious method involved message boards. These were wooden tablets coated in wax, with messages inscribed into the wax—a common means of communication at the time. Writing on the art of war in the fourth century BCE, Greek general Aeneas Tacticus proposed writing a secret message directly onto the wooden board and then coating it with the wax, into which an innocent message was then inscribed. This method was successfully used to convey intelligence of the proposed Persian invasion of Greece to the King of Sparta, giving him time to mobilize his forces.

THE ROMAN WAY

The Ancient Romans took enormous pride in their army, which established itself as one of the most deadly fighting machines in history. The Romans valued military virtue, and this tended to lead them to disparage deception or other forms of trickery. There were exceptions, however, and those who embraced spying proved to be Rome's most gifted commanders.

The Roman state faced possibly its sternest test in the Second Punic War (218–201 BCE). Their enemies the Carthaginians were led by the brilliant general Hannibal, who, in contrast to most Romans, understood the value of good intelligence. In 218 BCE, Hannibal secretly led his forces—complete with elephants—from Carthage in North Africa through Spain and France and over the Alps into northern Italy. The Romans were completely taken by surprise at this audacious move, and Hannibal capitalized on their confusion by winning a series of victories that almost destroyed Rome.

DEFEATING HANNIBAL

Suffering from shortages of men and material, Hannibal's forces were eventually forced back to Carthage, which was later invaded in 204 BCE by a Roman army under Scipio Africanus. Possibly influenced by Hannibal, Scipio did make good use of spies to gather information. After his intelligence-led victory over Carthage's ally, King Syphax, Scipio decisively defeated Hannibal at the Battle of Zama in 202 BCE, bringing the war to a successful conclusion.

SLAVISH DECEPTION

After his arrival in Carthage, Scipio faced King Syphax's powerful Numidian-Carthaginian army, defending a well-prepared camp. Scipio sent envoys to the camp to negotiate peace. Each envoy was accompanied by a number of slaves, who were, in fact, Roman centurions in disguise. While the negotiations were ongoing, the centurions reconnoitered the camp, noting the deployment of enemy troops and any possible weak points. Armed with this information, Scipio decided on a night attack. Just before the attack order was given, an advance guard infiltrated the camp, setting alight wooden barrack huts. The Carthaginians rushed out unarmed to extinguish the flames, only to be massacred by the Romans hiding nearby.

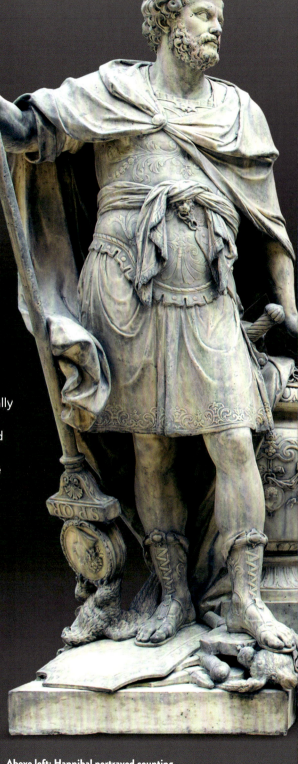

Above left: Hannibal portrayed counting the rings of fallen Romans.

Above right: This statue of Julius Caesar stands next to Hannibal at The Louvre in Paris.

WRITING HOME

The other Roman commander to integrate intelligence matters within an overall military strategy was Julius Caesar, whose conquest of Gaul (58–50 BCE) relied heavily on prior knowledge of the barbarian tribes he would encounter. A pioneer in the art of coded messages, Caesar also found the close interrogation of enemy prisoners a valuable information tool. While on campaign, Caesar regularly corresponded with his allies back in Rome. To prevent his letters being read by third parties, he used several coding systems, including a substitution cipher that still bears his name. The Caesar cipher replaced each letter of the alphabet with another letter at an agreed number of places from the original. Thus, if the key said to move each alphabet letter four letters forward, the word "CAESAR" would become "GEIWEV." Such a code would not have troubled a professional cryptographer, but it was sufficient to defeat untrained prying eyes.

CATASTROPHIC INTELLIGENCE FAILURE

Scipio and Caesar were exceptions to the Roman tendency to ignore intelligence gathering. This became apparent after Rome's transition from republic to empire. In 9 CE, a Roman army of three legions marched into territory held by Germanic tribes. The complacent Romans discounted information that the tribes were preparing a rebellion, and Varus, the Roman commander, even failed to conduct the most basic battlefield reconnaissance. Deep in the Teutoburg Forest, the Germanic tribes, led by Arminius, launched their ambush, and the Romans were annihilated in a savage battle that lasted for three days. Facing catastrophic defeat, Varus committed suicide.

Despite this warning, the Romans continued to show little interest in affairs outside the empire, concentrating their intelligence efforts on internal security. Roman leaders directed their energies towards personal protection, but despite a profusion of security measures—forming special guards, and spying on rivals—increasing numbers of emperors ended up being assassinated.

Above: The Battle of Teutoburg Forest involved fierce hand-to-hand fighting.

"NEVER WAS THERE A SLAUGHTER MORE CRUEL THAN TOOK PLACE IN THE MARSHES AND WOODS. THEY PUT OUT THE EYES OF SOME AND CUT OFF THE HANDS OF OTHERS."

Roman account of the slaughter following the Battle of Teutoburg Forest

THE RISE OF ISLAM

The extraordinary series of Islamic conquests that followed the Prophet Muhammad's seizure of Mecca in 630 CE owed much to the military abilities of his generals and the hardiness of his Arab soldiers. But behind these Arab victories lay the foundation provided by Muhammad's mastery of the covert arts of intelligence gathering, deception, and assassination.

After Muhammad had experienced the divine revelation that he was God's messenger in 610 CE, his attempts to convert his fellow citizens in Mecca to the new religion of Islam met with outright hostility. In 622, he was forced into hiding to avoid being killed by Mecca's dominant Quraish tribe. He fled by camel to Medina, where he established an Islamic outpost, its goal to overcome opposition to Islam in Mecca.

As well as building up his military forces, Muhammad waged an intelligence war against the Quraish. He sent hand-picked men to monitor trade routes into Mecca and establish a spy network within the city itself. The spies sent information about life in Mecca, including details of the arrival and departure dates of the caravans that provided the city's economic lifeblood. Muhammad attacked the caravans, and slowly but steadily wore down the enemy's resistance. He also sent assassins into Mecca, mainly to kill those who, he believed, had publicly blasphemed against Allah.

AGAINST TORTURE

Enemy troops captured by Muhammad's forces were closely interrogated. However, unusually, Muhammad discouraged his men from using torture to gain information. On one occasion, an enemy slave was captured. He readily gave his captors all they demanded except for the whereabouts of a Quraish leader named Abu Sufyan. They beat him, but he still didn't give the required information. The beatings continued until he invented information about Abu Sufyan's whereabouts. When Muhammad found out, he upbraided his men: "You beat him when he is telling the truth and stop and let him go when he tells you a lie." Muhammad's words revealed the inherent untrustworthiness of confessions extracted by duress—as relevant today as it was then.

In 630 CE, Muhammad decided to go on the offensive. He spread the rumor that his army was marching towards Syria, before secretly advancing on Mecca. When the surprised people of the city saw the powerful forces arrayed against them, their resistance crumbled. Muhammad promised to spare their lives if they converted to Islam, and they flung open the city gates—an almost totally bloodless victory, based not on brute force but on the skills of covert warfare, and reminiscent of the lessons in *The Art of War*.

Muhammad died two years later, but by then his Islamic armies were well on their way to subduing the Arabian peninsula. By 650 CE, most of the Middle East had been conquered by the Arabs, who continued to employ the arts of deception and subterfuge to outmaneuver their hapless enemies.

CODE MASTER

After its military conquests, the Arab world witnessed an extraordinary blossoming in both the cultural and scientific spheres. Among the foremost of the new Arab scholars was the polymath Yaqub ibn Ishaq al-Kindi (800–873 CE), who was also a master of making and breaking codes. Al-Kindi's key contribution to the study of cryptography was the development of the frequency principle, namely, that in every language some letters are used more than others. In English, for example, the most common letter is E, which is likely to be used 57 more times than the least common letter Q. This knowledge enabled cryptographers to locate key letters and open up the relatively simple substitution ciphers of the type used by Julius Caesar.

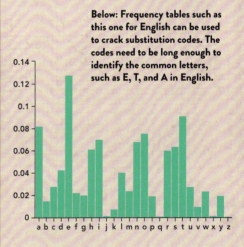

Below: Frequency tables such as this one for English can be used to crack substitution codes. The codes need to be long enough to identify the common letters, such as E, T, and A in English.

Left: Al-Kindi worked at the House of Wisdom, a renowned seat of learning in Baghdad at which many Islamic scholars and scientists pursued their studies.

VENICE: CITY OF SECRETS

Venice has long been a city of mystery and secrets. During the Middle Ages, its republican government—the Council of Ten—prohibited officials from having contact with foreigners. Among the city's citizens, the wearing of masks to conceal identities was commonplace, and secret denunciation was actively encouraged.

VALUABLE SECRETS

There was good reason for Venice's secrecy. It was first and foremost a trading state, and its specialty was the import of high-value goods—textiles, porcelain, and spices—from the East. These were sold on to the rest of Europe for large profits. Venetian merchants operated across the Middle East and India, and a few intrepid Venetian adventurers, such as Marco Polo, even reached China. Along with traded goods, the merchants brought back information from the Asian world, most of it unknown in the rest of Europe.

Venice jealously guarded this trade in goods and knowledge, hiding its activities behind a cloak of secrecy. Anyone found to have passed on secrets to foreigners faced severe penalties. On one occasion, a Venetian official in Constantinople was discovered to be selling intelligence to a foreign power. He was recalled to Venice and as his ship neared home, he was thrown overboard to drown in the Adriatic Sea.

CODED DEVELOPMENT

In the 1460s, the Italian polymath Leon Battista Alberti conducted a study of codes and codebreaking. Although he was unaware of the pioneering work of the Arab scholar al-Kindi, Alberti also understood the frequency principle (where some letters are used more than others) and he developed a cipher based on polyalphabetic substitution to minimize its effect. Whereas the simple Caesar cipher kept to one alphabet per message, Alberti developed a cipher disk, now known as an Alberti disk, on which the alphabetic keys were regularly changed during the coding of the message. This made it harder to locate common letters—such as E or S—as they were given different substitutions whenever the alphabet changed.

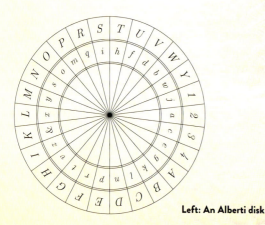

Left: An Alberti disk

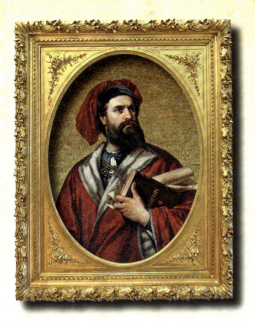

Above: Venice's wealth and power were based around its control of trade routes to the East, first opened up by earlier explorers such as Marco Polo, pictured.

Below: Map of Venice from the fifteenth century, when the city was the second-largest in Europe and at the height of its power.

FOREIGN AMBASSADORS

Venice introduced the system of resident ambassadors in the major cities of Europe. The ambassadors represented Venice and its commercial interests to the rulers of the host country, but they were also expected to send back intelligence to the Council of Ten. Many ambassadors developed their own spy rings, using foreign nationals to ferret out clandestine information.

By the early fifteenth century, Venice had become the foremost intelligence-gathering nation in Europe. It relied heavily on the correspondence sent by its merchants and ambassadors from around the world. To protect these letters from prying eyes, the Venetians developed some of the most complex codes yet formulated, and their codebreakers proved equally adept. Such was their skill that the leading Venetian codebreaker, Giovanni Soro, was sometimes "loaned out" to friendly foreign powers to help break especially difficult codes. Venice's reputation as a center for intelligence would last long after its economic importance declined after the opening of the Atlantic trade routes shifted power to the west.

"SWEAR, FORSWEAR, AND DO NOT REVEAL THE SECRET."

Oath taken by the Council of Ten

THE LION'S MOUTH

Venetian citizens were encouraged to inform on those they suspected of wrongdoing. Stone letterboxes were introduced throughout the city. They originally took the form of elaborately carved heads of wild beasts or people with an open mouth, and were called *bocche dei leoni* (lion's mouth). The letters posted through the mouth included accusations ranging from adultery and blasphemy to tax evasion and treason. The denunciations could not be anonymous, however, and had to be signed by at least two witnesses.

Above: This "lion's mouth," depicting a wild-faced official, is located by the Doge's Palace in Venice.

Plotting against the Queen

When Elizabeth I was crowned Queen of England in 1558, she faced many enemies. As a Protestant nation, England was threatened by the great Catholic powers of France and Spain, and within the country, Catholics secretly worked for the queen's downfall. Fortunately for Elizabeth, she was able to call upon the services of one of the most talented of spy chiefs.

In 1573, Sir Francis Walsingham was made Elizabeth's Secretary of State, an appointment that included running all aspects of espionage. A man of great intelligence and energy, Walsingham built up a spying organization that successfully defeated a series of plots intended to depose the queen.

THE BABINGTON PLOT

Elizabeth's main rival to the throne was her Catholic cousin, Mary Stuart, Queen of Scots. Mary was involved in many of the political intrigues of the period, which culminated in the Babington Plot of 1586. The plotters' intention was to free Mary, who had been imprisoned in England after fleeing from Scotland in 1568. This would be followed by an uprising of English Catholics, invasion by a Spanish army, and the assassination of Elizabeth.

At the center of the plot was Anthony Babington, a courier and former page to Mary. Unknown to Babington, however, his ring of conspirators had been infiltrated by two double-agents working for Walsingham. They discovered the details of the plot and were able to intercept correspondence between Mary and the plotters. The letters were deciphered by the English cryptographer-in-chief Thomas Phelippes. Although the messages were already highly damning, Walsingham unscrupulously forged an addition that "confirmed" Mary's involvement in the plot. The Babington ring were promptly arrested and its members executed. Mary was beheaded at Fotheringhay Castle on February 8, 1587.

Top left:
Sir Francis Walsingham

Bottom left:
Mary Stuart

Top right:
Elizabeth I

"THERE IS LESS DANGER IN FEARING TOO MUCH THAN TOO LITTLE."

Sir Francis Walsingham, Chief Spy to Queen Elizabeth I

GUNPOWDER PLOT

When Elizabeth died in 1603, she was succeeded by the Protestant king of Scotland, James VI, who became James I of England. A group of English Catholics, led by Robert Catesby and Guy Fawkes, planned to overthrow the new monarchy on November 5, 1605. Their aim was to blow up the House of Lords during the state opening of parliament, with James in attendance. The security of the plotters was poor, however, and an anonymous letter alerted the authorities to the plan. In a search of the House of Lords on the evening of November 4, Fawkes was discovered guarding thirty-six barrels of gunpowder. He was arrested, as were most of the other conspirators during the succeeding days. At their trial for treason, they were found guilty and sentenced to be hanged, drawn, and quartered. To this day, the foiling of the plot is celebrated each year on November 5 in the United Kingdom with a bonfire on which they burn an effigy called "the Guy."

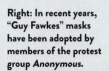

Right: In recent years, "Guy Fawkes" masks have been adopted by members of the protest group *Anonymous*.

DELAYING THE SPANISH ATTACK

The conclusion of the Babington plot did not remove the danger to Elizabeth's position, as the Spanish king, Philip II, had decided to invade England. Walsingham dispatched Anthony Standen—alias Pompeo Pellegrino—to Madrid, where he enlisted the help of the Florentine ambassador at Philip's court. Another source of intelligence was Sir Stephen Powle, who operated throughout Europe gathering information on Spanish intentions. By 1587, their intelligence provided Walsingham with detailed knowledge of the great fleet, or Armada, being prepared for the invasion of England.

Using his influence on the Continent, Walsingham was secretly able to delay the bank loans needed by Philip to finance the invasion. When the Armada finally sailed from Spain in 1588, the English were better prepared to withstand the assault, which famously ended in total disaster for Spain.

— CHAPTER 2 —
1600s–1800s

Europe's exploitation of Africa, the Americas, and Asia brought it enormous wealth. European nations fought one other over who would keep the best of these spoils. In the process, they carved out vast empires for themselves. The need for information about both their new conquests and rival imperialists drove the European powers to develop spy agencies. Increasingly, good intelligence went hand-in-hand with military and naval prowess.

The increasing professionalism of European intelligence services included the development, first in France, of "black chambers" for the interception of coded letters. This, in turn, encouraged the science of cryptography. Skilled cryptographers were now the single most important members of the intelligence world.

The success of the American colonies in breaking away from Britain in the late eighteenth century owed much to their skills in intelligence. Encouraged by George Washington, the spies of the republic gained a significant edge over their British opponents in North America. The British were more successful in Europe and, alongside Russia, became the new masters of intelligence matters.

THE AGE OF DISCOVERY

When Italian explorer Christopher Columbus sailed across the Atlantic in 1492, he laid the ground for European domination of the New World. Spain and Portugal were the early leaders in this colonial exploitation, soon to be joined by other European countries, all locked in bitter rivalry. Military and naval might went hand-in-hand with the covert battle for good intelligence.

The daring Spanish conquests of the Aztec (Mexico) and Inca (Peru) empires in the early sixteenth century relied on the cunning exploitation of the grievances of these empires' subject peoples. They provided the military support that allowed the conquistadors to overcome what would otherwise have been an overwhelming material superiority.

FIGHT FOR TERRITORY

The vast wealth in gold and silver taken from the Americas made Spain the most powerful nation in Europe during the sixteenth century. But the bullion fleets that regularly crossed to Spain were tempting targets for the privateers sailing out of England, France, and the Netherlands. These new arrivals also wanted a direct share of the New World's riches, and they founded their own colonies in the Caribbean and North America—lands already claimed by Spain.

Spain relied on its powerful army and navy and consequently paid limited attention to intelligence matters. Philip II of Spain held a typically aristocratic disdain for the grubby world of spying, and considered code-breaking to be a form of witchcraft. Spain's rivals were less scrupulous, and their superior handling of the arts of spying helped compensate for their lesser military strength.

THE RISE OF FRANCE

While Venice had long been preeminent in the intelligence world, this began to change in the late sixteenth century, with France gaining a new ascendancy. The mathematician François Viète, a pioneer in the development of modern algebra, broke the Spanish diplomatic cipher in 1590. This gave King Henri IV a vital edge in negotiations with Spain that led to the settlement of the French Wars of Religion.

Above: French mathematician and codebreaker François Viète

Above: Cortés, with Malinche by his side, is depicted holding court in the city of Xaltelolco in this drawing from the sixteenth-century manuscript *History of Tlaxcala*.

CORTÉS AND THE COURTESAN

The conquest of the Aztec Empire owed much to a young Aztec woman named Malinche. She came from a high-born Nahua family but had been sold into slavery as a child, and was part of a batch of female slaves gifted to the Spaniards by a non-Aztec leader. The Spanish commander Hernán Cortés took Malinche as his mistress. Malinche had a gift for languages and with the help of a Mayan-speaking priest, she soon had a good command of Spanish. She became Cortés' translator and provided him with intelligence. On one occasion, she discovered that the Cholulans, a powerful ally of the Aztecs, were preparing to fall upon the Spanish. On hearing this news, Cortés launched a forestalling attack that caught the Cholulans totally by surprise.

"FROM NOW ON THEY TOOK US FOR MAGICIANS AND SAID THAT NO PLOT COULD BE SO SECRET AS TO ESCAPE DISCOVERY BY US."

A Spanish comment on the Cholulans after their defeat

RICHELIEU'S SECRET SERVICE

During the early seventeenth century, the French monarchy under Louis XIII faced internal threats from a powerful nobility and external threats from the powerful Habsburgs, whose possessions included Spain, Austria, the Netherlands, and parts of Italy. Both of these threats were neutralized by Louis's formidable chief minister, Cardinal Richelieu.

Richelieu organized an effective national intelligence service that closely monitored the activities of the French aristocrats by intercepting their correspondence. In this manner, Richelieu thwarted plots against the King and re-established the power of the monarchy over the nation. Richelieu employed secret agents to further his policy of weakening the Habsburgs without involving France in costly wars. In one instance, Portugal and Catalonia were encouraged to rise up against their Spanish overlords, thereby weakening Spain's ability to wage war against France. By the time of Richelieu's death in 1642, his secret intelligence service had helped make France the most powerful nation in Europe.

Above: Cardinal Richelieu

SPYING IN THE ENGLISH CIVIL WAR

Right:
Oliver Cromwell

During the English Civil War (1642–1649), Oliver Cromwell's Parliamentary forces held the military advantage over the Royalists under Charles I. Unlike Charles, Cromwell understood the importance of good intelligence, employing the best spies to undermine the efforts of his enemies.

The Parliamentarians were able to call upon the services of John Wallis, a scholar at Cambridge University. Like many other cryptographers, Wallis was a brilliant mathematician (he also developed infinitesimal calculus). For him, codebreaking was an amusing intellectual diversion, and he had little difficulty untangling the codes used by the Royalists.

THE KING'S LETTERS

In 1645, Wallis deciphered the coded correspondence of Charles I to his wife in exile in France, as well as plans to encourage support from Catholics in Ireland and continental Europe. These letters were an invaluable propaganda coup for Parliament, who published their contents in order to discredit Charles. Firstly, they portrayed him as a king ruled by his wife, and secondly, they showed that a supposedly Protestant king was engaging in deals with foreign Catholics.

Wallis later worked for Thomas Scot, Oliver Cromwell's first intelligence chief. Appointed in 1647, Scot developed a spy network that infiltrated the Royal court-in-exile on the outskirts of Paris. One of his secret agents, Robert Werden, provided juicy details of the affairs of the royal princes Charles and James, much to the consternation of the straitlaced Scot.

Above: Charles I and his wife Henrietta Maria of France

"REALLY IT IS A WONDER THAT YOU CAN PICK AS MANY LOCKS LEADING INTO THE HEARTS OF THE WICKED MEN AS YOU DO, AND IT IS A MERCY THAT GOD HAS MADE YOUR LABORS THEREIN SO SUCCESSFUL."

Henry Cromwell (son of Oliver), writing to John Thurloe

FIGHT FOR THE CROWN

After the capture of Charles I in 1646, his eldest son Charles Stuart fled to the continent. When Charles I was executed in 1649, his son took the title of Charles II, and in 1650 he sailed to Scotland, assembling an army to invade England. The Royalist forces were decisively beaten by Cromwell at the battle of Worcester in September 1651, and once again Charles was forced to flee to France, briefly hiding in an oak tree to escape his pursuers. On his return to the English throne in 1660, he pardoned all his former Parliamentary opponents except for those who had signed his father's death warrant. Charles was determined on revenge, and one of the first of the regicides to be caught was Thomas Scot—his fate to be hanged, drawn, and quartered.

Right: Charles II

Left: John Thurloe

SPYING IN THE COMMONWEALTH

In 1653, Thomas Scot was replaced by John Thurloe, a lawyer and close friend of Cromwell. Thurloe extended Scot's spy network and helped Cromwell improve diplomatic relations with the rest of Europe. Among Thurloe's triumphs was his uncovering of the Sealed Knot, a small group of Royalist supporters in England who were liaising with the Royalist court in exile to instigate an uprising against Parliament. A message from the group to Charles II was intercepted by Thurloe's agents, leading to their arrest in 1654.

Above: John Wallis cracked codes for Cromwell but later worked for Charles II.

Such was Thurloe's skill that a despondent Charles II lamented that Parliament had "perfect intelligence whatsoever His Majesty [Charles] resolved to do, and of all he said himself." Thurloe also quashed internal rebellions in England. In 1655, he foiled the Penruddock uprising in York, and two years later he exposed a plot to assassinate Cromwell by members of the radical Levelers movement.

The Commonwealth collapsed following the death of Cromwell in 1660, and Charles II was invited to return to England and take the throne. Thurloe was arrested for treason, but such was his knowledge of spying that he was released. He was made a consultant to the monarchy on matters of intelligence.

WAR OF THE CODES

In intelligence battles, the side that has the best cryptographers usually comes off better. Code-making and codebreaking achieved a new importance in the semi-continuous warfare between the great powers of Europe from the sixteenth century onward. Each side attempted to crack the codes of adversaries and allies alike, while developing what they hoped would be impenetrable codes of their own.

The sixteenth and seventeenth centuries witnessed a steady growth in international post, and the correspondence of prominent individuals, embassies, and other state services were of great interest to national spy chiefs. France was the first country to develop a way to spy on letters with the formation of the *cabinet noir*, or black chamber. The function of the black chamber was to intercept, open, and decode a letter, then send it on to its destination such that the recipient would never find out that it had been tampered with. Other nations soon followed the French lead with black chambers of their own.

ENDING THE SIEGE

France's black chamber was run by the brilliant cryptographer-mathematician Antoine Rossignol. He established his reputation in 1626 during the Catholic siege of the Huguenot (French Protestant) city of Réalmont, when he broke a coded letter intercepted from the defenders, pleading for ammunition to replace their nearly exhausted supplies. The letter was then read out to the defenders. Realizing that help would not arrive and their plight was known to their Catholic besiegers, the defenders promptly surrendered.

Rossignol did much to improve the quality of the then-lax code-making practices of the French administration. He and his son Bonaventure developed the *Grande Chiffre* (Great Cipher) especially for Louis XIV. At the time, the system seemed impossible to break.

When the cipher key was lost in the mid-eighteenth century, it remained unbroken until the 1890s, when another brilliant French codebreaker, Étienne Bazeries, cracked it after three years of work.

BRITISH SUCCESSES

If France had taken the lead in advanced cryptography, then its main rival, England, was not far behind. John Wallis, who had started his career during the English Civil War, happily and productively worked for kings Charles II and William III following the restoration of the monarchy. On his death in 1703, Wallis handed over to his grandson William Blencoe, succeeded in turn by the able Edward Willes and his family. By the middle of the eighteenth century, France was losing the war of the codes, its standard ciphers regularly broken by cryptographers in Britain, Russia, and Austria.

QUICKTIME CODEBREAKING

Of all the black chambers in Europe, arguably the most efficient was the Austrian Geheime Kabinets-Kanzlei (Cabinet Office of Secrets), based in Vienna. During the middle of the eighteenth century, it came under the direction of Baron Ignaz von Koch, who insisted that all intercepted letters should be returned to the postal system with sufficient speed to prevent recipients from suspecting any interception had taken place. When the post arrived at 7 a.m., specialists melted the seals before a team of stenographers began copying relevant sections of the text. Up to four people might be working on one letter at a time. Once copied, the letter would be resealed and returned to the central post office by 10 a.m., ready for normal delivery. Translators and codebreakers would examine the copied letters, sometimes working around the clock to deliver fresh intelligence to the Austrian foreign ministry.

Above: A woman carefully reseals a letter at the Geheime Kabinets-Kanzlei.

A FAMILY AFFAIR

In 1716, Edward Willes assumed the position of Britain's royal decipherer and immediately proved himself by breaking coded correspondence between Jacobites (supporters of the deposed James II) and Sweden, a potential ally. Willes went on to break diplomatic codes from France, Austria, Prussia, and Spain—successes that brought substantial financial reward and the formation of the official Deciphering Branch. To assist him in his work, he enlisted the help of his three sons, and when he died in 1773, the youngest, Francis, took over the "family business." Although Francis lacked his father's ability, he maintained his position until his death in 1827. His nephew William Lovell took over the job prior to the dissolution of the Deciphering Branch in 1844.

GEORGE WASHINGTON: AMERICAN SPY CHIEF

Few of history's major military commanders were as well-versed in the art of spying as George Washington. In the secret intelligence war between the British and the fledgling American Republic, he ensured that it was the Americans who came out on top.

Washington's involvement as a spy chief during the American Revolutionary War (1775–1783) began as early as July 1775, when he sent an anonymous agent into Boston to "establish a secret correspondence for the purpose of conveying intelligence of the enemy's movements and designs." A year later, Washington agreed to allow a volunteer, Nathan Hale, to infiltrate British-held New York. Hale was an enterprising young man, but lacked the necessary skills of a good spy. He was arrested after just two weeks in the city and condemned to hang on September 22, 1776.

THE CULPER RING

In light of the Hale misadventure, Washington adopted a more professional approach, appointing Benjamin Tallmadge as his deputy in intelligence matters in 1778. Tallmadge created a spy network in New York that provided information in British movements and intentions. Known as the Culper Ring, after the code-names of the leading members, the spies were New Yorkers who were well known in the city and able to conceal their true sympathies.

The Culper Ring provided Washington with a steady stream of information, its most valuable contribution coming in 1780. The American spies discovered that the British were about to send a large force to intercept newly landed French troops, sent to help the Americans, in Newport, Rhode Island. This information was relayed to Washington, who promptly made bogus preparations for a full-scale march on New York. Hearing of this, the British commander countermanded the attack on the French in order to defend New York against an assault that somehow failed to materialize.

Above: Benjamin Tallmadge

Right: George Washington

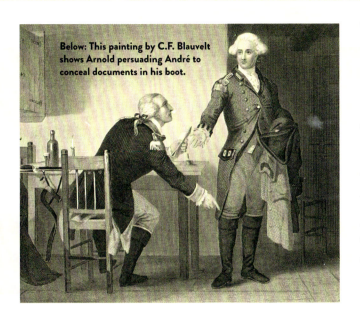

Below: This painting by C.F. Blauvelt shows Arnold persuading André to conceal documents in his boot.

TREASON IN HIGH PLACES

Major-General Benedict Arnold, one of the best commanders in the American army, became embittered after being passed over for promotion. Major John André, a British army officer, encouraged Arnold to change sides. In 1780, Arnold was given responsibility for the strategically important West Point on the Hudson River and agreed to hand over the position to the British in exchange for £20,000. André, however, was caught in civilian clothes while passing through American lines, and documents found on his person linked him with Arnold. Benjamin Tallmadge, Washington's intelligence officer, wanted to arrest Arnold, but a delay in executing the order allowed him to escape to the British side. André was less fortunate and was hanged as a spy.

FEEDING FALSE INFORMATION

During the winter of 1777–78, Washington's army was stationed at Valley Forge, Pennsylvania. Supplies were low and the whole force could have been swept away by a determined British advance. To forestall this, Washington prepared detailed documents referring to non-existent infantry battalions and cavalry regiments to give the impression that his army was strong and ready for battle. This information was forwarded to the British via double agents. Taken in by the deception, the British decided against any action, thereby sparing the Americans when they were at their most vulnerable.

On another occasion, one of Washington's officers came to him to seek permission to arrest a man believed to be a British spy. Instead of apprehending the spy, Washington sensed a useful opportunity and told the officer to invite him to dinner. At the ensuing dinner, the officer "carelessly" left unattended documents containing exaggerated figures for the strength of the American army. The spy stole the documents and handed them to the British, who, once again, were confused as to the real strength of their opponents.

Below: The execution of Nathan Hale

"I ONLY REGRET THAT I HAVE BUT ONE LIFE TO LOSE FOR MY COUNTRY."

Nathan Hale, final words at the gallows

FEAR OF SPIES IN REVOLUTIONARY FRANCE

The French Revolution, which began in 1789, can be seen as one of the turning points in history, as the monarchy of Louis XVI was overturned and replaced by a government of the people. During this radical transformation of society, the new republican government was beset by rumors of counter-revolution.

The revolution became increasingly violent with the passage of time. Although the revolutionaries had seized power with relative ease, their position was far from secure. The new French republic faced internal opposition from those still loyal to the king, as well as the threat of military intervention from the major foreign powers—Austria, Prussia, and Britain— who wanted to restore the French monarchy. Large numbers of the French aristocracy had fled the country, and these émigrés also plotted against the republic.

GROWING PARANOIA

The threats faced by the republic created an intense anxiety among the revolutionaries and the people of Paris. This turned into a corrosive paranoia with the outbreak of war against Austria and Prussia in the summer of 1792. Counter-revolutionary spies were seen at every turn and mass arrests became commonplace, most of those thrown into prison innocent of any crime.

As a Prussian army advanced into France in September 1792, mass hysteria descended on the capital, and many prisoners were brutally murdered by the Paris mob. The September Massacres, as they became known, were the prelude to a reign of state-sponsored terror that included the execution of Louis in January 1793. The establishment of the Committee of Public Safety in April 1793 formalized the Terror, with the creation of an early version of a police state, responsible for surveillance, investigation, and repression. The atmosphere of fear and suspicion this engendered could make loose talk or the telling of jokes against the Republic punishable by a visit to the guillotine.

Below: Louis XVI was executed in the Place de la Revolution in Paris on January 21, 1793, the day after he was convicted of conspiracy with foreign powers.

Right: Georges Danton was the first president of the Committee for Public Safety. Like many of the revolutionary leaders, he was himself later guillotined.

Far right: Maximilien Robespierre, who denounced Danton.

> "THE PEOPLE ASKS ONLY FOR WHAT IS NECESSARY, IT WANTS JUSTICE AND PEACE; THE RICH ASPIRE TO EVERYTHING, THEY WANT TO INVADE AND DOMINATE."

Maximilien Robespierre, French lawyer and revolutionary leader

SPREADING THE REVOLUTION

The French armies won a series of military victories in 1792–93, which encouraged republican leaders to make a summons for revolution throughout Europe. Their call was met favorably in many quarters. Fearful for their own futures, European monarchs instituted measures to snuff out seditious activity.

In Britain, developments in France led to the formation of the Aliens Office in December 1793, responsible for internal security and intelligence gathering abroad. Under the leadership of William Wickham, the agents of the Aliens Office penetrated many of the revolutionary groups, including the radical London Corresponding Society, but it turned out there was insufficient treasonable activity for successful prosecutions. Abroad, the Aliens Office provided support for the many émigré groups who promised to unseat the revolutionary government. Working from a base in Switzerland, Wickham held high hopes for their actions but despite generous British financial aid— known as the "cavalry of St. George"—the plots came to nothing. The revolution remained secure.

ESCAPE FROM PARIS

From the summer of 1789, King Louis XVI and his wife Marie-Antoinette and family were held under house arrest in the Tuileries Palace in Paris. By the summer of 1791, growing hostility towards the monarchy from the new republican government encouraged Louis to flee from Paris to the royalist stronghold at Montmédy on the Belgian border. The secret escape was well planned, and in the early hours of June 21, the royal family climbed into a coach and slipped past their guards. Louis, who knew nothing of France outside Paris, believed the countryside supported the monarchy, and once clear of Paris he foolishly began to reveal his true identity. News of this was reported to the authorities, who arrested the royal family at Varennes. Louis was returned to prison to await his eventual execution.

INTELLIGENCE IN THE ERA OF NAPOLEON

Like other national leaders, the French emperor Napoleon received a mass of intelligence reports. He consequently faced the perennial problem of what to judge as valuable information and what to discard as rubbish or outright disinformation from the enemy. It was a conundrum he was never able to properly solve during a series of conflicts with France's neighbors, known in the English-speaking world as the Napoleonic Wars.

Napoleon Bonaparte, the most successful general of the French Revolution, crowned himself Emperor of the French in 1804. In doing so, he became the undisputed leader of the most powerful country in Europe. With a large and highly experienced army at his disposal, Napoleon immediately began to prepare for war against his neighbors. He also inherited an efficient intelligence service, but he held ambivalent views about the importance of espionage, often preferring to trust in his own military ability over reports from his spies.

Below: Deceived Austrian general Karl Mack von Leiberich was forced to surrender his force of 30,000 men to Napoleon at Ulm after minimal fighting.

DECEIVING THE AUSTRIANS

For his first great campaign in 1805, which culminated in the decisive defeat of a combined Austro-Russian army at Austerlitz in 1805, Napoleon did rely on one of his more audacious spies, Carl Schulmeister, a businessman and smuggler from the Alsace region bordering France and Germany. Schulmeister ostensibly worked for Austrian intelligence, but he was in fact a double agent who had offered his services to the French.

Schulmeister managed to persuade the Austrians that French forces stationed in southern Germany were on the point of collapse. The Austrian commander in the area, General Mack, advanced toward them in anticipation of an easy victory, only to find his troops surrounded by the main French army at Ulm. Mack was forced to surrender, and the Austrians never fully recovered from this setback.

SPIES IN THE FRENCH COURT

Later in his reign, Napoleon was less receptive to good intelligence, whether from spies or decryption, and by 1810, France had fallen behind Russia in intelligence-gathering capability. The Russian Minister of War, Mikhail Barclay de Tolly, had created an efficient black chamber.

Russia had been at peace with France since 1807, but by 1810, Tsar Alexander and his government were increasingly fearful of a French invasion. Fortunately for them, they had two spies at the heart of Napoleon's court in Paris. Carl von Nesselrode, deputy head of the Russian embassy, gained detailed information on French strategic intentions. Prince Alexander Chernyshev, the Tsar's personal representative to Napoleon, operated a ring of agents in the French government. One agent provided Chernyshev with a monthly audit of the strengths and positions of every unit in the French army. Together, the two spies gained a detailed picture of French preparations for the invasion of Russia in the summer of 1812. The ensuing military disaster was the beginning of the end of Napoleon's empire.

Above: Prince Alexander Chernyshev

Above: Sat astride his distinctive white horse, Napoleon watches as Moscow burns. Russian troops had already abandoned the city to retreat to the east. Napoleon's invasion would end in a disastrous retreat.

IMPERIAL INTELLIGENCE

Napoleon was clear in laying out his demands for the acquisition of military intelligence: "Carrying out of a rapid reconnaissance of passes and fords, making sure to obtain reliable guides, questioning the priest and the postmaster, making rapid contact with local inhabitants, sending out spies, translating and analyzing postal correspondence, and finally responding to the questions of the commander-in-chief." In real-world circumstances, however, he was less happy with the intelligence he received: "Nothing is so contradictory and nonsensical as this mass of reports brought in by spies and officers sent on scouting missions. Often they do not even report their own eyesight, but only repeat what they have heard from panic-stricken or surprised people."

"A GREAT PART OF THE INFORMATION OBTAINED IN WAR IS CONTRADICTORY, A STILL GREATER PART IS FALSE AND BY FAR THE GREATEST PART IS OF DOUBTFUL CHARACTER."

Carl von Clausewitz, Prussian military theorist and officer in the Napoleonic Wars

CHAPTER 3

NINETEENTH-CENTURY INTELLIGENCE

The transformation of Europe and North America from mainly rural societies into industrial powerhouses gave them the means to dominate the rest of the world in a manner never seen before. Although the United States largely abstained from empire-building, the major European powers engaged in an orgy of territorial conquest in Asia and Africa. The Europeans used both armed might and intelligence agencies to oversee their subject peoples.

Within the Western nations, the pace of change was bewildering, not least for spy chiefs and their agents. Advances in communications transformed the spy's role, allowing them to travel hundreds of miles in a day on the new railroads and transmit intelligence reports via telegraph over even longer distances in a matter of minutes.

The nineteenth century also witnessed a dramatic expansion in population, leading to the creation of a new social order in the form of a middle class that helped organize the new industrial system and a working class that provided its labor. Both classes rocked the old order, and the establishment devoted much time and effort to suppress or at least subvert movements for change. Spies and secret agents offered their services to all sides in these conflicts.

REACTION, REFORM, REVOLUTION

The great upheavals caused by the French Revolution and the Napoleonic Wars permanently changed European society. However, in the early years of the nineteenth century the crowned heads of Europe were determined to set the clock back to the pre-revolutionary world of 1789.

After Napoleon's defeat and abdication in 1814, a conference was organized in Vienna to decide the future of Europe. The major nations at the Congress of Vienna were Britain, Austria, Russia, and Prussia—along with the defeated France. They were joined by diplomatic missions from across Europe.

MONARCHIES RETRENCH

The conservative monarchies had been shaken by the French Revolution, and at the Congress they made it clear they would stamp out radical change in the future.

Above: Prince Klemens von Metternich

Consequently, the half-century after Napoleon's abdication would see a battle between the forces of reaction and those of progress, the latter demanding fundamental reform or even revolution.

The monarchies had a tendency to believe they were facing a mass, Europe-wide revolutionary conspiracy. Prince Klemens von Metternich, the influential foreign minister and later Chancellor of Austria, was particularly affronted by the rise of radical and nationalist German student societies in southern and western Germany (areas then under partial Austrian control). In concert with Prussia, Metternich suppressed political activity in Germany's universities and sent in police spies to report on any possible sedition.

In Russia, in December 1825, a group of reformist army officers and their soldiers rose up in protest against the reactionary Tsar Nicholas I. Lacking popular support, the Decemberist revolt was soon crushed, and autocratic rule continued in Russia throughout the century. The failure of reform in Russia pushed progressive elements underground into a covert and increasingly intense revolutionary struggle against the regime and its secret police.

Below: Delegates from across Europe gathered for the Congress of Vienna, which was coordinated by Prince Metternich, pictured standing in front of his chair, sixth from the left.

YEAR OF REVOLT

Reformers had greater success in France. In 1830, the repressive regime of Charles X was overturned in favor of the somewhat more enlightened rule of King Louis Philippe. But his government collapsed in the face of the 1848 revolution, a mass uprising demanding better economic conditions and greater popular involvement in government. Louis Philippe fled to Britain and a new French republic was established.

The revolt in France was the first of a series of uprisings that swept through Europe in 1848, and although the other monarchies held on to their thrones, the beginnings of a new social order was emerging. The middle classes had enjoyed great economic success but they were faced by an expanding working class, whose desperate poverty saw the emergence of a new political movement: socialism and its new champion, Karl Marx.

Above: Revolutionaries enter the throne room of the Tuileries Palace, Paris. The 1848 revolution established the French Second Republic.

SEX, SPIES, AND DIPLOMACY

The Congress of Vienna was a hotbed of intrigue. As organizers of the event, the Austrians had obvious home advantages and their chief statesman, Prince Metternich, ensured that the servants drafted in to serve the foreign monarchs and their retinues contained suitable numbers of informers. The Viennese black chamber worked overtime to covertly open and decrypt the vast amount of correspondence that flowed to and from the city. The major participants were often accompanied by their mistresses, and the Congress became infamous for congress of another type, complete with the swapping of partners and pillow talk. Metternich's former mistress, Princess Catherine Bagration, gave both sexual favors and her old lover's correspondence to Tsar Alexander I of Russia.

"WE CANNOT GET INTO AN OMNIBUS OR ENTER A COFFEE HOUSE WITHOUT BEING FAVORED WITH THE COMPANY OF AT LEAST ONE OF THESE UNKNOWN FRIENDS."

Karl Marx, on the activities of police spies

MARKING MARX

Britain's greater tolerance of political dissent turned it into a safe haven for European revolutionaries forced to flee their home countries. The most famous of these was German Karl Marx, who arrived in England in 1849 and lived there for the remainder of his life. Marx was a focus for the activities of police spies from continental Europe, most notably Wilhelm Stieber of the Prussian police. Stieber was totally unscrupulous and sent back fraudulent reports to his masters in Prussia. In one instance he claimed—without any evidence—that Marx was planning to assassinate Queen Victoria and her family. The credulous Prussian foreign ministry fell for the report and swiftly informed the British government, who, with greater knowledge of the actual situation, filed the warning in the waste basket.

Right: Karl Marx

NEW TECHNOLOGY, NEW INTELLIGENCE

The rapid pace of technological progress that followed from the Industrial Revolution transformed the world. This was especially the case in the field of communications, in which technological advances changed the nature of spying.

Left: During the American Civil War (1861–1865), President Abraham Lincoln traveled the country in his own presidential car. The railroads had been taken over for the war effort.

AGE OF THE RAILWAY

The first passenger rail system was developed in Britain in the 1820s, and railways quickly spread around the globe. The steam train enabled secret agents to travel virtually unnoticed to wherever they were needed in a matter of hours, or, at most, a couple of days. Spies also found it advantageous to catalog the movements of trains, especially during wartime. Armies now traveled to the battlefield by train, and astute observers—perhaps camouflaged as a lady painter near the railroad—could work out the numbers of soldiers being transported to the front and where that likely destination would be.

One byproduct of this transport revolution was the emergence of the foreign correspondent—a journalist sent to report from hot spots around the world, most usually wars or other violent struggles. Like the spy, the foreign correspondent was looking for information, and it was not long before spies were using the cover of journalism to go about their covert activities.

INVENTION OF THE TELEGRAPH

The other great breakthrough in communications was the electric telegraph, the first practical examples of which developed on both sides of the Atlantic in the 1830s.

The system invented by Samuel Morse in the United States became the standard that others followed, and during the 1840s thousands of miles of telegraph lines were laid across America and Europe. During the Crimean War (1854–1856) undersea cables were laid in the Black Sea to provide a direct link between London and the British Army in the Crimea. A message could be sent in a few hours rather than the three weeks of normal postal correspondence.

By the time of the outbreak of the American Civil War in 1861, a network of rail and telegraph lines spanned the country, enabling commanders a control over their forces otherwise impossible. But the telegraph had one fundamental weakness—the lines could be tapped by outsiders and its messages read.

President Lincoln was so enamored of the information provided by the telegraph that a special telegraph office was installed in the White House, complete with a team of cryptographers to break coded messages. One of the major successes of the cryptographers came from their listening in to private correspondence between a source working for the Confederate states and another in New York. The decoded

Left: This map from 1871 shows the scale of the ambitious scheme to completely encircle the globe with telegraph lines.

MORSE CODE

American Samuel Morse—working with Joseph Henry and Alfred Vali—developed an early electrical telegraph in 1837 by sending electrical pulses along a wire. It was a simple system that used a hand-operated key. When the key was pressed, the signal was "on" and when released it was "off." The central feature of this invention was the development of a code to read these electrical pulses. In Morse code, the twenty-six letters of the English alphabet were each given an individual code made up of dots and dashes (the dash was three times longer than a dot). It was soon found that skilled operators could transmit and receive messages with great speed and accuracy, and Morse code spread around the world. It was used in radio messages throughout the twentieth century—and every secret agent would be trained in its use.

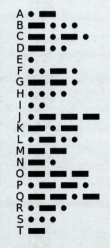

Right: HMS Agamemnon laying the Transatlantic telegraph cable. It was completed in 1858 after four years of work, but only functioned for three weeks. A second, more durable cable was laid in 1866.

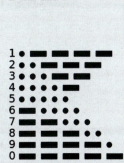

messages revealed that the New York source was engraving printing plates for the manufacture of Confederate bank notes. When the workshop was raided by the police, notes totaling several million dollars were seized.

The early telegraph systems were large and cumbersome and demanded a powerful source of electricity. This began to change in the twentieth century with the development of portable batteries, glass valves, and the ability to transmit wirelessly by radio waves. The advent of the suitcase radio during World War II was invaluable for secret agents, able to transmit and receive messages wherever they wanted and without outside help (see pages 170–171).

THE AMERICAN CIVIL WAR

Amateur spies came to the fore during the American Civil War. They proved highly effective, none more so than the female secret agents who made their mark in the history of espionage.

Both the Unionists and the Confederates developed ad hoc intelligence agencies to gather information. Spying was carried out on a wide scale because the nature of the war made it easy to do so. Both sides spoke the same language and they looked alike, while political affiliations were mixed and did not rely entirely on geography, meaning that pro-abolitionists favoring the Union lived in the South and Confederate sympathizers were based in the North. The scarcity of fixed military positions enabled spies to move between the lines with comparative ease.

ELIZABETH VAN LEW

Living in the Confederate capital of Richmond, Virginia, Elizabeth Van Lew was a convinced abolitionist who had freed her own slaves in 1843, including Mary Jane Richardson (or Bowser). Once war had broken out, Van Lew assisted in the welfare of Union prisoners. She then set up a spy ring—the Richmond Underground—that included Richardson, her most important source. Van Lew managed to have Richardson taken in as a servant in the house of Jefferson Davis, the Confederate president. The Richmond Underground ran five intelligence "depots"; the spies delivered reports to Van Lew, who then assigned them to couriers to slip through enemy lines to her Union handlers.

Above: Elizabeth Van Lew

Above: William A. Jackson, a slave in the house of Jefferson Davis, who spied for the Union

UNIONIST FIELD AGENTS

In the Unionist North, notable spy chiefs included Alan Pinkerton—who later created the Pinkerton Detective Agency— and Colonel George H. Sharpe, who provided intelligence to generals Hooker and Grant and set up the Bureau of Military Information.

The Bureau had as many as seventy agents in the field, and it collated their reports along with intelligence from captured prisoners and enemy documents retrieved from the battlefield. Sharpe acted as a handler for Elizabeth Van Lew, considered to be one of his best spies. Another excellent source of information came from slaves or former slaves, who were intimately acquainted with the Confederate South, their reports known as Black Dispatches. Leading black spies included George Scott, John Scobell, and Mary Jane Richards, as well as Harriet Tubman, who had already achieved fame for her part in the Underground Railroad for escaped slaves.

Right: Having herself escaped from slavery, Harriet Tubman guided dozens of people to escape to freedom along the Underground Railroad before the Civil War. During the war, Tubman was a scout and spy for the Union Army.

ROSE O'NEAL GREENHOW

A well-known society hostess in Washington, D.C., the widowed Rose O'Neal Greenhow was staunchly pro-slavery. Remaining in Washington after the outbreak of war, she was recruited as a Confederate agent. In July 1861, she forwarded vital information about the movements of General McDowall's Union army, which helped secure a Confederate victory at the Battle of First Bull Run. Alan Pinkerton tracked the leak back to Greenhow and had her placed under house arrest. Greenhow continued to supply intelligence to the Confederacy until she was deported to the South in June 1862. She sailed to Britain in 1863, acting as an unofficial agent for the Confederate government, but drowned on her return after her ship ran aground while attempting to run the Union blockade off North Carolina.

Right: Rose O'Neal Greenhow and her daughter pictured in prison in Washington, D.C., in 1862.

CONFEDERATE SPIES

On the Confederate side, Captain Thomas Jordan had established a spy ring in the Washington area even before the war began. Jordan soon transferred operational control to his star agent, Rose O'Neal Greenhow, and acted as her handler before he moved on to a more conventional military career.

The Confederacy sent secret agents to Britain—officially neutral—to negotiate covert deals. This was more difficult than it seemed, especially when the North established a naval blockade of the South. Confederate spy James Bulloch set up an office in Liverpool to buy cotton from the South in exchange for armaments and other war supplies. He also arranged for the purchase and construction of the famous commerce raider, CSS *Alabama*. According to Northern officials, Bulloch was "the most dangerous man in Europe."

THE GREAT GAME

The confrontation between Russia and Britain in Central Asia during the nineteenth century became known as the Great Game. The term was later popularized by novelist Rudyard Kipling, and described the covert efforts by both sides to influence local rulers and discover more of each other's activities.

As Russia expanded its territories eastward in the 1830s, it dispatched secret agents to sow division among the warring peoples of Central Asia and exploit any ensuing differences to its advantage. Among these agents was the charismatic multi-linguist Captain Jan Prosper Witkiewicz, a Polish-Lithuanian adventurer and explorer in Russian service. Witkiewicz and his Cossack guard advanced to Bukhara in Turkestan in 1836 and persuaded its Emir to remain neutral while Russia attacked the nearby khanate of Khiva. A year later, Witkiewicz was in the Afghan capital of Kabul in an attempt to win over the Afghan ruler.

MUTUAL MISTRUST AND RESPECT

Britain viewed developments in Turkestan with mistrust, anxious that the Russians had designs on India, the "jewel in the crown" of Britain's empire. As a result, the British authorities in India tried to create a buffer zone in the areas to the north of India that included Persia, Afghanistan, Tibet, and southern parts of Turkestan. The Russians, for their part, were irritated by British expeditions into Turkestan and feared the prospect of British control of Afghanistan acting as a staging post for further advances into Central Asia.

The fears of both sides were unfounded. Russia had no interest in India, while British expeditions into Central Asia were without intent to acquire territory. But this did not stop them from conducting reconnaissance to map this uncharted region and check out each other's activities.

When Russian and British explorer-agents encountered one another, relations were generally cordial. Captain Francis Younghusband was advancing along the Yarkand valley in Chinese Turkestan in 1889, with his escort of Gurkha soldiers, when he encountered Captain Bronislav Grombchevsky, accompanied by a troop of Cossacks. The two men dined together. Younghusband congratulated Bronislav on the horsemanship of his Cossacks, while Bronislav praised the shooting skills of the Gurkhas.

Above: This political cartoon from 1878, by British humorist John Tenniel, shows Emir Sher Ali of Afghanistan trapped by his "friends," a Russian bear and a British lion.

LOCAL KNOWLEDGE

As part of the geographical survey of India, the British used locals from the Indian border states in areas where Europeans would have been denied entry. Although the survey was a genuine mapmaking operation, its agents on the ground were also expected to supply any useful intelligence they could find. The mountainous country of Tibet was forbidden to Europeans on pain of death, and it was here that the agents—called pandits or "owners of knowledge"—were most effective.

The pandits were typically disguised as Buddhist holy men, and were given a modified Buddhist rosary with one hundred beads (instead of the usual one hundred and eight), which helped them count out the regular steps they used to measure distances. They were trained in the use of sextants (hidden in their travelers' chests), and had compasses concealed in their prayer wheels, which were also used to hold scrolls of paper for recording measurements. Those pandits who were caught by the authorities faced an uncertain fate, but those who returned brought back valuable information.

PANDIT NUMBER ONE

To preserve secrecy, pandits were referred to by numbers rather than names. The most famous of them, Nain Singh Rawat, was assigned as Pandit Number One. Born into a mountainous village in the Himalayas, Nain Singh had already traveled through Tibet and was familiar with its language and customs. He was hired by the British and given the mission of conducting a full survey of Tibet—a journey of 1,580 miles (2,540 km) that took eighteen months. He spent three months in the Tibetan capital of Lhasa and even met the country's ruler, the Dalai Lama, all the while gathering intelligence about a place virtually unknown to Westerners. He also managed to survey the Thok Jalung goldfields before fears for his safety led him to slip out of Lhasa and return to India.

Above: Nain Singh Rawat

"PROPAGANDA OF THE DEED": ANARCHIST BOMBERS

Above: Carlo Pisacane

A spectacular series of terrorist attacks swept through Europe and the United States during the late nineteenth and early twentieth centuries. They were carried out by radical anarchists, who described their actions as "propaganda of the deed."

The philosophy of anarchism at its simplest argued for the dissolution of the capitalist state. Most anarchists adopted peaceful means in their attempts to achieve their goals but a few adopted the more aggressive methods pioneered by the Italian anarchist Carlo Pisacane. In 1857, Pisacane wrote: "Ideas spring from deeds and not the other way round," insisting that the "deeds" must be violent in order to draw popular attention to the cause and to rally the masses behind revolutionary activity. These acts of violence were to be focused against the chief representatives of the state—such as monarchs and presidents—although a few anarchists went even further to include all members of the middle-class bourgeoisie.

ATTEMPTS AGAINST THE TSAR

In 1866, Russian revolutionary Dmitry Karakozov attempted to gun down Tsar Alexander II, and although the attempt failed, it set a pattern for further anarchist and revolutionary activity. In 1880, Stepan Khalturin used the new explosive dynamite in a further attempt to kill Alexander. The tsar escaped unharmed but a section of the Winter Palace was destroyed, with eleven killed and forty-five seriously wounded. Two years later, a bomb was thrown into the café of the Bellacoeur Theater in the French city of Lyons—the first in several other similar indiscriminate attacks against general targets that caused fear and revulsion.

Above: Dmitry Karakozov

"I REGARD ALL GOVERNMENTS AS INSTITUTIONS FOR COMMITTING THE MOST REVOLTING CRIMES."

Leo Tolstoy, Russian novelist and anarchist supporter

SPREAD TO THE UNITED STATES

Anarchist actions spread through Europe and then across the Atlantic to North America. In 1886, a bomb was thrown at police during a Chicago demonstration that had been protesting against the shooting of striking workers. The authorities clamped down hard, with four anarchist supporters rounded up and hanged in a rigged trial. The Chicago repression was typical of the authorities' responses around the world, although brutal repression only tended to produce further violent reaction from the radical anarchists.

Police spies and informers unmasked several anarchist gangs, but the outrages continued well into the 1920s, with a final flurry of action taking place in the United States as a result of the execution of the Italian anarchist immigrants Sacco and Vanzetti in 1927. But in the end violent anarchy died out because radical interest had turned elsewhere, towards socialism and the possibilities offered by the communist Soviet Union.

SOME MAJOR ANARCHIST OUTRAGES

1866 First of several attempts on life of Tsar Alexander II
1878 Kaiser Wilhelm I of Germany survives an assassination attempt
1881 Tsar Alexander II killed in bomb blast
1892 US industrialist Henry Clay Frick badly wounded in shooting attack
1893 Bomb thrown into a Barcelona opera house, killing eleven people
1894 President Sadi Carnot of France stabbed to death
1897 Spanish prime minister Antonio Cánovas gunned down
1898 Empress Elizabeth of Austria stabbed to death
1900 King Umberto of Italy shot and killed
1901 US President McKinley fatally shot
1909 Argentinian police chief blown up by a bomb
1911 Russian prime minister Pyotr Stolypin killed
1920 Wall Street bombing kills 38 people

Above: Artist's rendition of the bomb thrown in the French National Assembly by the anarchist Auguste Vaillant on December 9, 1893.

TECHNICAL ASSISTANCE

The insurrectionary anarchists would never have made such an impact without two technological developments: the revolver and dynamite. The revolver was a reliable handgun that could easily be concealed in a coat pocket and was capable of firing multiple shots in quick succession—invaluable when a single shot might not kill the target outright. Dynamite was an explosive developed by the Swedish chemist and inventor Alfred Nobel in the late 1860s. It was more powerful than gunpowder and more stable than the notoriously unreliable nitroglycerin—and it could be detonated with a simple blasting cap. The revolver and the dynamite bomb became the weapons of choice for the violent anarchist.

Left: Assassination of President McKinley

THE GROWTH OF PROFESSIONAL INTELLIGENCE

Prior to the 1800s, most intelligence services and spy networks were formed ad hoc to deal with rising issues or conflicts, and disbanded in peacetime or after their investigations ended. But after the near-constant warring periods of the eighteenth century, wherein at least two major powers were in conflict with one another at almost any given moment, intelligence groups likewise began to expand and develop.

As tensions continued to rise between European and other nations throughout the nineteenth century, so too did each power's investment into permanent intelligence services. The Austro-Hungarian Empire was the first to create a truly permanent office for military intelligence—the Evidenzbüro was founded in 1850, with a subordinate group, known as the Kundschaftsbüro, established to keep an eye on foreign nations. Britain followed Austria, with the Topographical and Statistical Department created during the Crimean War in 1854 (later reorganized into the War Office's Intelligence Branch in 1873); next came the French Ministry of War's Deuxième Bureau in 1871, supplemented by the national police.

THE RUSSIAN OKHRANA

Along with developments in standing intelligence departments, permanent counterintelligence offices also came into being. Spying on foreign powers was their main task, but sometimes they also suppressed internal dissent. One example was the Department for Protecting Public Security and Order, or Okhrana (the Russian word for "security"). This office was formed in 1866 in St. Petersburg, and later expanded to offices in Moscow and Warsaw in 1881, after Tsar Alexander II

was assassinated. The Okhrana cracked down hard on the terrorist group responsible along with leftist organizations, engaged in union-busting. It also allegedly drafted *The Protocols of the Elders of Zion*, a text of antisemitic propaganda.

The Okhrana's activities extended well beyond the Motherland. Its Foreign Agency spied on revolutionaries outside Russia, sent agents to foment disorder, and intercepted private letters, even deciphering British and German military and diplomatic codes. However, divided between military counterintelligence and suppressing anti-Tsarist activity during the 1904–1905 Russo-Japanese War, the Okhrana failed in both arenas. Ultimately, Russia ceased hostilities months before Japan would have entered an economic crisis, and growing revolutionary forces were emboldened by the Okhrana's attempts to stop them. Japan ultimately gained greater dominance over the western Pacific. The Okhrana itself was dissolved after its headquarters were looted and burned by revolutionaries in 1917.

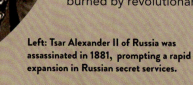

Left: Tsar Alexander II of Russia was assassinated in 1881, prompting a rapid expansion in Russian secret services.

THE DREYFUS AFFAIR

In 1894, French Army captain Alfred Dreyfus was imprisoned in French Guiana on espionage charges. Dreyfus's conviction was based on a single message found by a spy in the German Embassy in Paris, mentioning delivery of French military secrets. It was never established that it was written by Dreyfus, who maintained his innocence throughout. Nationalism and anti-Semitism were both motivating factors behind the prosecution of Dreyfus, an Alsatian Jew, and he was also linked to rumors of homosexuality. In 1896, the real traitor, Major Ferdinand Esterhazy, was discovered by Lieutenant Colonel Georges Picquart, head of the Deuxième Bureau, who refused to conceal the truth despite pressure from military officials who simply wanted the whole matter to go away. Dreyfus was pardoned after several years in prison, but the scandal was badly divisive to French society, and had repercussions internationally. After covering the trial, and disgusted by the anti-Semitism that accompanied it, the Austro-Hungarian journalist Theodore Herzl created the Zionist Congress, with the ultimate goal to establish a Jewish state.

Above: Alfred Dreyfus

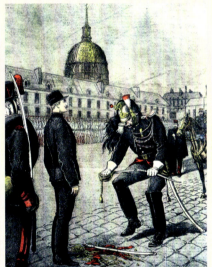

Above: This image of Dreyfus's degradation appeared on the cover of Paris newspaper *Le Petit Journal*, captioned "The Traitor."

> **"IT IS A CRIME TO POISON THE MINDS OF THE MEEK AND THE HUMBLE, TO STOKE THE PASSIONS OF REACTIONISM AND INTOLERANCE, BY APPEALING TO THAT ODIOUS ANTI-SEMITISM THAT, UNCHECKED, WILL DESTROY THE FREEDOM-LOVING FRANCE OF THE RIGHTS OF MAN."**

Émile Zola, *J'accuse!*, an open letter in defense of Alfred Dreyfus

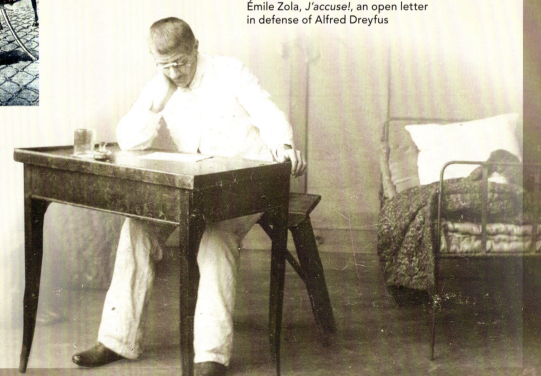

Right: Dreyfuss in his quarters at the notorious Devil's Island penal colony in 1898.

BRITANNIA CHALLENGED: THE CREATION OF MI5 AND MI6

Throughout most of the nineteenth century, the powerful Royal Navy had seemed sufficient to protect British interests. But in the early 1900s, a new anxiety arose in Britain that its security was being undermined by threats at home and abroad.

The rapid expansion of the Imperial German Navy in the early years of the twentieth century caused alarm in Britain, its position of naval supremacy under threat from a potentially hostile power. This alarm grew into a paranoia—stoked by the popular press—that Germany was preparing to invade Britain, and that there must be an army of German spies already operating in the country to aid the invasion attempt. It was against this background that Britain created an organized intelligence and security service.

The Secret Intelligence Bureau was formed in 1909, with military and naval sections. A year later, they were divided into two separate organizations. The military section became a security service responsible for counterespionage in Britain (later designated Military Intelligence 5, or MI5), and the naval section was uprated into a secret intelligence service, running agents abroad (subsequently MI6).

Right: Kaiser Wilhelm II came to the throne in 1888 with a long-term plan to expand Germany's navy.

MONITORING GERMANS

The first head of MI5 was Captain Vernon Kell, a man of limited intellectual horizons but an efficient administrator with a knack for empire building. MI5 initially consisted of a single office, a desk, and one filing cabinet—plus Kell and seven assistants. Working closely with the police, who provided much of the manpower, Kell set about compiling an "Alien Register"—a list of foreigners in the country that, by 1914, had grown to a figure of 16,000 (11,000 of them German). MI5 received its first lucky break in 1911 when the police became suspicious of a German journalist named Max Schultz.

Above: Vernon Kell

Below: The SMS König Albert, pictured in 1913, a heavily armed Kaiser-class battleship that strengthened the German navy.

Shultz's correspondence was intercepted. He had been sending reports about the Royal Navy to a German intelligence officer in Berlin, Gustav Steiner, via a forwarding agent in London. The agent was found to be Gustav Neumann, a German waiter. From then on, Neumann's mail was read by MI5, and many spies were identified. Twelve were arrested in 1912, and many others monitored for eventual arrest on the declaration of war in August 1914.

SPYING IN EUROPE

The secret intelligence service, or MI6, got off to slower start than MI5. Its first chief was Mansfield Cumming, a retired Royal Navy officer. Cumming was something of an eccentric. He wrote only in green ink, loved wearing disguises, and, after losing a leg in a motor accident, dashed around the corridors of Whitehall with his wooden leg balanced on a child's scooter. Establishing a network of spies in continental Europe was a time-consuming and difficult business, and on more than one occasion MI6 spies were duped by mercenary agents exploiting their lack of field experience.

Despite the setbacks, by 1914, the beginnings of a spy network had been established in Rotterdam and Brussels, with British businessmen abroad also providing information gleaned from their German clients. Thus, on the eve of the great conflict, MI6 joined MI5 in being ready to exploit the intelligence opportunities that a total war would provide.

Above: Mansfield Cumming

GERMAN SPIES IN BRITAIN

The idea that Britain was swarming with German spies was a figment of popular imagination. German military intelligence had little interest in Britain and there were no plans for an invasion. While the German army was focused on war with France and Russia, German naval intelligence did, however, demonstrate a lively curiosity in technical information about the Royal Navy and news of any fleet movements. Intelligence officer Gustav Steinhauer organized a small but significant espionage operation around Britain's naval ports and dockyards. Most of his spies were drawn from Germans already resident in Britain, although their intelligence was of limited value. This changed with the recruitment of George Parrott, a Royal Navy gunnery officer. Parrott provided solid information of real value, but he was arrested by MI5 in its 1912 spy swoop. Thereafter, the supply of intelligence steadily declined.

THE ROAD TO WAR

Above: Franz Ferdinand and his wife Sophie

The most fateful assassination in history took place in the small Balkan city of Sarajevo on June 28, 1914. Archduke Franz Ferdinand—the heir to the Austro-Hungarian throne—and his wife were shot and killed by a Serb nationalist, setting in motion a chain of events that would lead to the outbreak of World War I.

In 1914, Europe was divided into two armed camps: France and Russia ranged against Germany and Austria-Hungary. Britain, the other major European power, remained outside the formal alliance system but maintained friendly relations with France.

Each state was keen to discover the military strengths and strategies and diplomatic intentions of its opponents (and allies), but at this time good intelligence was patchy and what existed was not always acted upon in the best manner. France and, especially, Russia had the superior intelligence services, gaining results from their black chamber decrypting departments.

The diplomatic crisis that engulfed Europe in July 1914 was a direct consequence of the events in Sarajevo. The new state of Serbia had been created from the collapse of the Turkish empire in the Balkans, although substantial numbers of Serbs lived in territories that remained under Austrian control, including Bosnia-Herzegovina. Serb nationalists were determined to incorporate these areas into Serbia, even though they contained many other ethnic groups as well as the Slavic Serbs.

TREACHERY IN HIGH PLACES

From a humble background, Alfred Redl used his ability and ambition to rise through the Austro-Hungarian army. In 1900, he was assigned to the Russian section of the army's intelligence bureau, and seven years later he became chief of its counterintelligence branch with the rank of colonel. Redl was a homosexual with a taste for the good life well beyond his modest salary, and in 1901, he was blackmailed by Russian intelligence to work for them as a spy. From then on, Redl provided the Russians with a massive array of intelligence, which included Austria's plans for invading Serbia and details of Austrian mobilization plans against Russia. In 1913, Redl's treachery was discovered. Admitting his guilt, he was left alone with a loaded revolver. He duly shot himself.

Right: Alfred Redl

MURDER IN SARAJEVO

Black Hand leader Dragutin Dimitrijevic assembled an assassination team during the spring of 1914. Armed with bombs and revolvers, six assassins lined the route that Archduke Franz Ferdinand's motorcade would take, from Sarajevo's rail station to the town hall. On the way to the town hall one of the assassins threw a bomb at the Archduke's motor vehicle but it bounced off and blew up the following vehicle. The Archduke, however, carried on to the town hall to give his speech. On his return, his driver took a wrong turn and was forced to come to a halt near one of the other assassins, Gavrilo Princip. Seizing his moment, Princip leapt onto the car's running board and fired two shots that mortally wounded Franz Ferdinand and his wife.

Above: Dragutin Dimitrijevic

Right: Gavrilo Princip

Below: Archduke Franz Ferdinand and his wife leave the Sarajevo Guildhall on June 28, 1914. They were assassinated five minutes later.

STRIVING FOR A GREATER SERBIA

The Black Hand, a secret society devoted to forging a Greater Serbia, was formed in 1911. One of its leading lights was Dragutin Dimitrijevic, an army intelligence officer, who drew up the plans to assassinate Franz Ferdinand. The Archduke planned to grant a degree of autonomy to the Serbs in Bosnia. This would have weakened the nationalists' demands for the incorporation of Bosnia into a Slav-led Serbia.

Following the death of Franz Ferdinand, Austria accused the Serbian government of responsibility. A harsh and humiliating ultimatum was delivered to the Serbian government, which, to the surprise of many, met virtually all the terms. This was insufficient for Austria, however, which declared war on Serbia on July 28, 1914.

This marked the beginning of a wider conflict. Russia, an ally of Serbia, mobilized its army on July 30, while on August 1, Germany came to the aid of Austria by mobilizing its forces and declaring war on Russia. Two days later, Germany declared war on France and advanced into Belgium. Britain, a co-signatory to Belgium's neutrality, declared war on Germany on August 4. Europe was at war.

"WE DESTROYED A BEAUTIFUL WORLD THAT WAS LOST FOREVER DUE TO THE WAR THAT FOLLOWED."

Vaso Cubrilovic, a conspirator's subsequent regret over the Archduke's assassination

— CHAPTER 4 —

DECEIT AND DIRTY TRICKS

World War I marked the beginning of a new era of mechanized warfare. A conflict that both sides had believed would be "over by Christmas" dragged on for more than four years, leaving tens of millions dead. As the technology of war developed, so did the technology of espionage, with radio and telegraph messages and, for the first time, reconnaissance from the air. Behind the lines, resistance groups in occupied Belgium and France kept a clandestine record of German troop movements via rail. The speed and quality of the intelligence proved so good that it contributed to the stalemate, preventing either side from mounting a decisive surprise attack.

Improved cryptography was key to intelligence in this new kind of war. With the volume of transmissions possible via new technology, teams of talented individuals were recruited to decode them. In 1917, British intelligence triggered a decisive change in the course of the war by decoding a German telegram that provoked the United States to join the Allies' cause. That same year, the Germans secretly colluded with Bolshevik revolutionaries in order to take Russia out of the war. By November 1918, Europe was exhausted by the carnage, and an armistice was declared. By then, Russia had been through a communist revolution, while Germany seemed on the brink of one.

A NEW TYPE OF WAR

World War I involved dozens of nations in conflict on an unprecedented scale. Various technologies developed rapidly, including machine guns, air combat, chemical weapons, and trench warfare, all of which left their devastating mark. The impact of this "war to end all wars" extended well beyond new methods of fighting. The growing complexity of military data that accompanied the new hardware was such that espionage needed to develop to match it, from more secure forms of cryptography to the interception of new forms of communication.

STARTING TRANSMISSION

Prior to the twentieth century, espionage had largely been based on human intelligence (HUMINT)—the gathering of data from in-person observation. However, with the development of new methods of communication, including radio, the gathering and deciphering of intelligence from communications signals, or SIGINT, became increasingly important. Electronic communication was a nascent technology, and the first known SIGINT success had been recorded with the British interception of Russian radio messages during the Russo-Japanese War in 1904. In 1914, Germany's encrypted declaration of war was almost immediately decrypted by the French. This was a sign of what was to come.

NEW TECHNIQUES, NEW TROUBLES

Radio and telephone messages were deemed vital by all sides in the conflict for effective command. However, most soldiers and politicians underestimated the extent to which their messages could be intercepted and decoded, or disrupted. Telegram and telephone lines could be severed, and the British broke German undersea cables at the outbreak of the war, thus forcing messages to go through networks that could be more easily eavesdropped, such as Britain's own telegram system. Wireless connections afforded by the new radio technology could also be tapped into. The German "Moritz" apparatus was a signal amplifier connected to a set of copper terminals. British soldiers crept into No Man's Land under cover of darkness, and attached the Moritz to telephone or telegram lines leading to directly to British command centers. Unencrypted radio transmissions could easily be picked up by simply tuning into the right channel, if one had a wireless, knew the frequency, and could understand the language being spoken. Instructions to encode messages were often lost or not followed due to a lack of understanding of its importance.

Above: A German soldier talks on a telephone attached to a tree.

Below: Three British and French soldiers observe German positions with binoculars while a fourth communicates with artillery via a field telephone.

HUMAN ERROR

In the first month of the war, the outcome of the Battle of Tannenberg between Russia and Germany was decided in part by a combination of technological shortfalls and human error. Russian command had limited supplies of cable to lay down for telephone and telegram communications, and had to rely on radio, but they were also short on copies of their new codebooks. Messages were sent in the clear, uncoded, with nothing protecting them but the hope that they would not be picked up. The combined equipment shortage and poor comms discipline meant that enough Russian messages were intercepted to determine their troop movements and, ultimately, a German victory. This devastating defeat led to the almost complete destruction of the Russian Second Army, causing the Russians to retreat from East Prussia.

PARANOID DELUSIONS?

As intelligence work gained greater priority, various nations likewise increased their anti-spying efforts. Spies were arrested, imprisoned, and even executed, sometimes in retaliation for defeats that were blamed on espionage. However, these anti-espionage efforts often spilled over into paranoia. For example, shepherds northeast of Paris were arrested by the French authorities for moving their flocks in patterns thought to be signals for German observers, while artists were interrogated for daring to sketch the countryside. In England, renowned Irish artist John Lavery was arrested for painting a naval port, having been commissioned to do so by the Admiralty as an official war artist!

That said, to misquote Philip K. Dick, just because you're paranoid doesn't mean they're not after intel. In an innovative move, Dutch windmills were stopped and started in a seemingly haphazard fashion that concealed Morse code signals to German forces, while Belgian train engineers opened and closed their engines' fireboxes at night to send light-based Morse code messages to British agents in the Netherlands. The idea of spy-sheep wasn't quite as ridiculous as it might have sounded.

ROOM 40

From 1914 onward, British cryptography was centered around a group of gifted civilians operating in high secrecy from cramped offices in London. Known as "Room 40," they provided a stream of reliable intelligence to the Royal Navy, and helped to change the course of the war in 1917 by decoding the Zimmerman letter that brought the US into the conflict (see pages 74–75).

Above: Reginald "Blinker" Hall

The day after declaring war on Germany on August 5, 1914, Britain sent out ships to cut its new enemy's undersea telegraph cables. This left Germany highly reliant on radio communications, which could easily be tracked by British listening posts. The messages were secured by codes, which needed to be broken. This led to the formation later that year of a dedicated codebreaking team, based in a set of interlocking offices called "Room 40" in the British Admiralty in London.

SOLVING PUZZLES

The British military had largely dispensed with codebreakers since the Crimean War sixty years earlier, meaning that they had to start from scratch in 1914. This gave them the chance to select gifted individuals from the civilian world. At its peak, Room 40 employed 800 wireless operators and ninety codebreakers, led by the idiosyncratic Captain Reginald "Blinker" Hall, nicknamed after his pronounced facial twitch. Hall collected some of the most inventive puzzle solvers from a wide variety of fields, including scientists, lawyers, schoolteachers, and professors.

Room 40's first task was to break German naval codes. In this, they were helped by a stroke of good fortune when British naval intelligence acquired three German naval codebooks. They supplemented this information with coded German maps

Below: A German U-boat

passed to the Admiralty by the Russians. The first notable success came in January 1915, when Room 40 decoded messages outlining plans to attack British fishing boats in the North Sea, information that contributed decisively to the British victory in the ensuing Battle of Dogger Bank.

TRACKING GERMAN MOVEMENTS

In addition to breaking codes, analysts at Room 40 developed a system of traffic analysis to track the movements of German ships. They did this by locating the origin of radio signals. By pinpointing the positions of U-boats, Room 40 was able to identify the British ships most vulnerable to attack. However, this left the Admiralty with a dilemma, as acting on every piece of information would tip off the Germans to Room 40's existence. Such misgivings often led to delays in relaying information to the fleet admirals, who missed the chance for a number of possible victories in the North Sea. Nevertheless, its highly reliable information continued to prove vital throughout the war.

LOUD AND CLEAR!

By the end of the war, Room 40 had decrypted around fifteen thousand German communications. The huge volume of messages available had been aided by the German ships' habit of communicating frequently and transmitting at full power. British ships, by contrast, were instructed to use the radio only sparingly and to keep transmission power to a minimum. The Germans finally changed their habits in 1917, suspecting that the British were using signals to locate ships but still unaware that their messages were being read. The success of Room 40 came from the combination of the brilliance of its members and the strict secrecy that kept its very existence under wraps.

Left:
Alfred Ewing

UNASSUMING AMATEURS

The cryptographers at Room 40 could best be described as gifted amateurs. Initially, the group was managed by Scottish physicist Alfred Ewing, who worked on the properties of metals before the war, constructing ciphers as a hobby. The three men who successfully decoded the Zimmerman letter were a typically eclectic group. William Montgomery had made his name translating theological works from German. Alfred "Dilly" Knox was a classics scholar at King's College, Cambridge, specializing in the study of ancient manuscripts written on papyrus. Book editor and linguist Nigel de Grey, meanwhile, was so small and shy that he was nicknamed "the dormouse." These unassuming, bookish individuals set the gold standard for wartime cryptography departments—highly gifted civilians working in top secret— that would famously be repeated in World War II at Bletchley Park (see pages 126–127), at which de Grey would also work.

AN EYE IN THE SKY

World War I was the first major conflict in which aircraft played a leading role. Ace fighter pilots engaged in daring one-on-one dogfights to become national heroes, and later in the war, the first bombing missions were undertaken. However, the key strategic value of aircraft lay in reconnaissance and observation, and it was here that they had a profound effect on the course of the war. Aircraft provided intelligence on enemy positions in close to "real time." This new level of information was a major factor in creating the drawn-out stalemate of trench warfare.

Above: A birdlike German Taube aircraft flying over French positions.

> **"VICTORY SMILES UPON THOSE WHO ANTICIPATE THE CHANGE IN THE CHARACTER OF WAR, NOT UPON THOSE WHO WAIT TO ADAPT THEMSELVES AFTER THE CHANGES OCCUR."**

Giulio Douhet, Italian general and theorist on air power

Before World War I, reconnaissance was generally carried out by the cavalry. However, it could take up to two days for the information from cavalry scouts to reach headquarters, and cavalry could not cross enemy trenches. That time delay was cut to a matter of an hour or so using aircraft, which could also report on activities many miles behind the lines.

At the start of the war, the Germans and the Allies both had several hundred reconnaissance aircraft. They matched one another for aerial intelligence on the Western Front, and this quickly led to stalemate—each side able to anticipate and counter any moves on the flanks. The utility of the planes was quickly recognized, and aircraft production was placed into overdrive by both sides—by the end of the war, more than two hundred thousand had been made, and technological advances for these new machines were rapid.

RACE TO THE SEA

Between September and November in 1914, the trenches at the front extended for more than four hundred miles (650 km) from the Swiss border to the North Sea in a grim

"Race to the Sea." Casualties were enormous, but neither side could gain an advantage. It was clear that the war was going to be a long and bloody affair, due in no small part to the new "Eyes in the Sky."

From 1915 onward, the reconnaissance planes were equipped with the latest photographic technology, and they returned thousands of images, which could later be assembled as a mosaic showing a complete picture of the enemy lines. New images would be compared with photos from previous missions to identify any changes in position. In addition to cameras, the planes were equipped with radio, transmitting messages via Morse code to direct artillery fire to targets up to ten miles (16 km) behind the front lines. These heavily equipped aircraft were large and slow and made easy targets, so they were accompanied by armed fighters for protection.

LIGHTER THAN AIR

Lighter-than-air craft of various kinds played an important role in World War I. Observation balloons were used in large numbers along the static Western Front. These tethered balloons were filled with hydrogen gas and rose up to a mile (1.6 km) above the ground. Crews of observers reported to the ground via radio, directing artillery fire.

The static observation balloons were sitting targets and required constant protection from antiaircraft guns on the ground and fighter aircraft in the skies. Fighter pilots were awarded "aces" for shooting down balloons, and pilots with five or more aces were known as "balloon busters." Filled with highly flammable hydrogen, the balloons would explode into flames when hit, and the observers wore parachutes in case of the need for a hasty abandonment. (By contrast, aircraft pilots did not wear parachutes—they went down with their planes, and the average life expectancy for pilots during the war has been estimated at just 92 flying hours.)

In addition to balloons, both sides also used airships for reconnaissance. The German navy initially deployed Zeppelins on scouting missions. Later in the war, these huge dirigibles, which were capable of covering long distances, would carry out bombing missions over Britain, providing a foretaste of the terror that would be inflicted on civilian populations in World War II. The Zeppelins were also equipped with cameras to conduct reconnaissance.

Above: Lt. A. De Bathe Brandon attacking Zeppelin raiders over England on March 31, 1916. The New Zealand pilot Brandon was awarded the Military Cross for the action.

Left: A German Parseval-Siegsfeld balloon from 1916. The kite shape made the balloons more stable in poor weather than spherical balloons.

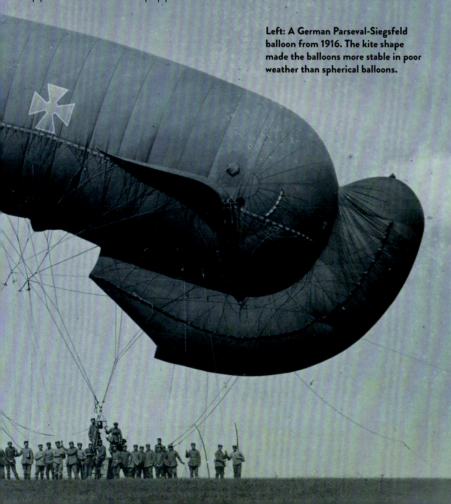

AERIAL INTELLIGENCE AT THE BATTLE OF MONS

The aerial arm of the British Army at the start of World War I was known as the Royal Flying Corps (RFC). The RFC's initial squadrons, comprising 60 aircraft, flew into France on August 13, 1914. Within days, the planes were making vital contributions to military intelligence, observing on August 22 the approach of the Germans toward the flank of the British Expeditionary Force in Belgium. This information allowed the British to realign troops around the town of Mons. While the British were forced to retreat following the Battle of Mons the next day, information from planes flying behind the lines helped them to inflict heavy casualties on the advancing German army, then allowed them to fall back in good order despite being outnumbered by three to one. With improved intelligence from the air preventing a decisive victory to either side, this first major encounter between the British and Germans set the tone for the rest of the war.

Above: An RFC C-Type aircraft reconnaissance camera

THE ARAB BUREAU

In 1915, British forces were fighting the Ottoman Empire on several different fronts in the Middle East, with lines of command through both the UK and India and little exchange of information between battlefields. The Arab Bureau was set up in 1916 to remedy this situation. The Bureau was also charged with disseminating propaganda among the Arab forces that were rebelling against Ottoman rule. It proved itself to be a first-rate intelligence unit, adeptly synthesizing information from a variety of sources to provide accurate information about the complex situation in the Middle East.

Left: T.E. Lawrence (left) worked on digs in Syria before the war alongside prominent archaeologist Leonard Woolley (right).

The Bureau worked out of the Savoy Hotel in Cairo, Egypt, then under the control of the British. Led by Brigadier Gilbert Clayton, the Bureau drew upon a wide range of talents both military and civilian, including several archaeologists, such as T.E. Lawrence, Gertrude Bell, and David Hogarth. Archaeologists have a skill set that could have been tailor-made for spying. Their day job provides the perfect cover story, while they have detailed knowledge of the local culture and speak the local languages fluently. Moreover, archaeologists are readymade experts in cracking codes—from hieroglyphics to cuneiform inscriptions—and indeed the Arab Bureau proved adept at intercepting Ottoman messages and breaking their codes.

THE ARAB BULLETIN

The Arab Bureau assimilated the information from intercepted messages with human intelligence from agents in the field. They condensed this intel into a series of concise reports called the Arab Bulletin. In total, 114 issues of the Arab Bulletin were produced between 1916 and 1919. Just thirty copies of each issue were printed, to be distributed among a small number of high-ranking officers, and not to be quoted under any circumstances to maintain its secrecy.

LAWRENCE OF ARABIA

Immortalized on celluloid in David Lean's lavish epic *Lawrence of Arabia*, the story of T.E. Lawrence (1888–1935) is an intriguing mix of fact and legend, much of the mythology created by Lawrence himself. Having worked in Syria before the war as an archaeologist, Lawrence was recruited to the Arab Bureau for his expertise in Arab culture. In Cairo, he supervised the preparation of maps, edited the bulletins, and interviewed prisoners.

Along with several other British officers, Lawrence also liaised directly with Arab forces fighting the Ottomans, working closely with Emir Faisal, the third son of the Sharif of Mecca who would later become the first King of Iraq. Lawrence took part directly in a number of military operations during the Arab Revolt, including the capture of Damascus in October 1918, but his influence on the outcome of the conflict was probably limited. His subsequent fame rests largely on footage shot by American broadcaster Lowell Thomas, who also took iconic photographs of Lawrence in Arabian dress. Lawrence also wrote about his war experiences in the book *Seven Pillars of Wisdom*.

Above: T.E. Lawrence in 1918

SUPPORTING THE REVOLT

The first Bulletin, edited by Lawrence, appeared in June 1916, a few days after the uprising that became known as the Arab Revolt had begun in Mecca. This military revolt, led by the Sharif of Mecca Hussein bin Ali, was intended to expel the Ottomans from Arab lands and create a single Arab state stretching from Syria in the north to Yemen in the south. The British backed Hussein's army, providing it with weapons and training, and promising that they would recognize the unified Arab state once the Ottomans had been defeated. However, it was a promise that the British secretly planned to break right from the start, and former Ottoman provinces would be divided between Britain and France following the war.

Above: Sharif Hussein in 1916, at the time that he started the Arab Revolt.

Unaware of the intended betrayal by the British, Lawrence and others in the Bureau ran intelligence operations in support of the Arab Revolt and documented its progress in the Arab Bulletin. They saw their documents not only as invaluable military intelligence but also as an important historical record of the events unfolding in the peninsula. However, they were regarded as pro-Arab idealists and dilettantes by many within the British establishment, and the Arab Bureau received a great deal of blame for the chaotic events in the region following the war. Nevertheless, the information provided by the Arab Bureau was to prove crucial in some of the final battles of the war, including aerial reconnaissance to support the successful Megiddo offensive of 1918. Among the innovations championed by the Bureau, it pioneered the use of aerial photography as a means of charting unknown territories. At Lawrence's suggestion, aerial photography would be used after the war to chart the British Mandate of Palestine and resolve issues of land registration.

"THE PRINTING PRESS IS THE GREATEST WEAPON IN THE ARMORY OF THE MODERN COMMANDER."

T.E. Lawrence

Above: Gertrude Bell on an archaeological dig in Iraq in 1909

GERTRUDE BELL

Like T.E. Lawrence, explorer and archaeologist Gertrude Bell (1868–1926) graduated with first-class honors in history from the University of Oxford before embarking on a career of Orientalism. Fluent in Arabic, Turkish, and Persian, Bell was the only female political officer in the British forces during World War I. She would travel the desert visiting the courts of various sheikhs, taking with her an extravagant retinue with her own bath and bed, a Wedgewood dinner service, and couture gowns for the evening—plus concealed guns and secret camera films. Beneath the exterior of a privileged British colonialist, Bell demonstrated an intricate understanding of the Arab tribal system and gathered a wide range of intelligence. After the war, Bell was instrumental in the formation of the new state of Iraq.

THE FRENCH CONNECTION

When some people think of spies in the modern era, they might envision suave European agents and operatives bent on seduction and stealing secrets. James Bond himself may be fictional, but the style of his exploits goes all the way back to World War I and France's Second Bureau.

GETTING A "SECOND" OPINION

No war is fought by combat alone. Effective military actions must be backed by effective intelligence efforts. As *The Art of War* states, "If you know yourself, and know your enemy, you need not fear the results of a hundred battles." This maxim was particularly proven by France's intelligence services: the First Bureau, which dealt with domestic and allied troop data, and especially the Second Bureau, which handled cryptanalysis and enemy intelligence to both great and ignoble effect.

SHAKY BEGINNINGS

Founded in 1871 to research enemy operations, the Second Bureau was named similarly to other continental nations' intelligence "desks" (with the first handling personnel, the second working with foreign intel, and so on). It was later closed in 1894 and its duties assigned elsewhere after it, along with many other French governing offices, was affected by the "Dreyfus Affair"—a highly politically divisive antisemitic scandal involving the imprisonment of, Alfred Dreyfus, a Jewish French artillery captain falsely accused of selling military secrets to Germany (see page 57).

Reopened in 1907 by Prime Minister Georges Clemenceau and reassigned its original counterespionage duties, the Second Bureau was headed by Commandant George Ladoux from 1914 on through the Great War. The bureau proved itself in several cryptographic triumphs, including deciphering German diplomatic codes. This victory led to another

Left: French prime minister Georges Clemenceau

massive scoop: the interception of Germany's war declaration before even the German ambassador in Paris could decode the telegram himself. The business of cryptography was a vital part of the war effort for every nation involved, and solving Germany's declaration of war was only the beginning for the French Second Bureau.

CODE CRACKERS

Two of the best cryptologists in France were Étienne Bazeries and Georges Painvin, both of whom went on to further accomplishments in both the creation and breaking of encryption.

Bazeries was a veteran of the Franco-Prussian War (1870–1871) who became interested in codes after solving cryptograms in the local newspaper. After solving French military codes in 1890 and forcing the War Ministry to adopt a new system, he exposed more flaws in French ciphers, and decoded "Le Grand Chiffre," the "Great Cipher" developed in the 1600s. In 1891, he was made part of the Ministry of Foreign Affairs' Bureau de Chiffre. He retired from military service in 1899 and, in 1901, published *Les Chiffres Secrets Dévoilés* ("The Secret Ciphers Unveiled"). The book is considered a landmark text in cryptography to this day, and was one of the reasons he was called up from retirement after the Second Bureau was reassembled.

Georges Painvin was one of Bazeries' contemporaries in the Bureau, and his cryptanalysis ultimately saved Paris near the end of the war. In June of 1918, the German army was only sixty miles (100 km) from the city, and the Allies were still uncertain of the details of the incipient offensive. Germany was using a cipher called ADFGVX, and Painvin had been hard at work trying to break the code—such was his focus and the stress of the task that he lost 33 pounds (15 kg) before he finally solved one short message: "Rush munitions. Even by day if not seen." This fragment was the key to determining the location of Germany's attack, which was repelled by Allied forces.

DOUBLE AGENTS . . . OR NOT

Spy fiction and fact alike wouldn't be complete without the presence of yet another archetype, this one known for working multiple espionage angles. The Second Bureau's head, George Ladoux, and one of history's most famous figures, Mata Hari, were both accused of double-agency during the war. Ladoux was responsible for recruiting Mata Hari as a spy after meeting her in 1916, and was later accused of being a double agent himself, before being cleared of all charges.

Mata Hari was less fortunate than her boss. Born in Holland as Margarethe Zelle, she married a Dutch Colonial Army captain and moved to Indonesia with him. She left her husband after years of domestic violence and infidelity, remaking herself as Mata Hari, an avant-garde dancer who had studied "sacred temple dances." Her sensual performances across Europe led to affairs with several wealthy suitors desiring an "exotic" mistress, but after the war began, her belongings and bank accounts were confiscated in Germany following a trip to France. Mata Hari was first offered money to be a spy for the Kaiser, then later, when she crossed paths with Ladoux, given the same offer on behalf of France. She apparently never performed any spy missions, but was found communicating with her German handler in February 1917 and arrested in Paris. The prosecution's evidence was just circumstantial, but with her many affairs with German and other officers, Mata Hari was used as a scapegoat for thousands of Allied casualties, and she was executed by firing squad in November of the same year.

Left: Mata Hari

A LEG UP ON THE KAISER

American mining engineer and adventurer Howard Burnham worked for French intelligence during World War I. With just one leg and suffering from tuberculosis, Burnham made an unlikely spy. In 1917, he crossed enemy lines to find out whether Germany intended to open a new southern front in the Alps. Using the cover of his illness, Burnham toured sanitoria in search of information. He put his engineering skills to good use, converting household goods into surveying instruments, which he hid inside his wooden leg. As his health worsened, Burnham crossed from Germany into neutral Switzerland. From there, he was taken to Cannes, where he revealed on his deathbed that Germany was not preparing an Alpine front.

THE ZIMMERMANN TELEGRAM

Above: German Foreign Minister Arthur Zimmermann

At the height of World War I, in early 1917, the Germans decided to restart their U-boat offensive against Allied shipping in order to force Britain and France to terms. However, the Germans understood that this action could provoke the United States into joining the Allied cause. In an effort to prevent this, German Foreign Secretary Arthur Zimmermann sent a coded telegram to the Mexican premier, Venustiano Carranza, via the German Embassy in Washington, D.C. He proposed an audacious plan to distract the Americans. Intercepting and decoding the telegram was a major coup for the British, as it drew the hitherto isolationist United States into the war against Germany.

AN AUDACIOUS OFFER

The scheme concocted by German Foreign Minister Arthur Zimmermann (pictured above) was to distract the United States by supporting Mexico in launching a cross-border offensive to recapture its nineteenth-century losses in the American Southwest. Further, the Mexicans would also invite Japan to launch an offensive against the United States across the Pacific. He proposed an alliance between Germany and Mexico, with Germany promising to help Mexico regain Texas, Arizona, and New Mexico in return for supporting the German side should the US enter the war.

Once the contents were revealed, Zimmerman eventually admitted, on March 3, that the telegram was authentic and this helped to inflame anti-German sentiment in the US. This decryption was not only one of Britain's greatest intelligence triumphs during World War I but, indeed, one of the first occasions in which a piece of signal intelligence would influence world events to such a degree.

PULLING TOGETHER A NETWORK OF CLUES

The route of Zimmermann's telegram was his undoing. The British had severed Germany's transatlantic cables at the beginning of the war, meaning that the telegram was sent to Washington via Sweden and Britain. The intercepted telegram was passed to Room 40, the British decoding office under the command of Captain Reginald Hall, where the Presbyterian Reverend William Montgomery and Nigel de Grey, a peacetime publisher, were the first to attack it. The specific code used had first been issued in July 1916. To add to the difficulty, it was enciphered. Room 40 had been working on the code through intercepts for about six months. However, they had some clues. Their Russian allies

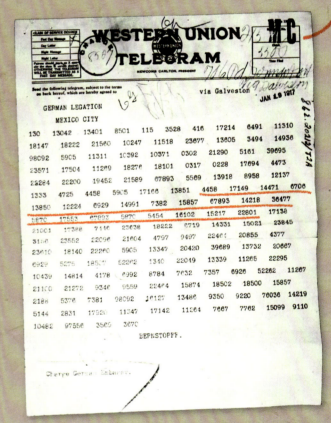

Above: Zimmermann's telegram

had captured a German codebook early in the war, having sunk the German light cruiser *Magdeburg* in the Baltic, and had shared its contents. Also, Wilhelm Wassmuss, a German agent planning to foment an anti-British rising among the Turkish tribes in Persia, had been briefly arrested in Behbahan in 1915, and his belongings had been returned to London. Room 40 now possessed the

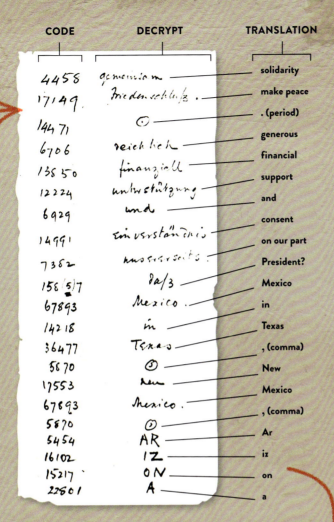

CODE	DECRYPT	TRANSLATION
4458	gemeinsam	solidarity
17149	Friedenschluss.	make peace
14471	⊙	. (period)
6706	reichlich	generous
13850	finanziell	financial
12224	unterstützung	support
6929	und	and
14991	einverständnis	consent
7382	unsererseits.	on our part
158/5/7	da/3	President?
67893	Mexico.	Mexico
14218	in	in
36477	Texas	Texas
5870	⊙	, (comma)
17553	New	New
67893	Mexico.	Mexico
5870	⊙	, (comma)
5454	AR	Ar
16102	IZ	iz
15217	ON	on
22801	A	a

Right: The scratch pad

Magdeburg military codebook and Wassmuss's diplomatic codebook, which contained an earlier version of the cipher used in the Zimmermann telegram. But these provided only partial clues.

DECIPHERING THE TELEGRAM

Arthur Zimmermann's telegram used a standard military numeric code, which relied on the receiver possessing the correct codebook for that day. Room 40 had to piece together scraps of information from the two captured codebooks. To crack the code, Hall's team in Room 40 concentrated on attempting to identify strings of consecutive numbers that appeared on the telegram.

The scratch pad produced by de Grey and Montgomery was based on partial clues provided by the Magdeburg and Wassmuss codebooks. Much of their interpretation was based more on deduction and lateral thinking than cryptanalysis. Nevertheless, they decrypted enough (for example, 67893 denoted Mexico) to deduce that the telegram was of paramount importance.

The string of numbers Room 40 focused on revealed sufficient clues to enable the rest of the telegram to be unraveled and translated. It spelled out in detail Zimmermann's plan, setting him up for the big fall.

A CODE-BREAKER'S DILEMMA

The translation of the telegram presented a dilemma to the code breakers: how could they tell the Americans about it without revealing to the Germans that they had cracked their latest code? Hall realized that the German embassy must have sent the telegram across public telegraph lines from Washington to Mexico, so a British agent in Mexico City was dispatched to steal a copy. To the delight of Room 40, it was encoded not in the newer Code 0075, but in the older 13040, so the Germans would assume that the British had learned of the plot using the stolen telegram and the captured codebook. Now the British could keep their secret and send a full version of the telegram to the Americans. Isolationist US President Woodrow Wilson received the decrypted telegram on February 25. It was published on March 1, and the US declared war on Germany on April 6, 1917.

Below: The decrypted telegram

TELEGRAM RECEIVED.

FROM 2nd from London # 5747.

"We intend to begin on the first of February unrestricted submarine warfare. We shall endeavor in spite of this to keep the United States of America neutral. In the event of this not succeeding, we make Mexico a proposal of alliance on the following basis: make war together, make peace together, generous financial support and an understanding on our part that Mexico is to reconquer the lost territory in Texas, New Mexico, and Arizona. The settlement in detail is left to you. You will inform the President of the above most secretly as soon as the outbreak of war with the United States of America is certain and add the suggestion that he should, on his own initiative, invite Japan to immediate adherence and at the same time mediate between Japan and ourselves. Please call the President's attention to the fact that the ruthless employment of our submarines now offers the prospect of compelling England in a few months

BEHIND THE LINES

Belgium, Luxembourg, and parts of northern France were occupied by Germany during World War I. Resistance movements in these occupied territories made contact with the Allies, helping escaped Allied prisoners to reach neutral Holland, but their most important role involved spying on the railways. In this way, they provided crucial intelligence from behind the lines about German troop movements to and from the front.

Above: A wounded soldier is carried from a German hospital train.

At the start of the war, Germany's invasion strategy—known as the Schlieffen Plan—was to overwhelm France within a matter of weeks, deterring Britain from becoming involved before transferring troops to face Russia on the eastern front. The plan depended upon the rapid movement of troops via rail. Once it became clear that France would not be overwhelmed and both sides had dug in to their trench positions, the Allies quickly realized that intelligence about train movements would be crucial. It was a reliable way to ascertain German intentions, such was the German military's dependence on rail. However, this intelligence could not be gathered directly across the heavily fortified front. Agents living and operating behind the front were needed.

LA DAME BLANCHE

In Belgium, an extensive network of spies was established in 1916 by Walthère Dewé, a telephone engineer in Brussels. Named "La Dame Blanche" ("The White Woman") after a character in German mythology whose appearance was said to signal the fall of the king, the network comprised more than one thousand agents across Belgium and occupied France. It was an eclectic group, including several hundred women and dozens of priests. The agents secretly watched the railways day and night, producing reports that were transmitted to British intelligence agents based in Rotterdam.

Above: Walthère Dewé

By 1918, the network had grown so extensive that it was impossible for a German military convoy to reach the front without being spotted.

The head of MI6, Mansfield Cummings, estimated that seventy percent of all Allied intelligence during the war had come from La Dame Blanche. When Belgium was occupied by Germany once more in World War II, Dewé set up a similar network. He was killed attempting to avoid capture in 1944.

SPYING FROM NEUTRAL TERRITORY

Both the Allies and the Germans set up spying operations in Rotterdam during World War I, and this busy international port was briefly the spy capital of the world. As a neutral country, travel into the Netherlands was relatively easy from either side, while Dutch citizens enjoyed relatively free movement in both directions. Meanwhile, censorship in the Netherlands was minimal, and newspapers were available from both Britain and Germany.

British MI6 spies operated out of the offices of the then-defunct Uranium Steamship Company (USB), under the leadership of Richard Bolton Tinsley, a retired naval captain who had been a director of the USB. From there, Tinsley liaised with Dutch agents who brought back information from inside Germany, while army captain Walter Landau took charge of contacts with Belgian resistance fighters in La Dame Blanche. From an office just a few blocks away, German intelligence agents also recruited Dutch spies, sending them across the North Sea to track the movements of warships in British ports.

THE ALICE NETWORK

In occupied Lille in northern France, the "Alice" spy network was set up by French housekeeper Louise de Bettignies. Fluent in English, German, and Italian, de Bettignies efficiently coordinated a group of about a hundred spies and liaised with British agents, using the pseudonym Alice Dubois. The Alice Network monitored troop movements and helped Allied soldiers to escape to the Netherlands. It is thought to have saved more than one thousand British soldiers in its nine months of operation. The Alice network was brought down in October 1915 when de Bettignies was arrested. One of her final messages warned of German attack on Verdun in early 1916. Unfortunately, this intelligence was ignored by French commanders, and the Battle of Verdun would turn out to be one of the longest and bloodiest of the war. De Bettignies was sentenced to life imprisonment with forced labor, and died in prison in Cologne aged 38 on September 27, 1918, just weeks before the end of the war.

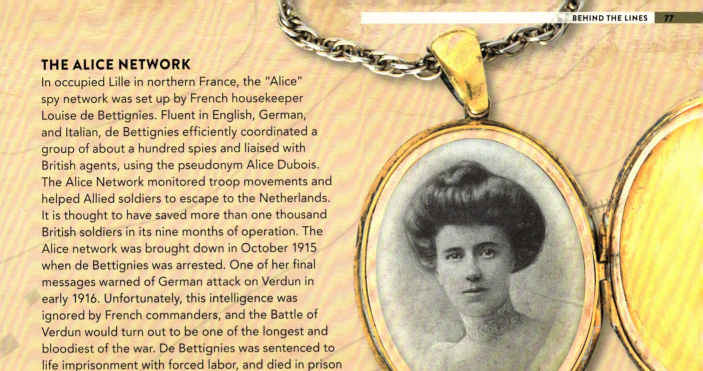

Right: Louise de Bettignies

CODED NEWSPAPER MESSAGES

In 1995, three decades after his death, the children of George Bruce, Lord Balfour, discovered among his papers documents that told a remarkable story of World War I espionage. Then a captain in the British army, Bruce had been assigned to military intelligence in Paris. There, he had recruited a woman from Luxembourg named Lise Rischard, persuading her to return home to operate as a railway spy. Rischard was joined by a Polish-Belgian soldier named Baschwitz Meau, who was flown into Luxembourg by hydrogen balloon. By 1918, Luxembourg had become a crucial rail hub for the German army. Rischard and Meau reported on train movements using, among other means, coded messages planted in newspapers. Their information helped the Allies to counter the German spring offensive that year, concentrating their forces where an attack was most likely.

Below: Rischard communicated messages about rail movements by taking out notices in newspapers.

SUPPORTING THE BOLSHEVIKS

The year 1917 saw two momentous revolutions in Russia. The first revolution removed the tsar, and shook the country. The second revolution installed a communist government, and shook the world. Victory to Lenin's Bolsheviks also saw Russia removing itself from World War I. Following the doctrine that "my enemy's enemy is my friend," the communist Bolsheviks had found an unlikely ally in their struggle for power—imperialist Germany.

By the start of 1917, Russians had grown weary of war, with casualties numbering six million. There was widespread hunger at home, and soldiers were deserting by their thousands at the front. Tsar Nicholas II had taken personal control of the war in 1915, and was personally associated with its failures. At home, his wife the Tsarina Alexandra—herself a German—had been left in control. She had proved a weak, ineffective, and distrusted ruler, seen as under the spell of her personal confidant, the strange mystic Grigori Rasputin.

THE TSAR FALLS

Having lost support from all sectors of society, the monarchy fell in the February Revolution, replaced by a broad-based Provisional Government. A few days later, news of the revolution reached Zurich, Switzerland, where a group of radical exiles planned their return home. They were led by Vladimir Ilych Ulyanov—better known by his *nom de guerre* Lenin. Lenin's communist Bolsheviks promised an end to the war, and he found a willing ally in the German government, which was eager to ease the burden of fighting on two fronts.

Above: Lenin in Switzerland

Above: Tsar Nicholas II under arrrest

Above: Alexander Kerensky

Just days earlier, the US had entered the war, bringing renewed urgency to the German desire to end fighting on the Eastern Front. The Americans had been swift to recognize the Provisional Government of Alexander Kerensky, and were keen to keep Russia in the war. Lenin, by contrast, promoted a strategy of "revolutionary defeatism," in which Bolsheviks would join the army and encourage the men to mutiny. This idea suited Germany just fine—a means to defeat an enemy from within.

"LENIN'S ENTRY INTO RUSSIA WAS A SUCCESS. HE IS WORKING ACCORDING TO YOUR WISHES."

Note to German High Command on Lenin's arrival in Petrograd

LENIN'S RETURN

On April 9, Lenin and thirty-one comrades boarded the train that would take them across Germany to eventually enter Russia via Finland. A band of Russian emigrés had gathered at Zurich station to denounce the revolutionaries as spies and traitors. And they had indeed negotiated a safe passage through Germany with German high command.

The extent to which Germany directly bankrolled the Bolsheviks remains disputed, but it is known that German financiers secretly funneled money to Russia. The idea that Germany might bankroll a revolution had first been proposed by Russian exile and communist Israel Lazarevich Gelfand, better known by his revolutionary name Alexander Parvus. He presented his plan in Berlin in February 1915—a twenty-three-page document detailing how a foreign-backed coup could overthrow the tsar. Parvus was provided with funds and put his plan into action, cultivating the division that he believed would lead to revolution. He smuggled money, goods, and weapons into Russia to support the Bolsheviks and other groups of dissenters, including separatists in various Russian regions. With the help of weapons and dynamite from Germany, ships were sunk and ports set alight. While it is disputed whether Parvus directly funded Lenin, he played a direct role in negotiating the safe passage for his homecoming.

A SECOND REVOLUTION

Following a summer of political turmoil, in which Lenin was accused by the government of being a German collaborator, the Bolsheviks seized power, overthrowing the Provisional Government in the October Revolution. Lenin immediately sent a telegram to German military headquarters on the Eastern Front offering an unconditional ceasefire. However, the cost of peace would be high. The resulting Treaty of Brest–Litovsk forced Russia to cede important industrial centers in Ukraine and the Baltic states. Lenin was denounced by his enemies once again as a "German spy" for accepting these terms, but the resulting peace had been a key promise of the Bolsheviks and it saved the revolution.

In the following year, facing growing opposition from both inside and outside Russia, the Bolsheviks cracked down ruthlessly. Lenin called for a "mass terror" as the country descended into civil war, and tens of thousands of deserters and peasants were massacred. In December 1917, he had established the Cheka, a secret police force charged with investigating "counterrevolutionary crimes." The force bore an uncanny resemblance to the Okhrana of the tsarist era, which had suppressed communist dissent. The hated institutions of the old regime had been replaced with mirror counterparts in the new, one form of fear replaced by another.

Left: German and Russian delegations meet for preliminary armistice negotiations in December 1917. The resulting Treaty of Brest-Litovsk was signed three months later.

— CHAPTER 5 —

BETWEEN
THE WARS

With the end of World War I came the start of the division of Europe into communist East and capitalist West. These two ideologically opposed camps would grow to define the nature of covert activity in the twentieth century. While the nations of the West reduced the size of their intelligence organizations post-1918, the Soviet Union greatly increased the size and scope of its services.

Western security agencies were well aware of the Soviet threat, but they looked for it in the wrong places, devoting much of their effort to undermining left-wing social-democratic political parties that had little connection with Soviet communism. Although the Soviets used the various national communist parties to further their ends, they also recruited middle-class sympathizers to secretly infiltrate the major government departments in the West.

As Western democracies focused on the Soviet Union, their intelligence agencies failed to take into account the rise of fascism during the 1920s and 30s. The emergence of Nazi Germany would pose the greatest threat—a threat that was only taken seriously by Western spy agencies after the outbreak of war in 1939.

SIDNEY REILLY: ACE OF SPIES?

"A MAN OF INDOMITABLE COURAGE, A GENIUS AS AN AGENT, BUT A SINISTER MAN I COULD NEVER BRING MYSELF TO WHOLLY TRUST."

Mansfield Cumming, head of MI6, on Sidney Reilly

Known as "The Ace of Spies" by his admirers, Sidney Reilly (1874–1925) was a master of the delicate art of serving multiple masters. In 1906, he was rubbing shoulders with Russian revolutionaries while simultaneously working for both the Tsar's intelligence service and Britain's MI6. Reilly was a colorful self-publicist, but his inability to distinguish fact from fiction would ultimately prove his undoing.

Reilly claimed to be the son of an Irish sea captain, but in reality he was born to a Jewish family in Russia, and his real name was Sigmund Rosenblum. He left Russia as a young man and traveled the world seeking his fortune in the armaments and petroleum industries. During his travels, he spent time in Britain. It was at this time, in the 1890s, that Reilly came to the notice of MI6, who employed him as a part-time secret agent.

SPYING ON THE BOLSHEVIKS

At the outbreak of World War I, Reilly was working in New York as an arms agent for the Russian government, but he was persuaded by MI6 to resume spying. In April 1918, he was sent to Russia as part of a covert campaign to overthrow the new Bolshevik regime and replace it with a government prepared to continue the war with Germany. Reilly joined up with British consular official Bruce Lockhart, who was financing Russian anti-Bolshevik groups, while British spies Ernest Boyce and George Hill ran their own agents and engaged in sabotage missions.

In the summer of 1918, Reilly and Lockhart were approached by two Latvian officers from the elite Kremlin guard. They claimed their men were ready to rise up against the Bolsheviks. Reilly hastily formulated a plan for the guards to stage a coup that would coincide with the Allied military invasion through the northern port of Archangel.

The Latvian officers were, in fact, agents of the Cheka, Russia's new secret security service. The Cheka swiftly moved against the so-called "Latvian plot." Boyce was shot dead and Lockhart and the other conspirators were arrested, but Reilly managed to flee the country aboard a Dutch freighter. Lockhart was subsequently released in an early version of a "spy-swap."

DUPED AGAIN

Back in Britain, Reilly maintained contact with agents in Russia, notably an anti-Bolshevik organization known as "the Trust," which in reality was another front organization set up by the Cheka. While MI6 doubted the authenticity of the reports coming from Russia, Reilly still believed the Bolsheviks could be overthrown. In 1925, he accepted an invitation from the Trust to return to Russia. After crossing the border from Finland, he was arrested and taken to Moscow, where he was interrogated and shot—an ignominious end to the "ace of spies."

With a few notable exceptions, British covert involvement in Russia had been amateurish, in marked contrast to the cold professionalism displayed by their opposite numbers in the Cheka.

Above: The Cheka was run by Felix Dzerzhinsky (seated, center), pictured in a meeting with his deputies in 1919.

Below: The coastal motorboat operated in the Baltic by Augustus Agar.

SPYING IN SHALLOW WATERS

While Sidney Reilly was the spy who caught the public's imagination, St. Petersburg-based music student Paul Dukes (1889–1967) was a more effective one. A master of disguise, Dukes was dubbed "the man with a thousand faces." He proved a highly capable undercover agent for MI6, sending accurate reports back to London via a contact in Finland. Dukes' information proved invaluable to Royal Navy officer Augustus Agar, a coastal motorboat commander also working for MI6. Operating in the Baltic, Agar helped lead two successful naval missions in the summer of 1919 during the Russian Civil War, sinking a Soviet cruiser and damaging two battleships, exploits that led to the award of a Victoria Cross. Dukes was knighted after his escape to Britain later in the year—he remains to this day the only person to receive such an honor purely for spying.

Above: Paul Dukes

SOVIET TERROR: HOW THE CHEKA BECAME THE KGB

The secret security and intelligence services of the new Soviet Union were infamous for their brutality, and were responsible, directly or indirectly, for the deaths of millions of Russians. They deliberately created an atmosphere of secrecy and suspicion, with an army of informers at the ready. The knowledge that a critical remark might be reported to the authorities—with the firing squad or labor camp as punishment—was highly effective in discouraging dissent.

Like those of many of his victims, Nikolai Yezhov's face was airbrushed out of official photographs following his execution in 1940.

Felix Dzerzhinsky expanded the Cheka rapidly in the aftermath of the Red Terror of 1918, and by 1921, it had a strength of over 250,000 personnel. The following year, it was renamed the GPU (State Political Directorate) and then the OGPU (Unified State Political Directorate), further establishing itself as the main secret security force.

The OGPU was not the only security force. The NKVD (People's Commissariat for Internal Affairs) had also been formed in the aftermath of the Revolution. It was initially responsible for policing and the creation of a prison-camp system for political dissidents who had not been executed. These camps spread across the Soviet Union, becoming part of the infamous forced-labor system known as the Gulag.

MILITARY INTELLIGENCE

In 1918, the Bolshevik government formed a powerful military intelligence service known as the GRU (Main Intelligence Directorate). Operating alongside and in competition with the NKVD, the GRU operated its own spy networks abroad. It proved highly successful during 1930s and 1940s, especially in Germany and the United States, but from the 1950s onward, corruption limited its effectiveness. Since the breakup of the Soviet Union, the GRU has undergone extensive reorganization, with Russia's Special Forces (Spetsnaz) coming under its command.

Following Lenin's death in 1924, Josef Stalin seized control of the Soviet Union. Stalin took a personal interest in the NKVD, and in 1934 it absorbed the OGPU within its ranks. Under the successive leaderships of Genrikh Yagoda and Nikolai Yezhov, the NKVD took the lead in the Great Purge of 1936–38 (see below). It also waged an espionage war against enemies abroad, assassinating anti-communist emigrés and covertly recruiting foreigners in the West to spy for the Soviet Union.

AFTER THE PURGE

From 1938, the NKVD came under the control of Lavrentiy Beria. One of Beria's first acts was to ensure the arrest and execution of his predecessor Yezhov. The NKVD played a key role in World War II, not least in stiffening the resolve of Soviet troops, with the ever-present threat of execution at any sign of battlefield cowardice. By the end of the war, the NKVD had been renamed the MVD (Ministry of Internal Affairs). After Beria's execution in 1954 following the death of Stalin, it took the title of the KGB (Committee for State Security). The KGB assumed responsibility for all aspects of intelligence and security in the Soviet Union.

Grigory Zinoviev, a member of the first Bolshevik Politburo in 1917, was one of the Great Purge's first victims when he was tried and executed alongside 15 other prominent old Bolsheviks in August 1936. He had been in prison since 1934. This photograph was taken by the NKVD on his arrest.

Among the victims of the Great Purge was head of the Red Army and hero of the 1917 Revolution, Marshal Tukachevsky, who was arrested for treason and shot in 1937.

"THERE WILL BE SOME INNOCENT VICTIMS IN THIS FIGHT AGAINST FASCIST AGENTS. WE ARE LAUNCHING A MAJOR ATTACK ON THE ENEMY. BETTER THAT TEN INNOCENT PEOPLE SHOULD SUFFER THAN ONE SPY GET AWAY."

Nikolai Yezhov, NKVD chief 1936–38

THE GREAT PURGE

The Great Purge was initiated by Stalin in 1936 to curb dissent within the Soviet Union. Under the direction of the NKVD and GRU, the purge began with the elimination of Soviet officials and then Stalin's old comrades from the Revolution of 1917. Torture was routinely employed to induce confessions, which were used as evidence of guilt in show trials held in Moscow. The purge extended to attack the more prosperous peasants (kulaks) and the leadership of the Soviet armed forces. By the time the killing stopped in 1938, over a million people had died.

WHO WROTE THE ZINOVIEV LETTER?

In the period between the two world wars, British intelligence feared what it described as the Soviet "Red Menace," focusing its attentions on the Communist Party of Great Britain and communist sympathizers within the Labour Party. Codebreaking work by the GC&CS (the Government Code and Cypher School, later renamed GCHQ) indicated a degree of covert Soviet involvement in British left-wing circles, but British intelligence officers were unable to uncover sufficiently incriminating documents to make public their suspicions—until the arrival of the Zinoviev Letter.

At the end of World War I, cost-conscious politicians saw little need for expensive intelligence agencies, and both MI5 (Britain's internal security service, roughly equivalent to the FBI) and MI6 (the secret intelligence service, comparable to the CIA) found their budgets savagely cut, with many staff laid off. Efficiency was further compromised by the quality of those left behind, former army and police officers whose bluff "King and Country" attitudes were poorly suited to the complexities of espionage.

In 1923, MI6 had the good fortune to take control of the cryptographers from Room 40, the cryptanalysis section of the Admiralty, which they renamed GC&CS. MI6 relied on the intelligence provided by Alastair Denniston's codebreakers, vastly superior to MI6's sources in the field.

VOTE FOR MACDONALD AND ME

ON THE LOAN TRAIL.

Left: Following the release of the Zinoviev Letter, satirical magazine Punch published this cartoon depicting a caricature of a Bolshevik urging people to vote for MacDonald. MacDonald's government lost the election later that year.

Right: Protesters carry the flag of the Soviet Union on a march organized by the Communist Party of Great Britain in 1927.

UNDERMINING LABOUR

The election of the first-ever Labour government in January 1924 rang alarm bells through British intelligence, some of whom saw it as the first step on the road to communism. Renewed efforts were made to find a damning link between Labour and Soviet intelligence. As the country prepared for another general election in November, MI6 received a copy of a letter allegedly written to the Communist Party of Great Britain by Grigory Zinoviev, head of the Soviet Communist International (Comintern). The letter encouraged militant action and subversion of the army, and made explicit references to cultivating links with the Labour Party.

No attempt was made to verify the accuracy of the document before senior figures within British intelligence released it for newspaper publication a week before the election. Labour lost and were replaced by a Conservative government. Although there were other factors to account for Labour's defeat, the Zinoviev Letter certainly played its part. It subsequently turned out that it was a fake, concocted by Russian emigrés and passed to MI6 via Sidney Reilly.

COMMUNIST SPY RING

MI5 was also busy fighting the "Red Menace," enjoying genuine success in breaking the Woolwich Arsenal spy ring, using a long-term undercover agent named Olga Gray. She joined the Communist Party in 1930 and acted as a secretary, gaining the trust of Percy Glading, co-founder of the Communist Party of Great Britain. Glading was a Soviet spy, and was photographing weapon designs from the Woolwich Arsenal in London. Once MI5 had sufficient evidence, Glading and his accomplices were arrested in January 1938.

Top: Ramsay MacDonald, the first Labour Prime Minister.

Above: Stanley Baldwin, the Conservative leader who succeeded MacDonald as Prime Minister in 1924.

THE ARCOS DEBACLE

In 1927, the British Conservative government decided to break off diplomatic relations with the Soviet Union. In order to justify this action, the government once again looked for incriminating evidence of Soviet espionage, ordering a police raid on the London offices of the All Russian Co-operative Society (Arcos), an Anglo-Russian trading company that was suspected of acting as a front for Soviet spying. When nothing of importance was discovered in the raid, government ministers instead justified breaking relations by publicly quoting Soviet telegraph messages decoded by GC&CS. This immediately alerted Soviet intelligence, who replaced their now-broken codes with ultra-secure one-time pads, cutting dead a valuable source of information. GC&CS was bitter at this intelligence blunder and vowed that it would never happen again.

THE LEAGUE OF (RELATIVELY) EXTRAORDINARY GENTLEMEN

In the aftermath of World War I, the US government had no standalone agency dedicated to protecting the country against foreign spies, relying instead on the FBI to supplement Army and Navy intelligence-gathering departments. However, they could also call on the services of a top-secret and completely unofficial group of amateur enthusiasts, inspired by a passion for spycraft, known simply as "The Room."

Kermit Roosevelt

Franklin D. Roosevelt

Vincent Astor

Frederic Kernochan

The Room was established in 1927 by two pillars of New York society—Vincent Astor, a millionaire publisher and philanthropist, and Kermit Roosevelt, Jr., an amateur explorer (and grandson of Theodore Roosevelt). The group was a mix of wealthy hobbyists and former intelligence officers, united by their love of secrecy and all the clandestine features of the spy world, whether writing in invisible ink or coding the letters they sent to one another.

A number of members went on to serve as national security officials, including Roosevelt, who later became an intelligence officer in both the OSS (Office of Strategic Services) and its successor the CIA. Other members already had a background in intelligence, including banker Winthrop W. Aldrich, Judge Frederic Kernochan, and David Bruce, a foreign service official who also joined the OSS. Associated with the club were two future intelligence chiefs, Allen W. Dulles and William Donovan.

PRESIDENTIAL APPROVAL

Franklin D. Roosevelt was another well-heeled spy enthusiast, and when he became US president in 1933, he welcomed whatever information The Room was able to provide. He also enjoyed the club's boys-together conviviality, complete with alcohol-fueled trips on Astor's yacht.

As well as entertaining guests, Astor sailed his yacht through the Pacific and gathered details of Japanese naval expansion in the Marshall Islands. He also used his position as a director of the Western Union Cable Company to eavesdrop on telegrams that revealed the presence of secret agents from Mexico and Spain's growing ties with Nazi Germany.

When war broke out in Europe in 1939, The Room was renamed The Club and began to take its work more seriously. The Anglophile tendencies of most of its members led to attempts to develop links with Britain, in defiance of the country's official policy of neutrality. Donovan conducted a tour of Britain in July 1940, at a time when Joseph Kennedy, the US ambassador to Britain, was reporting back to Washington on Britain's imminent destruction. Donovan came to the opposite conclusion and urged Roosevelt to provide support. This advice was accepted, a first step in America's growing involvement in the war against Germany.

THE BLACK CHAMBER

Above: Herbert Yardley

A former head of the US Army's cryptology section, Herbert Yardley was an able code-breaker. In 1919, he established a cipher bureau, giving it the grand name of the Black Chamber. The Chamber cracked an important Japanese diplomatic code just before the start of the Washington Naval Conference in November 1921. The conference was an attempt to place a limit on the size of the world's major navies. Armed with crucial knowledge of Japanese intentions, the American negotiators pushed hard and successfully persuaded the Japanese to accept US terms. Funding for the Black Chamber remained precarious, however, and in 1929 the arrival of Secretary of State Henry Stimpson (who disapproved of spying) led to its closure.

"GENTLEMEN DO NOT READ EACH OTHER'S MAIL."

Henry Stimpson, on his reasons for closing the Black Chamber

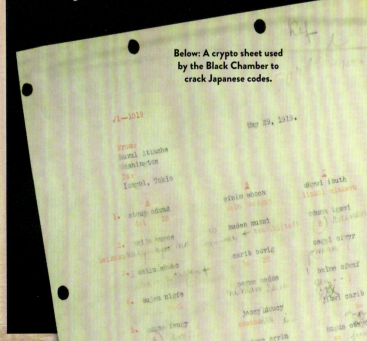

Below: A crypto sheet used by the Black Chamber to crack Japanese codes.

STALIN'S MOLES

After the Russian Revolution, America was gripped by what we now refer to as the First Red Scare. It is easy to dismiss the paranoia of the time, particularly in light of the better-known excesses of McCarthyism that characterized the Second Red Scare of the 1950s. And indeed, much of the paranoia at home and abroad about Russian infiltrators working to destroy the West was almost comically overwrought. But it was nonetheless based in fact, and there were several very successful Soviet operations in both the US and the UK.

In the years between the two world wars, Soviet intelligence was able to recruit from people in the West who were ideologically attracted to communism. The economic problems of the era—not least the desperate social cost of the Great Depression—led these youthful idealists to look favorably at the reform promised by communism. It was also widely believed that only the Soviet Union could stand against the rise of fascism in Italy, Germany, and Spain.

CAMBRIDGE SPIES

In Britain in the 1930s, Soviet recruiting officers began to extend their interests beyond the confines of the Communist Party of Great Britain and other mainly working-class socialist organizations. They focused their attentions on communist students from the major universities. The University of Cambridge proved the most fruitful source.

Harold "Kim" Philby was an early success, recruited in 1934 shortly after graduating from Trinity College, Cambridge, with a degree in Economics. He was quickly followed by Guy Burgess, Donald Maclean, and Anthony Blunt—like Philby, all drawn from the British upper-middle class and destined for great things. John Cairncross, a brilliant student from a more modest background, also joined this loose spy association from Cambridge, later known as "The Cambridge Five." All but Maclean had studied at Trinity College. They were part of a long-term Soviet strategy of creating deep-penetration agents, better known as sleepers or moles.

RECRUITING OFFICERS

During the interwar period, Soviet intelligence relied on the services of a group of ideologically inspired communists, many of Jewish descent from Central Europe, whose sophistication and international contacts made possible the enlistment of high-grade individuals in the West. Among these agents was Arnold Deutsch, a brilliant Austrian academic who recruited twenty spies in Britain, including the Cambridge Five. Deutsch instructed the fledgling Cambridge spies to immediately sever their links with communism and pursue a conventional career path inside the British establishment. Once they had risen to positions of trust and influence, they would then be ready to supply valuable intelligence to the Soviet Union.

Above: Trinity College, Cambridge—the "College of Spies"

Above: Kim Philby

Above: Richard Sorge

"COMMUNISM OFFERED ME WHAT NOTHING ELSE IN THE DYING WORLD HAD THE POWER TO OFFER, SOMETHING FOR WHICH TO LIVE AND SOMETHING FOR WHICH TO DIE."

Whitaker Chambers, Soviet spy who later abandoned communism and in 1948 testified against Alger Hiss and others

IVY LEAGUERS

In the US, the NKVD and GRU (military intelligence) competed with one another to secure the best agents. Many of the recruits were Ivy League graduates who would go on to work for the US government. Among these were State Department officials Alger Hiss, Laurence Duggan, and Noel Field, along with Harry Dexter White from the Treasury. Other notable Soviet spies included Duncan Lee. Lee was a lawyer and protégé of diplomat William Donovan. When Donovan took over the OSS, he was joined by Lee, who rose to the rank of major, all the while sending reports to his Soviet handler.

The degree of penetration achieved by these Soviet moles would subsequently send shock waves through the British and US establishments, but during the 1930s and 1940s, their activities went on unhindered and seemingly unnoticed.

SPYING ON JAPAN

German Richard Sorge started working for the GRU in the late 1920s. He operated in Scandinavia, the US, and China before moving to Japan in 1933. Engaged as a journalist, Sorge infiltrated both the German embassy in Tokyo and the Japanese general staff, managing to secure vital diplomatic and military intelligence. This included prior warning of the German invasion of the Soviet Union and information that Japan was going to attack the US and not the Soviet Union, enabling Stalin to redeploy his forces from the East. In October 1941, Sorge was arrested in Tokyo, suspected initially of being a German spy. He was executed three years later.

Above: Wilhelm Canaris

THE FÜHRER'S SPIES

It is usual for a spy chiefs in authoritarian states to be keen supporters of the policies of their leaders. But by a strange twist of circumstance, the head of German military intelligence turned against Adolf Hitler. Initially, he managed to disguise his anti-Nazi actions, but he was unmasked in the fallout from the Army's attempt to assassinate Hitler—and like many of his co-conspirators, his end was slow and painful.

Despite the restrictions of the Treaty of Versailles, the German armed forces covertly established an espionage unit in 1920. Known as the Abwehr, it developed into a full-scale security and intelligence-gathering institution. The Abwehr, however, faced competition when Hitler came to power in 1933, with Heinrich Himmler's SS determined to usurp it with its own secret intelligence force, the Sicherheitsdienst (SD).

When naval officer Admiral Wilhelm Canaris took command of the Abwehr in 1935, he came to an agreement with the SD—led by Reinhard Heydrich—to work in tandem. Both organizations continued to be bitter rivals, however, even to the point of working against one another.

CANARIS AND THE GENERAL

An example of Wilhelm Canaris's anti-Nazi attitude was demonstrated in his dealings with fascist Spain before World War II. A fluent Spanish-speaker, Canaris had become a friend of the Spanish dictator General Francisco Franco. Hitler sent Canaris to visit Franco in 1938 to encourage a military alliance between the two countries that, in the event of war, would allow German troops to transit through Spain and capture the British territory of Gibraltar. Canaris, however, advised Franco to stay clear of military entanglements and refuse any German rights of passage. Franco heeded his friend's advice, and maintained Spain's neutral policy.

Above: SS guards round up Jews in the Krakow ghetto to transport them to extermination camps in 1943.

Above: Reinhard Heydrich

PLOT AGAINST HITLER

Initially, Canaris had been a keen supporter of Hitler, but over time he became disillusioned with the whole Nazi system, shocked by its savage treatment of Jews and prisoners of war captured in the East. This led him to adopt a bizarre, contradictory set of policies. In some ways, he sought to further German interests, but he also developed his own covert anti-Nazi measures. Canaris allowed his senior officers, including chief assistant Hans Oster, to associate with the Army's anti-Nazi resistance, involving themselves in the 1944 July plot to assassinate Hitler. Both Canaris and Oster helped Jews escape to safety in Switzerland.

Hitler began to have doubts about the loyalty of Canaris and the Abwehr. He increasingly favored the SD, which operated not only in Germany and its conquered territories but also in neutral and enemy countries. The SD was just one of the many military and security organizations of the SS empire, and it worked closely with the Gestapo. As the status of the Abwehr declined—made worse by a number of intelligence blunders—so that of the SD rose. In February 1944, Hitler abolished the Abwehr, allowing the SD and Gestapo to take over its remaining intelligence functions. Canaris was arrested in July 1944 after the failed July plot, and was imprisoned in a concentration camp. He was executed, along with Oster, shortly before the end of the war, hanged from the gallows by a piano wire that slowly throttled him to death.

> ## "THIS IS THE END. BADLY HANDLED. MY NOSE BROKEN. I HAVE DONE NOTHING AGAINST GERMANY. IF YOU SURVIVE, PLEASE TELL MY WIFE."

Final message from Wilhelm Canaris, tapped out in Morse code to a fellow prisoner

THE GESTAPO

The Gestapo—or Secret State Police—was formed in 1933 by Hermann Göring, but the following year it taken over by the SS. It soon earned a reputation for brutality, arresting, torturing, and killing those deemed to be enemies of the state. During World War II, the Gestapo assumed security duties in the occupied territories, once again achieving notoriety for the ruthless methods used in suppressing resistance. It also played a major role in the administration of the Nazi concentration camp system and the destruction of European Jewry.

THE INTELLIGENCE WAR AGAINST HITLER

In 1935, Hitler repudiated the Versailles Treaty that had brought World War I to an end and whose terms were designed to keep Germany militarily weak. In retrospect, we can see that his plans for mass rearmament and territorial demands against neighboring countries made war in Europe a near certainty. However, the response from intelligence agencies in the West was slow and uncoordinated, and only the Soviet Union was able to place agents in key positions within the German state.

In Britain, many senior officers in MI6 favored appeasement with Germany, while a few openly supported Hitler and his stand against communism. Even when MI6 redirected itself to gathering intelligence of German military intentions, it lacked the time and resources to develop suitable contacts. It failed to provide advance warning of Germany's occupations of the Rhineland (1936) and Sudetenland (1938), or the invasion of Poland (1939). By contrast, MI5 adopted a robust approach to potential German espionage, monitoring the activities of almost all enemy spies in Britain.

Above: Harro Schultze-Boysen and his wife Libertas, pictured here in 1935, were hanged for treason in December 1942.

FRENCH INTELLIGENCE IS IGNORED

In the late 1930s, France's military intelligence agency, the Deuxième Bureau, supplied the French General Staff with information on German Blitzkrieg tactics, as well as details of the latest tank and aircraft designs. French military attachés operating out of the various European embassies alerted the authorities to the planned takeover of the remainder of Czechoslovakia in March 1939 and to the impending invasion of Poland. Unfortunately, the generals paid little attention.

SOVIET PENETRATION

In the late 1930s, Harro Schulze-Boysen, an officer in the Luftwaffe, formed a group of fellow-minded resisters. They made contact with Soviet agents operating in Germany, and Schulze-Boysen's position in the German Air Ministry provided a stream of intelligence that later included German preparations for the invasion of the Soviet Union in 1941. From 1940, Schulze-Boysen cooperated with a resistance group led by Arvid Harnack, an economist who supplied his Soviet contact with information on the German war economy. German diplomat Rudolf von Scheliha, who worked out of the German embassy in Warsaw, redirected information from his Polish contacts to Soviet intelligence. All three spies were captured by the Gestapo in 1942 and hanged.

THE VENLO INCIDENT

The intelligence arm of the SS was known as the SD. In November 1939, SD agent Walter Schellenberg, posing as an anti-Nazi German army officer, lured MI6 officers S. Payne Best and H. R. Stevens to Venlo, a Dutch town on the German-Netherlands border, for a supposed meeting with other anti-Hitler conspirators. As the two MI6 officers waited for the meeting, a car crashed through the border checkpoint. SD agents leaped out of the vehicle, firing wildly around them, and bundled Payne Best and Stevens into the car before fleeing back over the border to Germany. The two men were interrogated by the Gestapo, and the information they provided helped to wipe out much of the MI6 spy network in Western Europe. This was a triumph for the SD, and a painful blow to MI6.

Above: German troops march into Cologne to re-occupy the Rhineland in 1936, violating the terms of the Treaty of Versailles.

Above: Adam von Trott

GERMAN RESISTANCE

Another source of intelligence came from Germany itself, supplied by small, disparate groups who secretly worked against the Nazi system. They were spread around Germany, drawing upon all classes, occupations, and institutions, including the now-banned trade unions and political parties, along with small numbers from the Protestant and Catholic churches.

Of greater significance were those individuals operating in the German Army, the Abwehr, and the diplomatic services. They had access to high-grade information, some of which was forwarded to the West. German diplomats, among them Ulrich von Hassell and Adam von Trott, tried to involve British intelligence in their resistance work, but MI6—fearful of being double-crossed—failed to act before the onset of war, which made such cooperation much more difficult.

> **"WE CANNOT VIOLATE THE ALLEGIANCE WE OWE GOD. WE MUST THEREFORE BREAK OUR WORD GIVEN TO HIM [HITLER] WHO HAS BROKEN SO MANY AGREEMENTS AND IS STILL DOING SO."**
>
> Adam von Trott, member of the German resistance to Hitler

— CHAPTER 6 —

TRADECRAFT

Tradecraft involves the skills and equipment needed for covert operations. Governments train their operatives in all aspects of spy tradecraft in intensive courses at specialized—and highly secret—training camps. The operatives must then be able to train informants out in the field. It is critical to identify the right person to recruit. Are they in a position to access strategic information, and can they be trusted? Training in tradecraft includes the use of specialized technology, such as bugs or tiny cameras, plus counter-surveillance techniques to see if you've been detected.

Central to any spy's training is the art of deception. When operating in hostile territory, agents develop detailed cover identities to protect them as they go about their official and unofficial activities. Sometimes even dead spies may be given false identities in order to communicate disinformation. Training also involves more nefarious covert activities—breaking and entering, sabotaging the enemy, or state-sanctioned assassinations by highly trained operatives. Get caught, and you may cause an international scandal, as happened when the Watergate conspiracy brought down President Nixon.

RECRUITMENT

At the center of any government-led spy operation are a number of case officers. The case officers act as the sole point of contact with both the government and the spy. They are in charge of recruitment, often working out of a government's diplomatic office and operating with diplomatic cover. Typically, they will have a nominal job title within an embassy, conducting their espionage duties while "off duty."

Case officers need to have the skills to identify and recruit assets—informants and agents who are able to supply useful human intelligence (HUMINT). Once they have recruited the agents, the case officers will train them in spycraft, including a crash course in methods to cover their tracks and avoid detection. The case officer will also supply the audio recording technology, miniature cameras to photograph sensitive information, and any other spy gadgets they might need. From the agent's point of view, the case officer will be the only enemy employee they will ever contact. This means that the case officer also needs many of the skills of the social worker in order to reassure and encourage agents who may be feeling the heat.

KEY ASSETS

The targets for recruitment as assets include enemy intelligence officers, diplomats, senior politicians, civil servants, military personnel, scientists, and technicians. In addition, workers in more lowly positions, such as chauffeurs, guards, and secretaries in enemy embassies may be targeted. Information from idle gossip can be as valuable as intelligence from a leaked document. Many of the spy stories in this book start out with someone who is disgruntled with their work or their government's beliefs, or has financial problems. A case officer will monitor potential informants to understand their motivation and evaluate whether they can be encouraged to come to the other side.

Most spies start with something simple, sharing or selling one or two documents. Having avoided detection and appreciating the financial benefit—or maybe enjoying the adventure of spying—they continue down a slippery slope. If anybody finds themselves in over their head, the case officer can create a situation that confirms they will keep working for them, or gives them an out when they are caught.

According to current-day spies serving prison sentences, "money" is the number one reason Americans commit treason, with "ego gratification" ranking second. While recruitment happened in person in the past, today the internet makes it easy for case officers to identify strategic informants anywhere in the world.

THE ROMEOS OF EAST GERMANY

During the Cold War, East Germany used "Romeo" agents to seduce West German women working as secretaries in key government departments. Romeo spies were the brainchild of Markus Wolf, the head of East Germany's foreign intelligence service throughout most of the country's existence. Wolf saw that there was a shortage of men in Europe after World War II, and that Romeo spies could fulfill a need. He also realized that female secretaries had access to far more information than most male diplomats. They were responsible for private correspondence and were privy to most of the office gossip.

Not just anyone was cut out to be a Romeo spy. They had to be between the ages of twenty-five and thirty-five, well-educated, handsome, and to display good old-fashioned manners. Ninety-nine percent of the candidates failed the screening process. Those selected were given a cover identity and sent to West Germany to identify a "Juliet" who could provide the information they desired. From there, the Romeos would create a "chance" encounter, such as a meeting at a bus stop, from which they would develop the affair. Every time the Romeo met with his Juliet, he would write a report, which would be analyzed by psychologists who decided the next steps. In some cases, the "romances" lasted for decades (see below).

A SMITTEN SPY

In 1968, West German postgraduate student Gabriele Gast met Karl-Heinz Schmidt on a trip to Karl-Marx-Stadt, where she was researching her doctorate on the role of women in East Germany. Schmidt was her official driver, and as a thank you, Gast took him for a beer. From there, a relationship blossomed. Gast visited Schmidt in East Germany, which she could visit on a student visa. When this became difficult, Schmidt told Gast that he worked for the Stasi and that he suspected Gast was monitoring him for the West Germans. They could never meet again unless Gast offered to help the Stasi. She agreed.

Gast was given a forged passport and a handbag with a secret compartment. She also went through tradecraft training, learning how to use invisible ink, monitor numbers stations, and photograph documents. She was allowed to meet with Schmidt once every three months. The relationship only ended in 1990 at the fall of the communist system, at which point Gast was arrested for treason. At her trial, Schmidt testified that he had been a lure to recruit Gast.

TRAINING IN THE TRADE

Training in intelligence work was first formalized during World War II, setting a template that has since been developed by various agencies around the world. The CIA's training camp is known as "The Farm," or "Camp Swampy." Meanwhile the British Special Operations Executive (SOE) established a camp in the remote Scottish Highlands, while the KGB ran the Red Banner Institute just outside Moscow. These schools have become renowned—even infamous—for their rigorous and tough training.

DENY EVERYTHING: THE MOSCOW RULES

During the Cold War, spying in Moscow was notoriously dangerous, and every spy knew the harsh consequences of being caught. Although they were never formally written down, the Moscow Rules were a set of broad principles for spies to keep in mind when conducting activities in the Soviet capital.

- Assume nothing.

- Never go against your gut.

- Everyone is potentially under opposition control.

- Do not look back—you are never completely alone.

- Go with the flow and blend in.

- Vary your pattern and stay within your cover.

- Do not harass the opposition.

- Lull them into a sense of complacency.

- Pick the time and place for action.

- Always keep your options open.

The new intelligence schools have developed a demanding curriculum that continues to evolve as technology progresses. Spies use many skills that are useful in everyday life and business negotiation, such as assessment, observation, situational awareness, relationships, persuasion, and negotiation to execute operations. Spy schools help agents learn, practice, and hone these skills. Future case officers must also gain the knowledge and confidence to train their new recruits informally "in the field."

THE FARM

The CIA's covert training camp, "The Farm," is located inside Camp Peary located near Williamsburg, Maryland. Hidden away on the ten thousand acre site, the CIA created a fake town in which to carry out practice espionage games. Over the course of six months of intensive training, new recruits learn a huge range of physical skills, including evasion driving, use of firearms, martial arts, and hand-to-hand combat. They also acquire more cerebral abilities, learning how to identify and recruit sources; understand body language; gather data through elicitation; memorization; lying; conversational engineering, and counter surveillance; and maintaining their cover. In training exercises, they will be pulled over by police and undergo grueling interrogation. Trainees also learn how to work a cocktail party, lose a tail, set up a dead drop, pick locks, open mail, infiltrate computer systems, reconnoiter meeting places, and other ways to communicate with informants—basically everything they need to know to be a good intelligence agent. It is even reported that agents are trained in ways to kill themselves in case of capture. The standards are high, and many new recruits fail to complete the training.

SEXPIONAGE

Russian intelligence officers are trained at the Red Banner Institute, but there is a rumor that a special school once existed to train female Foreign Intelligence Service (SVR) "Sparrows." A sparrow was an agent trained to seduce her target. As the story goes, female soldiers were recruited and trained in physical fitness, handling firearms, sexual communication, elicitation, and even hardcore pornography to prepare them for their assignments. While the majority of the trainees were women, men also went through this specialized training, after which they were known as "ravens." The story of the Soviets' spying seductresses is told in the 2018 movie *Red Sparrow*, about a Russian ballerina-turned-spy, based on a novel by former CIA agent Jason Matthews.

GUNSLINGER'S GAIT

Sometimes you can see the result of someone's training in plain sight. Take the case of Russian President Vladimir Putin. Putin has a specific swaggering gait, in which he keeps his right arm stiff against his body while his left arm swings freely. Other Russian leaders have been noticed to have a similar walk. In a leaked KGB manual, firearms training includes the instruction not to swing the right arm and always to keep it close to the body to be able to draw your gun. Putin started his career at the KGB. Old habits clearly die hard.

Left: Vladimir Putin walking with his gunslinger's gait.

COMMUNICATIONS

Once in possession of valuable intel, a spy faces the tricky problem of passing on the information without being detected. This is the moment at which a spy can be most exposed, and a wide variety of methods have been developed to communicate covertly—from old-fashioned low-tech methods to sophisticated electronic encryption.

IN PLAIN SIGHT

Communications can be disguised in a variety of ways in order to hide them. Dead drops, invisible ink, numbers stations, and steganography all hide information in plain sight. If you don't know where you are looking, you're unlikely to find it. When KGB-British double agent Oleg Gordievksy was called back to Moscow, he took a book of Shakespeare sonnets with him. Hidden on the pages was a secret escape plan written in invisible ink in the event that British Intelligence needed to rescue him (see page 163).

BRUSH PAST

One way of passing information is to hand it over in person. In the classic "brush past," two agents pass each other closely in a busy area. One hands the other something concealed in a newspaper, or sets down a briefcase and walks away only to have another agent pick it up a moment later. However, the brush past requires person-to-person contact. Where that is not possible, some method is needed to conceal the message.

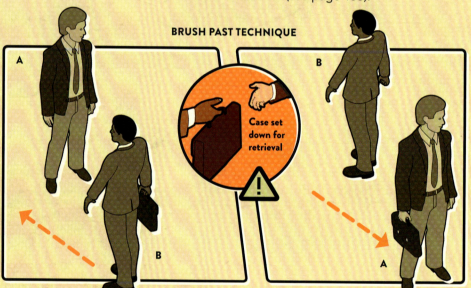

BRUSH PAST TECHNIQUE

A

B

Case set down for retrieval

B

A

DEAD DROPS

A dead drop is a way to pass information using a secret but public location. When there is something to pick up, the spy communicates a signal, which could be a chalk mark on a mailbox or a mark on a specific subway wall. The two parties can visit the dead drop at different times, increasing the safety of the transfer. A dead drop could be hidden under a footbridge in a public park, in the rocks off a hiking trail, or behind a loose brick in a wall. Dead drops were often made using purpose-built waterproof "dead drop spikes," which could be filled with microfilm and easily pushed into the soil near a specific tree in a public park. Dead drops are one of the safer exchange methods, but if either person is compromised, countersurveillance teams can follow a suspected agent to their dead drop. After the agent has left, they can retrieve the materials, gaining enough evidence to arrest them—this is how John Walker's spy ring was discovered (see pages 160–161).

Dead drop spike and lid

CORRECT USE OF SPIKE

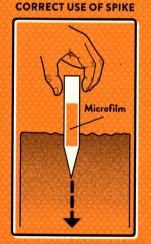

Microfilm

NUMBERS STATIONS

Countries can communicate with their spies over long distances using numbers stations. These were first used in World War I, and are still in use today. Numbers stations broadcast a series of numbers or a phrase on shortwave frequencies. Anyone can tune into the numbers station, but it won't make much sense. You might hear a list of numbers or phrases that seem like nursery rhymes, repeated several times until the broadcast ends.. The numbers correspond to one-time pads, the only mathematically unbreakable encryption method. Numbers stations communicate with spies deep inside enemy territory, and the spies can communicate back with a message from their one-time pad. The messages can be picked up using a simple shortwave radio.

Above: A shortwave radio

DIGITAL COMMUNICATIONS

Digital steganography is an increasingly common means of covert communication. In 2011, an al Qaeda agent was arrested in Berlin in possession of a memory card with encrypted files. German computer forensics experts eventually managed to open the files, which contained a pornographic video called "KickAss." Within the video, they found 141 text files detailing plans for future terrorist attacks. In its crudest form, digital steganography may involve simply opening a JPEG file in a text editor and adding the text at the end of the content. The image will still display, but the text can be easily discovered by analysis. More sophisticated methods involve distributing the code for your message across a range of bytes of data.

Shared email accounts can be used to communicate via email without actually sending the email. When an email is sent, data is attached to the message specifying the IP address of the sender, the date and time the message was sent, as well as information about the mail client and server—all incriminating information. However, if an online email account is shared between people, you don't need to press send on the message to communicate. You write the message and save it as a draft. Then the person you are communicating with logs into the same account online and reads the draft of the message.

They can delete the message (and clear out the trash), and even reply by saving another message in the draft folder. Apparently, this method was used between CIA Director David Petraeus and his biographer Paula Broadwell.

DRAFTS

LOG IN

USER NAME: ABC1234

PASSWORD: ************

LOG IN

USER NAME: ABC1234

PASSWORD: ************

SURVEILLANCE

Watching somebody without yourself being seen takes skills and training. Spies are taught how to keep tabs on a potential recruit or an enemy spy through human surveillance, visual monitoring, and listening devices. Spies use all kinds of technology to keep track of their opposition, including physically tailing a subject; covert listening devices such as wires or telephone taps; observation in person or via closed-circuit TV; and using the internet to gather information. When researching a potential source, case officers first gather data to learn what information they have access to, what motivates them, and any other important details, before approaching them.

THE GREAT SEAL BUG

In 1945, a few weeks before the end of World War II, schoolchildren from the Soviet Union presented a wooden replica of the Great Seal of the United States to the US Ambassador W. Averell Harriman. The Seal was hung in the study of the ambassador's residence in Moscow. Unknown to the Americans, the Soviets had inserted an audio bug into their gift, with the antenna directly under the eagle's beak.

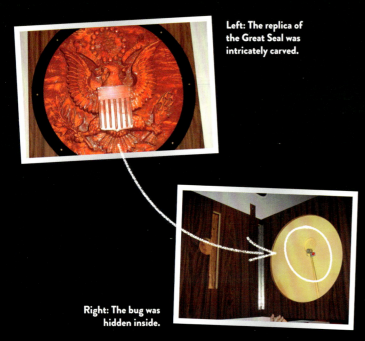

Left: The replica of the Great Seal was intricately carved.

Right: The bug was hidden inside.

The bug was only discovered in 1952 when a British radio operator accidentally overheard a conversation from the US Embassy. The bug was found in a sweep of the offices. It had been nearly undetectable because it used a passive technique to transmit the audio signal. This clever device had been invented by Leon Theremin, inventor of the Theremin electronic musical instrument, who was conscripted to create new radio technology while languishing in a Siberian gulag in 1940. It lacked its own power source, so it could only be detected when the Soviets transmitted the energy source—a radio signal sent from a remote transmitter.

The Americans did not announce that they found the bug, but reverse-engineered it with the help of MI5. Its discovery remained secret until U-2 spy pilot Gary Powers was shot down in 1960 (see page 175). Soviet leader Nikita Khrushchev used the U-2 incident to prove that the US was spying on the Soviets. In response, the Americans pulled out the great seal bug to show that the Soviets had been spying on them for fifteen years.

Left: Here, three people are tailing the target "X." "C" follows "X" closely. "B" follows "C." "A" keeps a close eye through binoculars from across the street. All three may switch roles at any time.

TAILING A SUSPECT

To covertly follow people, private detectives and CIA agents use specific techniques with names like Picket, Web, and Leapfrog. If you're serious about tailing someone, you need a team—you may have people in front of the suspect, across the street, or at various exits they may take. The goal of a tail is to gather information, find out where are they going, who are they meeting with, and whether they are making any dead drops.

The most basic tailing method is called ABC. Person A follows the target. Person B follows behind A, while person C across the street keeps an eye on the situation. These roles can change when the target crosses the street, turns a corner, or enters a store. Teams communicate with each other through hand signals. Followers may change appearances as they tail a subject—athletic clothing and a bike if they're blending in with exercise, or a business suit if they will be in a business environment. A good tail is called a "ghost" because no one can tell they are there.

UP CLOSE AND PERSONAL

In some cases, the tail gets to know the subject so well that they know all the special things about the person. Robert Hanssen, the FBI agent uncovered as a long-term Soviet/Russian spy in 2001, was initially revealed by information from a defector. To discover the evidence needed for a court conviction, Hanssen was placed under surveillance by being assigned a new assistant, young agent Eric O'Neill. Specially trained in surveillance techniques, O'Neill managed to steal Hanssen's Palm Pilot device for long enough for the FBI to download its contents. Hanssen was arrested after he was tailed making a final dead drop on February 18, 2001. He had clearly been entirely deceived by O'Neill as the documents in the dead drop included a note suggesting that O'Neill might make a good candidate to replace Hanssen as a mole when he retired.

Left: Robert Hanssen at the time of his arrest.

Right: Today, Eric O'Neill runs private security companies and gives lectures.

COUNTERSURVEILLANCE

Spies need to know when they are being followed—and what to do about it. Countersurveillance is the skill needed to detect if you are being tailed or observed, and if so, how to respond. If you are being followed on your way to meet a source, the obvious answer is to not meet the source—and to head to a safe area or return home. At other times, you will need to evade the tail or employ active countermeasures.

Training in countermeasures includes being aware of your surroundings, using code words and speaking discreetly, concealing your identity, and working out how to leave an area without being followed. Good ways to check without making it obvious are to stop and look at your reflection in a window to see who is behind you, take a meandering route, or stop in a store that has a window where you can look out. But it is all too easy to become paranoid and end up thinking perfect strangers are following you when they are just doing their errands.

SUSPICIOUS BEHAVIOR

An acronym used to help identify surveillance is TEDD: Time in different Environments and over Distance or one who displays poor Demeanor. Do you see the same face over a period of days in multiple places? Does someone look suspicious? And of course, spying isn't a solo activity despite the impression given in the movies—there are countersurveillance teams on hand to protect an agent from enemy surveillance at important times.

Countersurveillance also involves detecting any audio bugs or visual cameras. The bug inside the great seal of the US (story on page 104) took years to identify. The surveillance device lacked its own energy source, so it could only be detected when it was active—only when the Soviets hit the device with 1800Mhz radio waves. Other radio and visual surveillance devices can be detected by the radio waves or the energy their batteries give off.

Right: Spies can spend a lot of time looking in the mirror. The key to countersurveillance is to find a way to look around you without it being obvious what you are doing.

HIDDEN IN A ROCK

In 2006, the Soviet security service (FSB) revealed the presence of an MI6 radio transmitter hidden in a fake rock in Moscow. They had observed several men acting suspicious near it, walking slowly then speeding up, bending down to pick it up, or kicking it. It turned out that the rock was hollowed out and had electronic circuits inside.

CAUGHT VIA RADIO

Radio-Detection Finding (RDF) is a way to find the direction of a radio source. Eli Cohen was a spy for Mossad, the Israeli intelligence agency, who worked in Syria in the early 1960s (see pages 158–159 for the full story). He sent his collected intelligence back to Israel by radio, which would eventually lead to his capture. Syria used Soviet radio tracking equipment to detect radio transmissions, successfully triangulating a transmitter, and caught Cohen in his apartment in the middle of a transmission.

DECEPTION AND DISINFORMATION

Intel agencies often fool the opposition by spreading disinformation—intentionally false and misleading intelligence. The term "disinformation" was coined by Joseph Stalin in the early twentieth century, and the KGB were experts in the tactic, with a whole department specifically focused on "black propaganda." The most famous use of this tactic probably came in 1944, when the Allies successfully misled the Germans over the D-Day landings (see pages 136–137). "False flag" tactics involve operations by intelligence agencies with the intention of blaming a rival organization or country. Hitler used false flag operations to justify starting World War II.

THE GLEIWITZ INCIDENT

Above: Details about the Gleiwitz operation were provided at the Nuremburg Trials after the war by former SS officer Alfred Naujocks, who claimed to have led the operation.

As Europe edged to the brink of war in the summer of 1939, Nazi Germany sought justification for its military ventures, including the invasion of Poland. The Gleiwitz incident was a "false flag" operation intended to depict Poland as an aggressor and Germany as the aggrieved party. On August 31, 1939, German operatives dressed as Polish nationals seized the radio station in the city of Gleiwitz (then part of Germany, now in Poland and renamed Gliwice). They started to broadcast anti-German propaganda across the region. A local farmer, who had been arrested the day before, was killed by lethal injection then shot to make it look like he was an accomplice. Prisoners from the Dachau concentration camp were also shot and disfigured to make identification impossible. The killings were coordinated by the German SS to give the appearance of a Polish assault on Germany, and were coordinated with more than twenty similar attacks. The German army began the invasion of Poland the very next morning.

Page 2

Issued in lieu of N°

Surname MARTIN

Other Names WILLIAM

Rank (at time of issue) CAPT
(ACTING M

Ship (at time of issue) HQ
COMBINED C

Place of Birth CARDIFF

Year of Birth 1907

Issued by

At ADMIRALTY

Date 2nd February

"I WILL PROVIDE A PROPAGANDISTIC CAUSUS BELLI. ITS CREDIBILITY DOESN'T MATTER. THE VICTOR WILL NOT BE ASKED WHETHER HE TOLD THE TRUTH."

Adolf Hitler

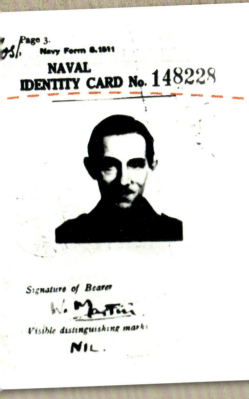

Left: Captain Martin's fake ID card.

Above: The photograph of Captain Martin's fake girlfriend "Pam."

OPERATION MINCEMEAT

Above: John Godfrey

In 1939, Director of British Naval Intelligence and avid fly fisher John Godfrey wrote *The Trout Memo*, which compared military deception to fly fishing. (Ian Fleming, creator of James Bond, was Godfrey's assistant at the time.) The book included more than fifty suggestions for deceiving the enemy, including the inspiration for a real operation called Operation Mincemeat: "The idea very simply was to get a dead body, to equip the dead body with false papers, and then to drop it somewhere where the Germans would find it."

On January 28, 1943, a Navy team headed by intelligence officer Ewen Montagu purchased the body of a man who had died eating rat poison. Montagu went to great lengths to create a believable identity for the corpse—now named Captain (acting Major) William Martin of the Royal Marines. They dressed him in the appropriate battle dress, filled his pockets with items including a picture of, and love letters from, his fake girlfriend, stamps, cigarettes, coins, matches, a receipt for a diamond engagement ring, and Royal Marine identification. They gave him a briefcase with a number of false intelligence documents containing plans for an Allied invasion through Greece and Italy. The body was kept in a special container filled with dry ice, which was labeled as

"optical instruments" to avoid detection. In the early hours of April 30, 1943, the body was released into the water off the coast of Huelva in neutral Spain. It was found by a fisherman later that morning and handed over to the Spanish authorities, who did a brief autopsy then buried "Major Martin" with full military honors in the local cemetery.

Major Martin's briefcase was sent to Madrid and thence on to London. But the Spanish had secretly removed and copied the letters before reinserting them into the sealed envelopes. The Spanish shared the intelligence with the Germans, with whom they sympathized—just as planned. German documents found after the war show that the false information had made it all the way to Hitler, prompting him to transfer forces from France to Salonika, Greece. This freed the Allies to launch their invasion through Sicily, as planned all along. Montagu later wrote a book about the operation called *The Man Who Never Was*.

Above: The grave of "William Martin" in Huelva, now with the man's real identity, Glyndwr Michael, added at the bottom.

BLACK BAG OPERATIONS

Black bag operations involve the collection of intelligence using criminal methods. The name comes from the bags burglars use to carry their tools, and indeed black bag operations very often involve breaking and entering a property. The skills needed reflect the criminal nature of the work, including lockpicking, cloning keys, and safecracking, plus specialist spy skills to quickly photograph materials or plant listening devices. And don't get caught in the act! In 1972, a black bag operation went wrong to bring down a US President.

Above: Anti-Nixon demonstrators march on the White House in 1973.

Covert listening devices, also known as bugs or wires, are a combination of microphone and radio transmitter placed in a room or phone—often in an embassy or diplomatic office. Those listening in need to be near the bug, such as in a nearby room or office, a hotel across the street, or a van parked in a nearby lot.

BRINGING DOWN A PRESIDENT

The scandal that would lead to the downfall of US President Richard Nixon in 1974 began when five burglars were found in the Democratic National Committee offices of the Watergate office complex in Washington, D.C., in 1972. The burglars first broke into the offices on May 27 to place bugs in the phones of the DNC Chairman Lawrence O'Brien and Executive Director R. Spencer Oliver. From a room in the Howard Johnson Hotel across the road, they could monitor conversations on Oliver's phone, but O'Brien's phone was not working, so they returned to fix the broken device late on June 17, taking the opportunity to copy more documents while they were there.

On his regular round, a security guard noticed that the locks of some of the doors from the underground parking garage had been taped over. He removed the tape, thinking nothing more of it. The locks had been taped to allow the doors to close without locking. On his second round, the guard discovered that the same locks had been retaped, and called the police. Alfred Baldwin, an accomplice of the burglars, was across the street in a hotel room at the time. Baldwin spent his days listening in to the conversations, and he was supposed to be on the lookout for any funny business while they were fixing the bug. However, he was watching TV instead, and missed seeing three plainclothes policemen arrive.

When the police arrived, they startled five men wearing surgical gloves

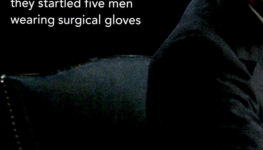

"I WANT IT IMPLEMENTED ON A THIEVERY BASIS. GODDAMN IT, GET IN AND GET THOSE FILES. BLOW THE SAFE AND GET IT."

President Nixon, ordering a break-in at the Brookings Institution in 1971

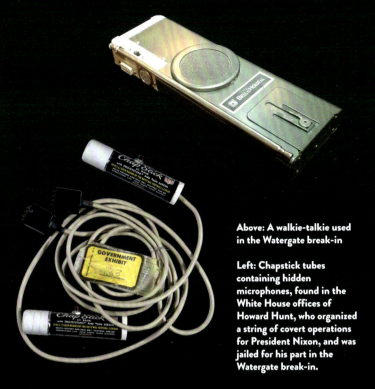

Above: A walkie-talkie used in the Watergate break-in

Left: Chapstick tubes containing hidden microphones, found in the White House offices of Howard Hunt, who organized a string of covert operations for President Nixon, and was jailed for his part in the Watergate break-in.

KEYSTROKE LOGGING

One of the more creative uses of bugs was discovered in 1984, when the Americans discovered that sixteen IBM Selectric typewriters in the embassy in Moscow and consulate in Leningrad had been compromised. The Soviets had been monitoring the machines for at least eight years using a "keystroke logger."

The monitoring device was installed in the hollow metal support bar in the typewriter. The device measured the magnetic disturbances caused by the rotation of the print ball, providing a best guess as to which letter had been typed. It would send the collected information to a listener through short radio bursts. While the data was not perfect, those listening in were able to reconstruct the text that had been typed using the probability of each letter. It likely took over an hour to install each bug, which probably took place during transit to the US embassy. The bug was undetectable to the eye, completely hidden inside the machine, and evaded detection because the radio transmission was only done in short bursts. The bugs were discovered after a tipoff from the French, who had discovered a similar device inside a teleprinter. Equipment was taken back to the US for analysis, and the bugs were discovered using X-rays.

in the process of photographing files. The police found lock picks, a shortwave receiver, forty rolls of film, two 35-millimeter cameras, three pen-sized tear gas guns, and $2,300 in serialized $100 bills. In Baldwin's room in the Howard Johnson Hotel, they found another $4,200, more breaking and entering tools, and six suitcases of bugging equipment.

NIXON IMPLICATED

The cash was later connected to the Nixon re-election campaign committee—Nixon successfully won re-election later that year. Subsequent investigations revealed that Nixon himself had directly conspired to cover up his administration's involvement in the break-in, and he was forced to resign. It had emerged that Nixon had secretly taped his own conversations in the White House. The tapes revealed that Watergate was not the first black bag operation he had organized. In 1971, he ordered the theft from the Brookings Institution, a think tank in Washington, D.C., of a report that Nixon thought would expose his own illegal actions to sabotage peace talks to end the Vietnam War in 1968, the year he was elected President.

Left: Richard Nixon announces the release of White House tapes relating to the Watergate scandal on April 29, 1974. He resigned four months later.

Below: The bugged typewriters were IBM Selectric Type II models like this.

COVER IDENTITIES

A convincing false identity is a must for any spy operating undercover in a foreign country. Spies operating in their own country (or even a friendly one) need only a fairly simple cover to disguise their identity, such as a false passport, official records of address, and type of work. But the more hostile the territory a spy is operating in for extended periods, the more developed the cover must be.

CREATING A LEGEND

The most detailed cover is known as a "legend." This is an entire fake life with details to maintain consistency. Typically, the spy will use the birth certificate of a child who died shortly after birth, and use it to develop a new identity with fake social security numbers, marriage certificates, family history, and more. The spy must memorize the details of their fictitious past life so that they become second nature.

There is an art to creating good cover, which must be a good enough background that the agent can back it up realistically. For example, if the cover identity speaks any languages fluently, the agent must be able to do so as well. With today's technology, it's harder to create good fake identities due to the digital nature of our world, where data about our activities is collected everywhere.

OFFICIAL COVER

A spy may be provided with official cover if they live in a country and work officially as part of an embassy or consulate. Unofficially, they engage in their real work: covert activities such as identifying and meeting with potential informants. If the real identity and activities of a spy with official cover are discovered, they have diplomatic immunity to somewhat protect them. Official cover agents are recognized by the government they serve, and that government may come to their aid should they need it. When spies with official cover are discovered, they are most often simply kicked out of the country.

Non-official cover (NOC) is the term used for a spy in a country for covert purposes who is not protected by diplomatic immunity. If a country discovers a spy in NOC, that spy can be arrested, tried, and imprisoned. These agents are also known as "illegals," and when discovered, they may deny any involvement by their government in order to maintain their legend. In 2010, the FBI uncovered a network of deep-cover NOC Russian agents (see page 229).

POCKET LITTER

Spies must be airtight with their cover stories, and one way to reinforce this is to carry items related to their secret identity in their wallets, purses, luggage, and pockets. "Pocket litter" is the term that describes small, throwaway objects giving credence to a spy's cover, including ticket stubs, receipts, letters, or coins. If the spy is stopped, the pocket litter lends authenticity to their identity.

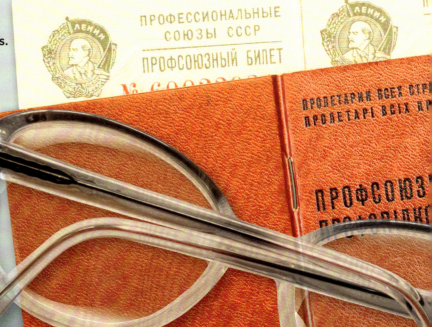

Left: Konon Molody

A LEGEND UNDONE

The Soviet spy Konon Molody successfully adopted the identity of a dead Canadian child, Gordon Lonsdale. He was the mastermind of the Portland Spy Ring in England from 1950 to 1961. His legend was flawless except for one small detail—the real Lonsdale had been circumcised at birth; Molody had not. "Lonsdale" was arrested along with four others in 1961, and sentenced to twenty-five years in prison. However, in 1964, he was part of a prisoner swap with the Soviets in which he was exchanged for British spy Greville Wynne. As part of the swap deal, the Soviets admitted that he was their spy and gave the British his real name.

SABOTAGE

Although intelligence gathering is the main purpose of intelligence agencies, they are also sometimes called upon to conduct sabotage operations. Sabotage involves the deliberate damage or destruction of equipment or infrastructure, or the deliberate misleading of targets. It can involve blowing up bridges and railways, or more modern acts such as computer ransom by malware. In 2010, intelligence agencies created a computer virus to sabotage centrifuges in Iran that could be used in uranium enrichment (see page 223).

During World War I, German agents sabotaged port installations in the US, and there was a mass sabotage of German communications by Soviet partisans during World War II. The British Special Operations Executive (SOE) was formed in World War II partly for sabotage purposes, followed by the US Office of Strategic Services (OSS).

SET EUROPE ABLAZE!

On July 16, 1940, British Prime Minister Winston Churchill established the Special Operations Executive (SOE), with the specific purpose of frustrating the enemy with acts of subversion—not just attacking infrastructure but morale as well (see also pages 122–123). The SOE blew up factories, kidnapped German generals and, in one clever attack, added itching powder to the water supply of a German laundromat. One of the SOE's most famous operations was the sabotage of the Heavy Water facility at Telemark in occupied Norway. Heavy water was a byproduct of nitrogen fixation, and the Germans were using it to develop atomic weapons. In 1942, SOE agents joined up with a group of Norwegian resistance fighters near the plant. In early 1943, they successfully destroyed the facility after several previously unsuccessful attempts.

Above: The SOE was headed from 1943 until it was disbanded in 1946 by Brigadier Colin Gubbins. Gubbins played a hands-on role, training agents and controlling them in the field.

Top: A vial of heavy water (deuterium oxide) produced by the Norsk Hydro plant.

Above: In 1944, Norwegian saboteurs blew up the ferry SF *Hydro*, on which the Germans were attempting to remove the remaining heavy water from the facility at Telemark.

SOE vs. MI6

During World War II, a bitter feud developed between the SOE and MI6, reflecting their very different operational methods. MI6 opposed the existence of SOE on the basis that its operations led to German counter-reactions that upset delicate, complex intelligence activities. SOE, meanwhile, complained that MI6 got in the way of direct-action missions.

Below: A train blown up by T.E. Lawrence in 1917 still lies where it fell in the sand at Hadiyah in modern-day Saudi Arabia.

DESTROYING THE HEJAZ RAILWAY

The Hejaz Railway was part of the railway system of the Ottoman Empire. At the outbreak of World War I, the line ran for 810 miles (1,300 km) from Damascus in Syria to Medina in the Arabian peninsula. During the Arab revolt from 1916 to 1918 (see pages 70–71), the railway became a strategic route for the Ottoman Army to move supplies and soldiers down the peninsula, making it a key target for sabotage. In 1917, T.E. Lawrence ("of Arabia") led half a dozen attacks on the railway, taking prisoners and destroying locomotives.

THE ART OF SIMPLE SABOTAGE

In the US, the Office of Strategic Services (OSS) was the precursor to the CIA. It coordinated espionage activities across US military forces. During World War II, the OSS published the Simple Sabotage Field Manual to train everyday citizens in the art of simple sabotage. For employers, the suggestions included acting like worst boss ever, giving inefficient workers praise, complaining about efficient workers, making systems overly bureaucratic, and referring all decisions to committees for "further study and consideration." For employees, suggested sabotage included working slowly, clumsily, and forgetfully, and making work take many more steps. Techniques to stymie travel involved making getting around as unpleasant as possible, with tactics such as issuing multiple tickets for the same seat and watching the argument that inevitably ensued.

ASSASSINATION

Assassination is the most extreme form of intelligence operation, widely used historically by authoritarian regimes such as Nazi Germany and the Soviet Union, though other powers have been known to engage in similar activities. Israeli intelligence uses "targeted killings" as a virtual arm of government policy, while in the US, former misgivings have recently fallen by the wayside in favor of more aggressive approaches, especially through the use of drones.

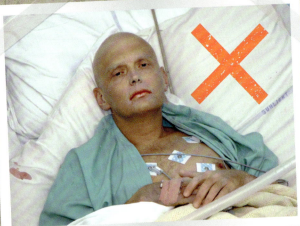

Above: Alexander Litvinenko, shortly before his death.

WETWORK

In spying circles, assassination is euphemistically known as "wetwork" due to the spilling blood. In 2006, Russia passed a law that allows the killing of "extremists" beyond its borders, which basically made it legal to assassinate anyone who was considered an enemy of the state, including former double agents. Several ex-KGB double agents have faced attempts on their lives, only sometimes surviving. Two high-profile Russian assassinations have involved the poisoning of former agents living in the UK. Alexander Litvinenko was killed in 2006 by poisoning with polonium-210, while former double agent Sergei Skripal and his daughter survived poisoning with the Novichok nerve agent in 2018 (see page 177).

"TO PROTECT CIVILIANS, THE STATE NEEDS SOMETIMES TO DO THINGS THAT ARE CONTRARY TO DEMOCRATIC BEHAVIOR."

Michael Bar-Zohar, author of *Mossad: The Greatest Missions of the Israeli Secret Service*

ELITE ASSASSINS

In the 1970s, Israel's intelligence agency Mossad developed a reputation for sleek wetwork operations, with a highly secretive division—the Kidon—that is dedicated to assassination work. Of all intelligence agencies, Mossad's assassins are perhaps the most feared—and most skilled, though they have made mistakes. Mossad's ruthless attitude is epitomized by the phrase "If someone comes to kill you, rise up, and kill him first."

Left: Qasem Soleimani

DRONE STRIKE

Since 2007, the US has been given an enhanced ability to engage in "targeted killings" by the introduction into service of the MQ-9 Reaper drone equipped with Hellfire missiles. One such target was Iranian general Qasem Soleimani, who was killed by a Reaper in Iraq in January 2020. There is controversy as to the effectiveness of drone strikes, as missile launches from a drone always carry a threat to innocent lives near the target. Internationally, the use of drones for targeted killing has also had an adverse effect on the reputation of the United States among the general populations of the parts of the world that have been targeted.

A specific chain of authority must be followed to authorize a drone strike in the US, and they must be personally signed off by the President. In other countries the chain of authority is not so clear—in Israel, for example, according to reports from Mossad, there is significantly more leeway lower down in the chain of command.

LILLEHAMMER AFFAIR

Mossad has long been known for the skill of its assassins, but in 1973 it all went wrong. The incident started with an assassination operation ordered as retaliation for the 1972 Munich massacre, in which a Palestine terror group kidnapped and killed eleven members of the Israeli Olympic team. Mossad responded with "Operation Wrath of God," with the intention to kill everybody involved. Ali Hassan Salameh was the chief of operations for Black September, the Palestinian organization responsible for the massacre. During their hunt for those responsible, Mossad thought they had found Salameh in the town of Lillehammer, Norway. Mossad agents tracked the man they thought was Salameh, a Moroccan waiter named Ahmed Bouchikhi, following him home from an evening out with his pregnant wife, then shooting him while she looked on. However, they had already aroused the attention of the local police, who arrived on the scene quickly. Two agents were caught, while several others escaped. Details of the operation emerged in subsequent interrogations, blowing much of Mossad's cover and revealing the locations of safehouses across Europe.

Below: MQ-9 Reaper drone

— CHAPTER 7 —
WORLD WAR II

Espionage played a decisive role in turning the tide of World War II (1939–1945). The British enjoyed considerable success with their SOE missions into occupied Europe, although their agents faced constant danger. The United States created its first permanent intelligence agency, the OSS, modeling it on Britain's MI6. Together, the British and Americans pulled off the extraordinary deception of Operation Fortitude, employing a range of tactics to mislead the Germans as to the location of the Normandy landings in 1944. This was one of several intelligence failures suffered by the Germans. Soviet spies enjoyed considerable successes, but Stalin's poor handling of good intelligence would cost countless lives.

The intelligence war was also fought at the level of technology. The success of British cryptographers in breaking the German Enigma code gave the Allies a crucial advantage throughout the war. Meanwhile, real-life "Q" departments in Britain and the United States created a wide range of gadgets and secret gear for spies. But the brave individuals who were parachuted into danger still had to live by their wits, relying on old-fashioned skills of deception in the knowledge that betrayal to the enemy meant almost certain death.

THE DUQUESNE SPY RING

Above: Duquesne was motivated by the harsh treatment of his family by British forces during the Second Boer War (1899–1902).

Below left: The Manhattan dockyards of the East River and Hudson were the main shipping points for Lend-Lease Aid to both beleaguered Britain and the Soviet Union.

Below right: Mugshots of all 33 operatives brought to justice in the Duquesne ring were published after they were sentenced.

One of the most important US counter-intelligence coups of World War II occurred before the nation had even entered the war. Between 1940 and 1941, the FBI succeeded in rounding up, trying, and imprisoning a ring of thirty-three spies and informants. The ring was led by the quixotic South African immigrant Frederick "Fritz" Joubert Duquesne, whose obsessive campaign against the British is as strange as anything in fiction.

ESTABLISHING THE RING

The Duquesne ring, largely based in New York, was established in 1940, with the approval of German military intelligence and the Gestapo. It was to provide information concerning supplies of arms and aid to the British war effort, including details of shipments—effectively providing a hunting map for the German U-Boat "wolf packs" prowling the Atlantic. Duquesne had recruited agents, largely German immigrants and WWI veterans, often members of the right-wing Bund, in various factories across the US and in the teeming dockyards of New York.

THE DOUBLE AGENT

The key to the detection of Duquesne's ring was a German immigrant to the US, WWI veteran and aircraft engineer William Sebold. While visiting his mother in Germany in 1939, Sebold's passport was stolen, and he was approached by the Gestapo. With threats being made to his

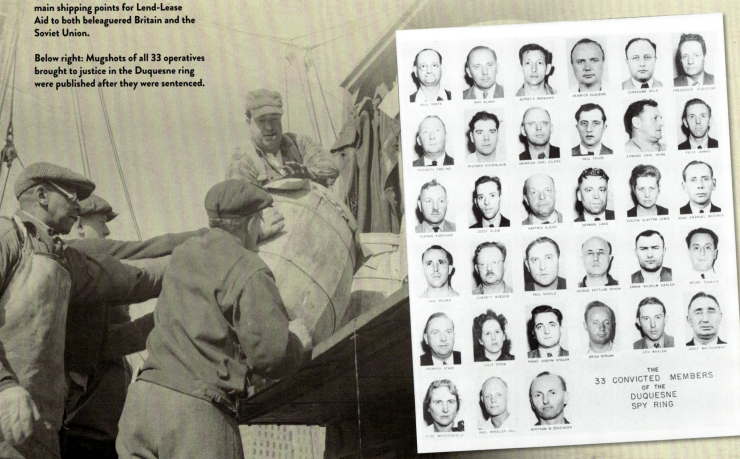

family in Germany, he agreed to spy for the Germans. However, when Sebold applied for a new passport at the US embassy in Cologne, he informed them of the situation, and agreed to become a double agent. Back in New York, furnished with a new identity ("Harry Sawyer," diesel consultant), he contacted Duquesne and offered his services as a radio transmitter.

BREAKING THE RING

The FBI made much of their success in cracking such a large Nazi spy ring (much-needed national security credentials that the Bureau needed after spending most of the 1930s swatting high-profile but essentially minor dustbowl hoodlums such as John Dillinger). But the fact is that, apart from a carefully controlled surveillance operation, the Bureau did little on-the-hoof detective work—the case was handed to them on a plate by Sebold. The FBI placed hidden cameras and recording devices in Sebold's office, and simply watched and waited as the operatives delivered all the evidence the FBI needed to arrest them. The Bureau was also able to monitor the radio traffic, as some five hundred messages in total were sent or received by an FBI short-wave radio transmitter on Long Island. Duquesne was sentenced to eighteen years' imprisonment.

Kitchener's success in the Boer War made him a focus for patriotism in World War I.

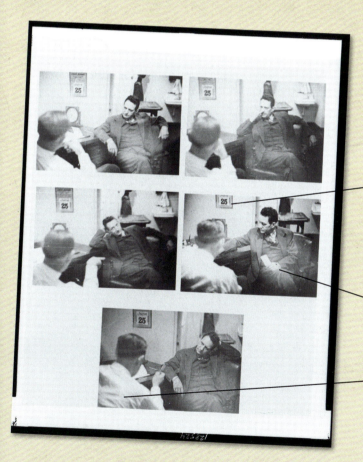

The FBI rigged Sebold's NY office with both film and sound recording equipment. The informants were completely at ease.

Second secret surveillance camera hidden behind picture.

Informer gives Sebold the information.

No notes were taken as it was too dangerous. Sebold memorizes interview before transmitting to Germany—and the FBI.

"THE MAN WHO KILLED KITCHENER"

During the Boer War, Duquesne became involved in anti-British activities in South Africa, leading to his internment on Bermuda. He emigrated to the US on his release in 1902. During World War I, he focused on maritime sabotage, and was implicated in several UK cargo ship sinkings, and was again imprisoned. Among other acts, he was blamed for the sinking of HMS *Hampshire*, in which Field Marshal Kitchener drowned. He traveled to Germany after his release and suggested setting up an information-gathering ring in the US. He opened his front for the infamous spy ring in New York, under the name of "Air Terminals Co."

"DON'T BE CONCERNED IF THIS INFORMATION IS CONFIDENTIAL, BECAUSE IT WILL BE IN THE HANDS OF A GOOD, PATRIOTIC CITIZEN."

Fritz Duquesne, in a letter to the US Chemical Welfare Service, 1940

SPECIAL OPERATIONS EXECUTIVE

Left: An SOE demolition class at Milton Hall, England.

Below: A Welrod pistol with silencer, used by the SOE from 1942.

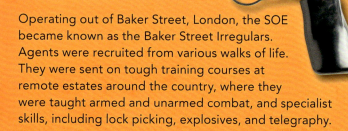

The Special Operations Executive (SOE) was set up by the British in 1940, following the fall of France, to wage a secret war behind enemy lines. The mission of the SOE was to link up with local resistance movements and spread sabotage and subversion in the occupied territories—in the worlds of British prime minister Winston Churchill, to "set Europe ablaze." Working out of uniform, the agents faced the prospect of torture and execution for spying if caught. Many lost their lives, and the average life expectancy of a radio operator sent to France was just six weeks.

Operating out of Baker Street, London, the SOE became known as the Baker Street Irregulars. Agents were recruited from various walks of life. They were sent on tough training courses at remote estates around the country, where they were taught armed and unarmed combat, and specialist skills, including lock picking, explosives, and telegraphy.

SPY EQUIPMENT

New equipment was developed specially for the SOE at research and development labs. Specialized tools included a radio disguised as a suitcase (see pages 170–171), silenced

Left to right: Odette Hallowes, Violette Szabo, Noor Inayat Khan

Below: SOE agents pose in uniform in southern France.

FEMALE OPERATIVES

More than three thousand women joined the SOE, many of them enlisting in the First Aid Nursing Yeomanry (FANY) to hide their true roles. Female agents proved highly effective, particularly in France, where young women could move around without attracting suspicion more easily than young men. Many female SOE agents were later decorated for bravery, including Odette Hallowes, who operated as a courier for the French Resistance for five months before her capture in 1943. She was tortured by the Gestapo before being sent to Ravensbruck concentration camp, and was ultimately one of the few SOE agents to survive capture. Violette Szabo was captured on her second mission to France and was also sent to Ravensbruck, where she was executed. Wireless operator Noor (Nora) Inayat Khan was executed at Dachau concentration camp following her capture in Paris. All three women were awarded the George Cross for bravery.

pistols, single-use firearms disguised as pens, limpet mines, and plastic explosives. Agents would be parachuted into place carrying the equipment and forged papers they needed.

Despite misgivings from MI6, who considered the SOE to be a bunch of dangerous amateurs, it achieved considerable successes. A daring sabotage mission destroyed the Norsk Hydro plant in Norway, thwarting the Nazis' attempts to build a nuclear bomb (see page 114), while the high-profile assassination in Prague of Reinhard Heydrich, one of the main architects of the Holocaust, sent shock waves across Europe. The killing of Heydrich provoked extreme reprisals in Czechoslovakia with the execution of thousands of civilians. Such brutal acts of revenge caused misgivings among many in the British Foreign Office, but Churchill remained a staunch supporter of the SOE, maintaining that the disruption they were causing was critical to build resistance in the occupied countries and help to coordinate an invasion. His continued faith in the SOE was to prove well placed.

CLEARING THE WAY FOR D-DAY

SOE operatives played a crucial role in the D-Day landings in 1944 through a mission codenamed Operation Jedburgh (see also page 139). Three-man teams were parachuted into France shortly before the landings to direct resistance actions toward delaying the deployment of German troops to Normandy. They sabotaged German transport trains by replacing the axle oil with abrasive grease that seized up the wheels. As Allied troops advanced, the SOE provided a link between the resistance groups and Allied command.

FORCE 136

Above: Douglas Jung

While the SOE initially operated in Europe, it expanded its operations in 1941 to territories in Asia that were occupied by the Japanese, under the cover name Force 136. Agents secretly recruited and trained local people in Burma, Malaya, China, and Thailand to perform sabotage operations and gather intelligence. One hundred and fifty Chinese Canadians served in Force 136. Their heroics helped to secure Chinese Canadians full voting rights after the war, and a former Force 136 agent, Captain Douglas Jung, became the first Canadian Member of Parliament from a visible minority when he was elected in 1957.

AIDING THE PARTISANS

In occupied Yugoslavia, SOE operatives initially joined forces with the royalist Chetnik resistance movement. However, following reports of Chetnik collaboration with the German and Italian occupying forces, they switched allegiance in 1943 to the communist Partisans, led by future Yugoslav leader Tito. The extreme resistance encountered by the Axis powers in Yugoslavia diverted huge resources from other fronts. By 1945, the Partisans were the most effective resistance movement of all. They numbered 800,000 members, and played a leading role in the liberation of Yugoslavia.

"THE DISRUPTION OF ENEMY RAIL COMMUNICATIONS, THE HARASSING OF GERMAN ROAD MOVES, AND THE CONTINUAL AND INCREASING STRAIN PLACED ON GERMAN SECURITY SERVICES THROUGHOUT OCCUPIED EUROPE PLAYED A VERY CONSIDERABLE PART IN OUR COMPLETE AND FINAL VICTORY."

General Dwight Eisenhower

US INTELLIGENCE IN THE PACIFIC

Just before 8 a.m. on Sunday, December 7, 1941, the Imperial Japanese Navy (IJN) mounted a surprise attack on Pearl Harbor, a US military base in Honolulu, Hawaii. President Roosevelt described it as "a date that will live in infamy." This sneak attack was intended as a preventive action to stop the US Navy's Pacific Fleet from intervening in Japan's planned offensive in Southeast Asia. It produced an immediate response from the Americans, who declared war on Japan the next day. It also galvanized the United States into organizing coordinated intelligence operations. This would quickly lead to decisive intelligence-led victories in the Pacific. Following the war, the memory of Pearl Harbor motivated the establishment of a permanent peacetime agency. The Americans were determined never to be taken by surprise again.

Above: US cryptographers built six reverse-engineered analogs of Japan's "Purple" cipher.

From 1939, Japan's high-level diplomatic communications had been encrypted with the help of Enigma machines supplied by Germany. That year, the US Army and Navy had set up a joint operation dedicated to breaking Japanese codes, called Operation Magic. The new code—named "Purple" by American cryptographers—proved hard to crack, but the formulaic nature of the messages, starting with the same phrase each time, allowed significant progress by 1941. Deciphering the messages was a laborious process, however, and the information was often out of date by the time it had been deciphered. In any case, none of the deciphered Purple messages gave a clue of the impending attack, as the Japanese were careful not to mention it on diplomatic channels. Instead, information about the plan was sent by the IJN using a new code, named JN25 by the Americans. JN25 was identified as a five-digit code, but it remained unbroken by December. The air raid on Pearl Harbor came as a complete surprise.

Above: Admiral Chester Nimitz, the Commander in Chief of the US Pacific Fleet, presents a Navy Cross to Steward's Mate Doris Miller. Despite a lack of training, Miller had manned anti-aircraft guns during the attack on Pearl Harbor. The first black American to be awarded the Navy Cross, he was killed in action in 1943.

RAMPING UP THE INTELLIGENCE EFFORT

Now formally at war with Japan and Germany, the US sought help from its British allies, who sent cryptographers from Bletchley Park (see pages 126–127). Six months later, US intelligence could decipher the Purple code far more swiftly. Meanwhile, the IJN's communications traffic increased considerably after Pearl Harbor, giving operatives at Operation Magic the raw material they needed to decipher JN25. By April 1942, about one in five words in JN25 was readable—enough to extract useful information. The Japanese had no idea either code had been broken.

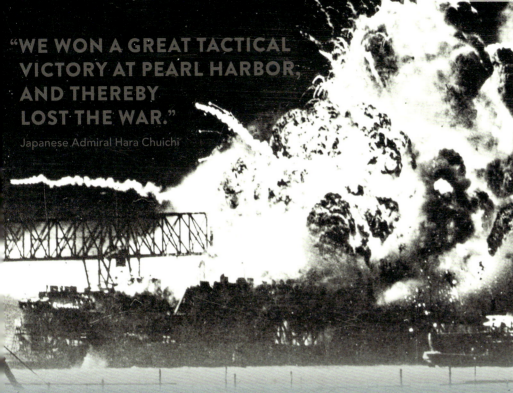

"WE WON A GREAT TACTICAL VICTORY AT PEARL HARBOR, AND THEREBY LOST THE WAR."

Japanese Admiral Hara Chuichi

Above: USS *Shaw* burns following the attack on Pearl Harbor.

Above: Marshal Yamamoto

DEATH OF YAMAMOTO

The architect of the attack on Midway, Marshal Yamamoto Isoroku, whose plans had been so comprehensively defeated by US intelligence, was himself to lose his life due to an intelligence failure. In early 1943, Yamamoto planned an inspection tour of the South Pacific aimed at improving Japanese spirits. Messages detailing Yamamoto's itinerary were intercepted and decoded by US intelligence, and the decision was made to take him out. On April 18, Yamamoto's flight from Rabaul to Balalae was shot down by American fighter jets. The loss of the commander-in-chief of the Combined Fleet proved a major blow to Japan's already flagging morale.

TURNING THE TIDE

The Japanese would continue to use the Purple code, which was also broken by the Soviets in 1941, right through the war. However, they never managed to break US codes, and this created an intelligence deficit that would prove critical. The Japanese once again planned a massive attack on a US base in the Pacific, with the intention of knocking them out of the war. This time the target was Midway Atoll. However, the contrast with Pearl Harbor could not have been more stark. With the help of partially broken JN25 messages, US intelligence officers determined both the location and the date of the planned attack, complete with an IJN order of battle that would allow the Americans to ambush Japanese fighter jets.

Four Japanese aircraft carriers attacked Midway base in the early morning on June 4, 1942. However, they did not know that a US fleet was waiting for them to the east of the island. Over the course of two days of fighting, the Japanese lost all four carriers, one cruiser, and hundreds of aircraft. It was a decisive victory to the Americans, and marked the point at which the Japanese empire started to retreat. Victory at Midway was the beginning of the end of the war in the Pacific, made possible by superior intelligence.

Left: US Navy Douglas SBD-3 "Dauntless" dive bombers in action during the Battle of Midway.

Above: An Enigma machine

THE ENIGMA MACHINE

At the start of the war, the Germans believed they had an unbeatable advantage in cryptology, in the form of a device called the Enigma machine. However, a group of brilliant British cryptologists used a combination of clever mathematics and brute force to crack the Enigma codes, providing the Allies with a secret ear on the German military throughout the war.

Invented by engineer Arthur Scherbius in 1918, the Enigma machine was first adopted by the German military in 1926. Externally, the machine resembled a typewriter; it was easily portable and simple to use in the field. Each time a key was pressed, three rotors inside the machine rotated. This kept the cipher continuously changing, and later models had a mammoth 103 sextillion (that is, a 1 with 21 zeros after it) possible settings. Even modern computers could not crack this number of possibilities in a reasonable timeframe.

THE POLISH BOMBA

Not surprisingly, the Germans believed the Enigma codes to be unbreakable. However, poor operating procedures produced cracks in the armor. Polish cryptographers were the first to exploit these weaknesses. The initial breakthrough came in 1932, when a spy in Germany's Cipher Office, Hans-Thilo Schmidt, passed German manuals and Enigma keys to the French, who in turn passed it to the Poles. The talented Polish mathematician Marian Rejewski used this information to work out the internal wiring of the Enigma machines and reverse-engineer them. By 1938, Rejewski had built a machine to crack Enigma ciphers, which he called the "bomba."

As war loomed, the Poles shared their Enigma work with the British and French in July 1939. However, as part of their preparations for war, the Germans increased the security of their encryption, adding complexity to the machines and changing the cipher

"THE KNOWLEDGE NOT ONLY OF THE ENEMY'S PRECISE STRENGTH AND DISPOSITION BUT ALSO HOW, WHEN, AND WHERE HE INTENDS TO CARRY OUT HIS OPERATIONS HAS BROUGHT A NEW DIMENSION TO THE PROSECUTION OF THE WAR."

General Harold Alexander, Supreme Allied Commander in Italy

Above: German troops using an Enigma machine in the field.

system daily. The codes once more became unreadable. Cryptologists working for the GC&CS at Bletchley Park, England, led by another brilliant mathematician, Alan Turing, built on the knowledge passed on from Rejewski's team to build their own Enigma-cracking machine, the "Bombe," which was ready for action by March 1940. The huge machine, contained 108 rotating drums, which simulated the scrambling actions of the Enigma rotors, and could be used to test possible starting positions of the Enigma machine used to encrypt a message.

Above: Marian Rejewski

FINDING "CRIBS"

The Bombe allowed Turing and his team to greatly narrow down the number of possible settings in the Enigma codes, but they still needed a starting input for the machines to test. This was provided by "cribs"—sections of plaintext that were thought to correspond to the ciphertext. Guessing the correct cribs was difficult, but the habits of the German Enigma operators provided a way in. Certain standard messages, such as "nothing to report," appeared often, while regular weather reports provided further clues. The Bombe was programmed in such a way that it would stop at each setting that was consistent with the crib. These stopping positions provided a set of possibilities that could be tested, and codes could often be broken within a matter of hours. By mid-1940, the Bletchley team was breaking keys on a daily basis. Eventually the British built 211 Bombes, and Turing later helped the Americans build their version. A workforce of more than ten thousand was employed at Bletchley Park. Despite the numbers involved, security was never breached. The Germans remained oblivious to their existence throughout the war.

Above and below: A working replica of the original Bombe is on display at Bletchley Park, which is now a museum.

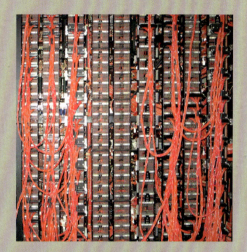

ALAN TURING

The wartime work of mathematician Alan Turing (1912–1954) was only revealed long after his death. He joined the GC&CS at the outbreak of the war. In addition to his work on the Enigma code, he worked out a procedure known as "Turingery" to crack the German Lorenz cipher. He also found the time to write two papers on probability and statistics in cryptography, which were considered so important by British intelligence that they were only declassified in 2012. After the war, Turing worked in computing, producing the blueprint for modern computers. He later turned his mind to problems in biology. At a time when homosexual acts were criminal offenses in the UK, Turing was convicted for "gross indecency" in 1952, and he died shortly afterward, apparently by suicide. His contributions to cryptography and computing are only now being properly recognized in his own country.

Below: This statue of Turing at Bletchley Park is made from half a million pieces of Welsh slate.

USING ULTRA

From 1941 onward, British signals intelligence was classified as "Ultra," signifying that this was the most secret intelligence operation of all. Intelligence gathered by the Bletchley Park cryptographers (see pages 126–127) was modified to disguise its original source, while elaborate ruses were devised to create alternative explanations for the Allies' knowledge, such as traitors within German command. As the war progressed, "Ultra" came to stand for all Allied intelligence as the British and Americans increasingly shared information and expertise. Its success was key to victories in the crucial Battle of the Atlantic.

PHANTOM SPIES

To create cover for the Ultra intelligence, a secret MI6 agent codenamed "Boniface" was invented. Reports from Bletchley Park were marked with the initials of different agents, giving the impression that "Boniface" was running a network of spies within Germany. Security was kept so tight that even senior members of the government were kept in the dark as to the real identity of "Boniface." While verbatim transcripts of decrypted messages were sent to the Admiralty, heavily paraphrased versions were sent to commanders in the field, disguising the true source of the intelligence in case the Germans intercepted the messages. Fortunately, the Germans had such faith in their Enigma encryptions that it took little to persuade them that they had been betrayed from within. Meanwhile, aerial reconnaissance patrols were routinely ordered over enemy positions—with instructions to make sure they were seen—whenever Ultra intelligence was about to be acted on. For every intelligence-led action, a plausible alternative source of the information needed to be provided.

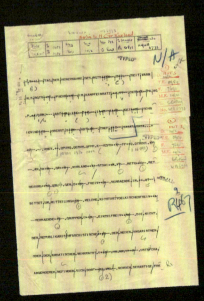

Above: A typical marked-up
Bletchley intercept sheet,

BATTLING FOR THE ATLANTIC

Ultra first proved its value in the Battle of the Atlantic, a continuous naval battle that lasted the length of the war, peaking in 1943. The British relied on merchant ships from the Americas to keep them supplied and capable of prosecuting the war. The Battle of the Atlantic involved Axis attempts to starve Britain of this materiel, deploying "wolfpacks" of U-boats to torpedo British convoys.

By spring 1941, the British were suffering heavy losses. This all changed from mid-May onward, when the British captured a German weather trawler and a U-boat, providing them with an Enigma machine and codes for the next two months. Armed with this information, the team at Bletchley had broken U-boat messages by the end of the month, and they would continue to break the transmissions for the next five months. This gave them detailed knowledge of the movements of the wolfpacks, which were controlled via extensive communications with command. The effect was immediate, and merchant ship losses dropped by more than two thirds,

Above: Admiral Karl Dönitz, seen here inspecting a U-boat, formulated the "wolfpack" tactic for the Battle of the Atlantic. He was bewildered when so many of his submarines were located and destroyed.

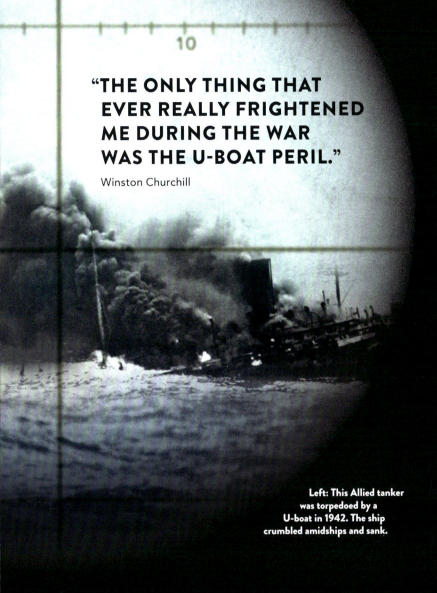

10

"THE ONLY THING THAT EVER REALLY FRIGHTENED ME DURING THE WAR WAS THE U-BOAT PERIL."

Winston Churchill

Left: This Allied tanker was torpedoed by a U-boat in 1942. The ship crumbled amidships and sank.

DEFEATING DÖNITZ

By 1942, the Germans had introduced a new Enigma key setting, ending British access to U-boat communications. The timing could not have been worse, given that the Americans had now entered the war, and the Allies on both sides of the Atlantic suffered heavy losses throughout the year. U-boat numbers were higher than they had been in 1941, and so many convoys were being attacked that Britain's ability to continue the war was once again being called into question. Another Ultra success turned the tide when the new codes were finally cracked by Bletchley Park. Following two months of intense fighting between March and May, 1943, U-boat losses amounted to a quarter of the entire fleet. The losses were so heavy that Admiral Dönitz, the commander of the German Navy, was forced to abandon operations in the North Atlantic. Dönitz ordered a review of signals security, but the review wrongly concluded that Enigma itself was secure. This decisive victory secured the supply lines that would be critical to the preparations for D-Day a year later.

DEFEATING ROMMEL

Above: Erwin Rommel

The Allied victory in the Second Battle of El Alamein in Egypt in October–November, 1942, was later acclaimed by Churchill as the decisive turning point in the war—the moment, he said, from which the Allies started to win. The German Afrika Korps, led by the "Desert Fox," Field Marshal Erwin Rommel, was repelled, and the Allies secured control of the vital Suez Canal and Middle Eastern oil fields. In the leadup to the battle, Ultra intelligence provided information about Axis shipping to North Africa. It was relentlessly attacked, with only thirty percent of ships getting through. Intelligence subsequently painted a picture of supply lines in total chaos. The Allied commander in North Africa, Field Marshal Bernard Montgomery, took decisive advantage of this situation, further using Ultra intelligence to plan surprise attacks. Ultra intercepts showed that Rommel had desperately pleaded with his superiors for more troops and supplies. However, with the war in Russia sucking in resources as the Battle of Stalingrad ground on, it had never been likely that Rommel would receive the men and arms he had begged for. On November 4, after twelve days of fighting, Rommel gave the orders to retreat. A week later, the Axis had been expelled from Egypt.

STALIN AND HIS SPIES

The Soviet Union operated an extensive network of spies around the world both before and during World War II, supplying Stalin with a stream of first-rate intelligence. Many Soviet spy rings were run by dedicated communists of diverse nationalities, eager to contribute to the cause. Unfortunately, Stalin's paranoid and authoritarian nature often led him to ignore their reports, most disastrously those forewarning of Operation Barbarossa—the German plan to invade the Soviet Union.

THE RED ORCHESTRA

The Red Orchestra was the name given by the SS to resistance groups across Europe assumed to be under the control of the Soviet Union. Sticking with the theme, SS counter-espionage agents called radios "pianos," operators "pianists," and organizers "conductors." Disparate groups, including German resistance fighters such as Harro Schultze-Boysen (see page 94), were included under the "Red Orchestra" umbrella term, but in reality they mostly had little or no contact with one another.

Among the most effective Red Orchestra groups were those set up by a long-standing NKVD agent, the Polish Jew Leopold Trepper. Trepper had worked closely with the French Communist Party in the years before the war, and he had a wide range of contacts with the communist resistance. Posing as a Canadian industrialist, he set up a series of cover companies, establishing groups in occupied France and Belgium. Through these groups, Trepper gathered a range of military and industrial intelligence. He even obtained information from high-ranking German officers at dinner parties where he posed as a German businessman.

Trepper's networks were betrayed in spring 1942, and had mostly been liquidated by the end of the year. More than six hundred people were arrested, most of whom were tortured and executed. When the Germans arrested Trepper, they tried to turn him into a double agent, sending misinformation to Moscow. However, he managed to escape, and sat out the war in hiding in Paris. On his return to Moscow in 1945, he was immediately arrested. Like many returning combatants, he was suspected of disloyalty by Stalin's paranoid regime, and he spent the next ten years in a gulag. On his release in 1955, Trepper moved to Poland, from where he emigrated to Israel, where he died in 1982.

THE RED THREE AND THE LUCY RING

The Soviet Union established its most efficient spy network in neutral Switzerland. Known as the "Rote Drei" ("Red Three"), the network was run out of Lausanne by Hungarian cartographer Alexander Radó, who communicated by radio directly with Moscow. Radó's network supplied a steady stream of information, averaging around five reports a day between 1941 and 1944. Despite the group's name, there were often four or five agents operating in the ring, all reporting to Radó. They included the Germans Ursula Hamburger and Rachel Duebendorfer. Another German joined Radó's ring operating under the code name "Lucy." Radó knew nothing of Lucy other than that he was operating

> ## "THEY WERE OFTEN NOT RUSSIANS AT ALL . . . THEY WORKED UNDERCOVER, OFTEN AT GREAT PERSONAL RISK, AND TRAVELED THROUGHOUT THE WORLD IN SEARCH OF POTENTIAL RECRUITS. THEY WERE THE BEST RECRUITERS AND CONTROLLERS THE RUSSIAN INTELLIGENCE SERVICE EVER HAD."
>
> Peter Wright, author of *Spycatcher*

Right: Leopold Trepper in later life

Below: Alexander Radó

out of Lucerne. The "Lucy Ring" was so secretive that many myths and legends became associated with it, including a rumor that it was run by the British as a means of communicating secrets to the Soviets. In reality, "Lucy" was German refugee Rudolf Roessler, who was relaying information from a number of sources inside Germany. The identities of Roessler's sources remain uncertain, but they included senior army officers and politicians. Whoever they were, they provided "Lucy" with timely information about German operations on the Eastern Front. Some, or all, of the Lucy sources are thought to have been involved in the failed plot to assassinate Hitler in 1944, after which the information dried up. Like Trepper, Radó received no thanks for his work. He was also sent to a Soviet labor camp in 1945.

IGNORING THE WARNINGS

The Soviets' spy operations demonstrated how intelligence is only useful if it is acted on appropriately. Stalin received prior warning of the German invasion in 1941 from a number of different sources, including Trepper, Radó, and Richard Sorge operating out of Tokyo (see page 91). This tallied with intelligence the Soviets had obtained from the Allies. However, Stalin chose to disbelieve the evidence, and German tanks were already deep into Soviet territory before he reacted to the invasion.

THE SOCIALITE SPY

Prior to the occupation of France, Belgian heiress and socialite Suzanne Spaak lived the high life in Paris with her husband and two children. In 1942, appalled by the occupation and the Nazis' racial ideology, Spaak offered her support to the newly formed National Movement Against Racism, a group set up with the primary aim of saving black French children from deportation. Via this group, Spaak was recruited to the Red Orchestra by Leopold Trepper. In her time with the Red Orchestra, she saved dozens of Jewish children from deportation, often sheltering them in her own home. Like many members of the Red Orchestra, Spaak was betrayed and arrested by the Gestapo. She was executed on August 12, 1944, just days before the liberation of Paris.

Left: Suzanne Spaak

THE DOUBLE-CROSS SYSTEM

One of Britain's most successful spying operations in World War II started with a German attempt to spy on the UK. In the early years of the war, the Germans smuggled hundreds of spies into Britain, but they were badly trained and poorly motivated, and British security services had little trouble in identifying them. MI5 decided that this was an opportunity not to be missed, creating the Double-Cross system, in which the Germans' entire spying operation in Britain was turned against them. The double agents fed their handlers a stream of carefully chosen misinformation and misdirection that would prove crucial to the defense of Britain and the success of the D-Day landings. The Germans never caught on that they were being duped.

In May 1940, German troops swept through Western Europe. With the Americans and Soviets yet to enter the war, Britain found itself isolated. Amid widespread public concerns that a "Fifth Column" of Nazi spies was preparing the ground for an invasion, MI5 received thousands of reports of suspected enemy activity. The vast majority of these reports were false alarms, but the Germans had indeed initiated an espionage campaign in Britain from July 1940. They would never realize how much that decision had cost them.

Left: Eddie Chapman

> **"CHAPMAN LOVED HIMSELF, LOVED ADVENTURE, AND LOVED HIS COUNTRY, PROBABLY IN THAT ORDER."**
>
> MI5 internal assessment of Eddie Chapman, AKA Agent Zigzag

TAKING OVER THE NETWORK

Records from after the war show that, of the 115 spies sent to Britain, 114 of them were identified by MI5, while the 115th committed suicide. They were swiftly picked up, and by 1941, British intelligence was confident that it controlled the entire network, turning Germany's spies against them in the highly successful Double-Cross system.

The system was operated by the Twenty Committee (so-named because the number 20 is written "XX" in Roman numerals), under the chairmanship of the academic John Masterman. Masterman later wrote a book in which he gave details of more than one hundred agents he had working for him. Captured spies underwent lengthy interrogations, after which those considered suitable were offered the chance to save themselves from prison or execution by turning double agent. The new agents were passed on to the control of MI5 operative "TAR" Robertson. Via his double agents, communicating via steganography or wireless, Robertson fed the Germans a carefully selected mix of disinformation and real (but harmless) intelligence.

AGENT ZIGZAG

Many of the Double-Cross agents proved difficult to handle, given their questionable loyalty and often checkered pasts. Eddie Chapman, an English safecracker who had been recruited by the Germans while in prison in occupied Jersey, was codenamed Zigzag by his British handlers for his erratic character. Chapman was already well used to the use of aliases from his criminal past. His spying activities took him right around Europe. He was given credit for a faked sabotage attack on an aircraft factory in England, and traveled to Lisbon in neutral Portugal to be debriefed by his German handler. In Lisbon, he convinced the Germans to give him two bombs with which to blow up a merchant ship. He promptly handed over the bombs to the ship's captain to pass on to the British for analysis. Chapman subsequently moved from Lisbon to an Abwehr safehouse in Norway, where he secretly photographed German agents, before he returned to Britain to continue his work. The Germans were so impressed with Chapman's faked sabotage actions that they awarded him the Iron Cross.

Above: A street lies in ruins in Camberwell, southeast London,
after a V-1 bomb has fallen short of its central London target.

DECEPTION AND CONFUSION

The Double-Cross system played an important role in
Operation Fortitude (see pages 136–137) in the lead-up
to D-Day. The agents fed their German handlers a steady
stream of disinformation about troop movements in
Southern England, creating the false impression that
the D-Day landings would be taking place at Calais.

One week after the D-Day landings, the Germans
commenced a sustained missile attack against Britain.
Between June and October 1944, nearly ten thousand V-1
rockets were fired at southeast England. The Double-Cross
agents were instructed to inform their handlers that the
rockets aimed at central London were overshooting their
targets. The Germans adjusted their aim, and the majority
of rockets fell short, hitting less-populated suburban areas
instead. By October, the launch sites of the V-1 rockets had
been taken by the Allies, but by then the longer-range V-2
rockets had taken their place. The Double-Cross agents fed
their handlers the locations for V-2 bomb impacts in central
London that could be verified by the Germans by aerial
reconnaissance, but with a time-stamp to identify the bombs
with earlier impacts that had fallen short. More and more
bombs fell short of their targets as the Germans once again
readjusted their sights. The strategy was controversial but
ethical objections were overruled, and there is little doubt
that the Double-Cross system saved lives during this time.

THE "GESTAPO SPIES"

Hundreds of Nazi sympathizers were interned
in Britain during the war, including the leader
of the British Union of Fascists (BUF) Oswald
Mosley. However, fear of a German invasion
persisted into 1942, when MI5 instigated an
operation to ferret out potential Fifth Columnists.
Armed with a fake Gestapo identity card under
the alias "Jack King," intelligence officer Eric
Roberts posed as a Gestapo operative seeking
to establish a network of spies. Roberts first
contacted known Fascist sympathizer Marita
Perigoe. Perigoe eagerly passed documents to
"King," including sketches she had made of the
security arrangements at various factories. She
also proved zealous in her mission to expand the
circle, regularly introducing King to potential
recruits. Perigoe's recruits passed on a variety of
military secrets. In fact, the imaginary spy ring
proved so productive that MI5 decided to award
two of its members—Perigoe and the Austrian-
born Hans Kohout, who had access to intelligence
through his role in the Civil Defence—with fake
commendations from the Gestapo. Roberts
maintained his spy ring throughout the war,
intercepting a wealth of information that might
otherwise have made its way into German hands.

GERMAN INTELLIGENCE

Germany's intelligence successes in World War II were certainly outnumbered by its failures. Intelligence operations were run by the Abwehr until 1944, when its functions were taken over by Heinrich Himmler's SD. The SD was more committed to the Nazi cause than the Abwehr. However, both services suffered from poor intelligence evaluation and limited success in code-breaking. Many of their efforts were used against them, as their operatives were turned into double-agents, including the entire cohort of spies sent to Britain (see pages 132–133).

The Abwehr was run by Admiral Wilhelm Canaris. Canaris was executed for his part in the plot against Hitler in 1944 (see page 92), but his opposition to the brutal manner of the Nazi war methods, including the persecution of Jews and the execution of prisoners, had been growing for years. He maintained strained relations with Heinrich Himmler's rival intelligence agency, the *Sicherheitsdienst* (SD), and his lack of commitment to the cause compromised his organization's effectiveness. Intelligence failures by Canaris's Abwehr included a disastrous underestimation of Soviet capabilities in the lead-up to the invasion of the Soviet Union in 1941. Partly as a result of the outcome of that invasion, Canaris had reached the conclusion as early as 1942 that the war could not be won, and was now often actively working against his own side.

FAILED US MISSIONS

In the US, the FBI had rounded up the Duquesne spy ring by the time the Americans entered the war (see pages 120–121). Canaris had made the US a primary target for espionage, but he suffered another major setback in 1942 with the failure of Operation Pastorius. He recruited eight Germans who had previously lived in the US for the operation. They were trained, given false identities, and smuggled into the

OPERATION BERNHARD

Named after its director, SS Major Bernhard Krüger, Operation Bernhard was a plan to destabilize the British economy by flooding it with counterfeit bank notes. In 1942, Krüger created a team of counterfeiters from the prisoners at Sachsenhausen concentration camp. By the time the camp was evacuated in April 1945, its printing press had produced nearly nine million notes, which were so well made that it was nearly impossible to distinguish them from the real thing. The original plan had been to drop the notes from aircraft over Britain, but in the end most were not used. Those that were used were either laundered to buy imported goods or paid to German agents. The slave laborers used to produce the notes were transferred from Sachsenhausen with the intention to exterminate them en masse. However, amid the chaos, many of them survived. Most of the notes ended up at the bottom of a lake in Austria, but they occasionally appeared in circulation for many years after the war.

Below: Holocaust survivor Adolf Burger holds up one of the bank notes he was forced to forge.

country, with orders to sabotage a series of high-profile economic targets. One of the first targets was to be the Hell Gate Bridge in New York City. However, the operation was sabotaged from within almost immediately. One of the agents assigned to Hell Gate Bridge, George Dasch, turned himself in to the FBI, and all eight saboteurs were captured before they could carry out a single mission. Six were executed, while Dasch and one other were given long prison terms.

Above: Hell Gate Bridge, one of the main targets of Operation Pastorius.

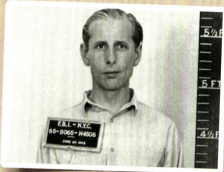

Above: George Dasch on his arrest by the FBI

THE ENGLAND GAME

One of the Abwehr's biggest successes came in the Netherlands in 1942. The British SOE had been training Dutch agents to help the nascent resistance movement. One of the first agents to be sent into the Netherlands, Huub Lauwers, was captured by the Germans on March 6, 1942. Under duress, he was instructed to continue to send messages to London. However, Lauwers was confident that the SOE would realize he had been compromised. In his messages, he left out the secret security code that was supposed to be included in all his messages. Surely this would be the sign the SOE needed? To his dismay, they disregarded the lack of a security code and continued to send agents into the Netherlands, where they were easily picked up in an operation that the Abwehr called the *Englandspiel*, or England Game. German agents sent further messages to London posing as the captured agents, again lacking the security codes, and received in return detailed plans for the SOE's operations in the Netherlands. More than fifty agents were captured over the course of two years, effectively decapitating the Dutch resistance movement. Nearly all of them were executed. Agents within the SOE had highlighted the lack of a security signature within the messages, but their concerns had been ignored. The *Englandspiel* was the Abwehr's greatest intelligence success, and the SOE's greatest failure.

AGENT CICERO

The Albanian Elyesa Bazna—codenamed Cicero by the SD—was Germany's most successful spy during World War II. He worked as the valet to the British ambassador, Sir Hughe Knatchbull-Hugessen, in Ankara in neutral Turkey. He managed to win the trust of the ambassador, who was in the habit of taking classified documents home with him. Bazna broke into the ambassador's document box and photographed the papers. He offered the films to the German Embassy in return for payment in pounds sterling. In total, he would be paid the princely sum of £300,000 for his services. Between October 1943 and February 1944, Bazna passed over a wealth of high-grade intelligence, including the codeword for for D-Day, Operation Overlord. However, the Germans distrusted Bazna and, lacking the ability to properly evaluate his intelligence, they mostly disregarded it. They had no idea what they had. Bazna's lucrative activities were eventually ended when he was identified as the leak in a "honey trap" operation by a US spy working as a secretary at the German Embassy in Ankara. Bazna promptly fled with a suitcase full of the cash he had been paid, only to discover that the Germans had paid him in worthless forged notes printed at Sachsenhausen.

Right: Elyesa Bazna

PROTECTING D-DAY

On June 6, 1944, 156,000 British, American, and Canadian troops landed on five beaches in Normandy, Northern France. This was D-Day—the start of Operation Overlord to liberate Europe. The coastline was heavily fortified, and for the invasion to have any hope of success, Germany's powerful panzer divisions had to be kept well away from the landing beaches. To this end, the Allies enacted a colossal deception plan to persuade the Germans that the invasion would take place farther to the east in Pas de Calais. Fake armies were invented, and their movements were reported to the Germans by fake agents. Dummy ships and tanks were built, and a mass of fake radio traffic was broadcast. The operation was so successful that the Germans held a large force back in Pas de Calais for months after the Normandy landings had taken place. It made the difference between success and failure.

The operation to mislead the German army as to the location of the landings was named Operation Fortitude. The Allies contrived to convince the Germans that they intended to invade anywhere but Normandy—through Norway (Fortitude North) or Pas de Calais (Fortitude South), or even both.

FAKE ARMIES

The Allies used a variety of "special means" to confuse the Axis forces. The British created six fictional divisions to maintain the illusion of Fortitude South, while a fictional field army—the British Fourth Army—was invented, with its headquarters at Edinburgh Castle, to keep the Germans worried about Norway. US "phantom forces" included FUSAG, the "First United States Army Group," a formidable military force comprising 150,000 men. FUSAG was stationed in Kent opposite Pas de Calais under the leadership of none other than General George Patton, well-known to the Germans as one of the Allies' best tank commanders.

Above: US troops wade ashore under enemy fire at Omaha Beach on D-Day.

GREAT BRITAIN

Dover

Southampton

Calais

Portland

Dartmouth

Cherbourg

FRANCE

Left: The Allied landings took place on five Normandy beaches, far from Calais, where the Germans were expecting them.

COMPLETING THE ILLUSION

The technological footprint had to match the type and location of each false operation in order to fool German aerial reconnaissance. Fake equipment was built for these fake armies, including dummy landing craft and aircraft, inflatable tanks, and fake airfields. Controlled leaks of disinformation were passed through diplomatic channels in order to be intercepted, while double agents sent false information to German intelligence. Wireless traffic was simulated to make it look as if a real operation was underway.

Above: An inflatable dummy FUSAG Sherman Tank

Right: Decoy dummy landing craft

Operation Fortitude was a spectacular success. It was reported that, just days before D-Day, Hitler expected the Allies to launch a multi-pronged attack against Norway, Denmark, and southern France in order to disguise a main attack on Calais. Normandy was not even on his radar. The deception was maintained for some weeks following D-Day. Fake intelligence convinced the Germans to maintain a reserve force around Calais awaiting an invasion there as late as September. This dilution of German defenses was crucial to the success of the D-Day landings, allowing Allied forces to secure a foothold in Normandy.

AGENT GARBO

Above: Joan Pujol

The most important Double-Cross agent during Operation Fortitude operated under the codename Garbo. His real identity was Joan Pujol, an unassuming man from Barcelona with a loathing of the Nazis, who had been running a wholly fictitious spy ring in Britain for three years. Pujol had first offered his services to the British in 1941, but was rebuffed. Undeterred, he decided to lay the groundwork for his plan himself. He presented himself to the Germans in Madrid, posing as a pro-Nazi government official with business in London. The Germans eagerly took him on. Rather than traveling to London, Pujol moved to Lisbon, where he invented an imaginary network of agents, filing reports using information about Britain that he gleaned from magazines.

In 1942, Pujol finally made contact with MI6. He was brought to London and assigned to Spanish-speaking officer Tomás Harris. Pujol and Harris constructed an imaginary spy network of twenty-seven agents spread across the country.

By 1944, through the careful provision of accurate, but harmless, intelligence, Garbo had built up a solid relationship with his handlers. It was to pay off spectacularly. Garbo reported that the Normandy landings had been a ruse to divert attention from the main attack at Pas de Calais, which was still to come. As a result, the Germans maintained a heavy presence in Calais throughout July and August. Garbo's standing was so high by this point that he was awarded the Iron Cross by Hitler himself.

THE OSS

On its entry into World War II in 1941, the US lacked a central intelligence service. This was quickly remedied with the formation in 1942 of the Office for Strategic Services (OSS), headed by William "Wild Bill" Donovan. Donovan built the service from scratch, combining the functions of intelligence gathering with direct action. He modeled the OSS on Britain's MI6 and SOE, and the service would work closely with its British counterparts in daring operations across German-occupied Europe.

Above: OSS agents were trained at camps in the US, Canada, and Britain.

RESEARCH AND DEVELOPMENT

The OSS Research and Development branch was headed by the maverick chemist Stanley Lovell, who was nicknamed "Moriarty" by Donovan after the devious villain in the Sherlock Holmes stories. Lovell's team worked closely with their British colleagues in the SOE to produce a wide range of innovative gadgets that were not what they appeared to be. They developed explosives disguised as lumps of coal or mule droppings, and created the "Beano" grenade, which was the size and weight of a baseball, created on the reasoning that American agents would be well-practiced at throwing them. Compasses were concealed inside buttons, and information was hidden inside playing cards, which would reveal maps when the top layer was soaked off. The R&D branch also created weaponry for the local resistance movements, including the simple one-shot FP-45 Liberator pistol, which was distributed in occupied France and Greece.

In addition to gadgets and weapons, the R&D team had to ensure that every detail of the agents' appearance was made to blend in. The clothing was sewn as if it had been made locally, and every personal possession, from eyeglasses to toothbrushes, had to be right for the area. The tiniest slip-up could betray an agent.

Left: The baseball-shaped "Beano" grenade was developed for the OSS by Eastman Kodak. It was designed to explode on impact.

UNCONVENTIONAL APPROACH

Donovan recruited agents from all walks of life, the main qualification being that they should be quick-witted and unafraid to use their initiative. The full list of names of all 13,000 OSS personnel was only released in 2008. Its agents included major league baseball player Moe Berg, former French Foreign Legionnaire Peter Ortiz, and professional wrestler "Jumping Joe" Savoldi. The photographic unit was headed by the Oscar-winning director John Ford. At first, recruits were trained at the British facility in Canada known as "Camp X." The OSS later opened its own training camps in the US and abroad.

Within a few months, Donovan built up a highly effective operation that could provide a range of services around the world. The OSS provided assistance and training for anti-German resistance groups in Europe and anti-Japanese resistance movements in Asia. In Vietnam, OSS officer Archimedes Patti liaised closely with Ho Chi Minh, the leader of the Vietnamese independence movement with whom the US would later be at war. Assistance was also provided to both the Kuomintang Nationalists and Mao Zedong's Communists in China.

RUNNING SPIES

In addition to helping resistance movements, the OSS also ran its own spies, finding particular success in Germany. Probably the most successful OSS-run spy was Fritz Kolbe, an anti-Nazi German

Above: The OSS Deer Team was established in 1945 to work in North Vietnam. OSS operatives are pictured here alongside Viet Minh independence fighters, including Ho Chi Minh (fifth from left).

"SURPRISE, KILL, AND VANISH"

Motto of the Jedburgh teams

JEDBURGH TEAMS

In the months leading up to D-Day, a notice appeared in American training camps asking for "Volunteers for immediate overseas assignment. Knowledge of French or another European language preferred." The soldiers who applied were put through a series of rigorous tests before they were even told of their mission—they were to be parachuted into France, Belgium, or the Netherlands in the dead of night to carry out sabotage behind enemy lines. The men received intensive training, including language instruction, espionage skills, explosives training, and hand-to-hand combat. Depending on the area they were to operate in, they also received specialist training in skills such as skiing or mountain climbing. They were to form the elite "Jedburgh teams"—small cells of between two and four men mainly comprising a mix of American, British, and Free French officers. Each team carried a radio, nicknamed the "Jed Set." They would act as the vital link between the resistance and Allied command, coordinating sabotage efforts to assist the Allied forces as they swept through occupied Europe.

The first Jedburgh teams were dropped into France on June 4, 1944, two nights before D-Day. Over the next six months, ninety-two more teams were dropped into French territory. One of these teams was led by 24-year-old American William Colby, a future Director of the CIA. Colby later described the objective of his mission as "to harass the Germans as much as possible."

diplomat. Despite refusing to join the Nazi Party, Kolbe had risen in the ranks of the German Foreign Office and gained access to important military secrets, including troop movements, supply lines, and spy operations. From 1941 onward, he had been working against the Nazi regime, forging passports to help Jews to escape the country.

When he was assigned to Bern, Switzerland, in the summer of 1943, Kolbe managed to make contact with the OSS. Given the codename "George Wood," he was run by Allen Dulles, the future director of the CIA. Dulles described Kolbe as "an intelligence officer's dream." Between 1943 and 1945, Kolbe would meet with Dulles in Bern twice a year, passing on more than one thousand six hundred Foreign Office documents, which included details of the V-1 and V-2 missile programs, information about German expectations for D-Day, espionage activities in Britain and Turkey, and Japanese plans in Southeast Asia. In addition, the documents Kolbe passed to Dulles proved invaluable to cryptographers, providing unencrypted original communications from which to work.

Right: A Jedburgh team preparing for departure.

THE LADY WITH A LIMP: VIRGINIA HALL

The full story of the wartime adventures of American Virginia Hall has only recently been told. Spying first for the British and later for the Americans, Hall managed to set up two separate spy networks in occupied France. Adopting a variety of disguises, she evaded capture on both operations, escaping the first time on foot across a treacherous mountain pass in the dead of winter. Remarkably, she achieved all this with just one foot, having lost her left leg in a hunting accident before the war.

Above: Virginia Hall

Born in 1906 to a wealthy family in Baltimore, Maryland, Virginia Hall hoped to pursue a career in diplomacy. She received an expensive education, studying in Paris and Vienna and becoming fluent in French, German, and Italian. However, she found entry into the diplomatic service blocked to her because of her sex. Instead, she became a clerk at US embassies, still hoping to become a diplomat by the back door. She lost her left leg below the knee in a hunting accident at the age of 27, and her dreams of foreign adventure appeared to be over. However, Hall was determined not to let either her sex or her disability defeat her. Following a long convalescence and walking with the aid of a cumbersome wooden prosthetic that she nicknamed "Cuthbert," she returned to Paris as a civilian in 1940. She drove ambulances for the French army before escaping to Britain when France fell to the Nazis.

OPERATING IN VICHY FRANCE

In London, Hall was recruited to the newly formed SOE following a chance meeting at a cocktail party with British spymaster Vera Atkins (supposedly Ian Fleming's model for "Miss Moneypenny"). Atkins was impressed by Hall's passionate hatred of the Nazis, while her language skills and encyclopedic knowledge of France made her a valuable potential asset. In 1941, Hall was sent to France as the SOE's first resident female agent. She posed as a reporter for the New York Post, establishing a base in Lyon, in France's Haute Loire Department. Her mission was to gather information on political developments and economic conditions in the unoccupied "Free Zone" of collaborationist Vichy France,

"MANY OF MY FRIENDS WERE KILLED FOR TALKING TOO MUCH."

Virginia Hall

but she soon established a network that provided detailed information on a great deal more, including German troop movements and a new submarine base being built in Marseilles. Hall's network, codenamed Heckler, comprised ninety agents spread across southern France. They offered support to local resistance groups, assisted downed Allied airmen, organized daring jail breaks, and provided a network of safe houses to hide escapees while safe passage from France was secured.

In her operations in Vichy France, Hall took advantage of the prejudices that had once held her back. As she moved around, she found that the authorities would treat her as a harmless disabled woman of little consequence. What threat could a female with one leg pose to them? However, the Gestapo and Abwehr enjoyed considerable success in infiltrating the resistance in Vichy France, and several members of the Heckler network were betrayed. As a result, Hall's activities came to the attention of Gestapo chief Klaus Barbie, the notorious "Butcher of Lyon." Barbie would never learn Hall's real identity, reportedly stating that "I would do anything to get my hands on that limping Canadian bitch." Barbie placed a bounty on Hall's head and circulated "Wanted" posters that described her as "The Enemy's Most Dangerous Spy." As a result, Hall constantly changed her appearance, often adopting several different identities in a single day. But the net was closing in.

THE FREEDOM TRAIL

Above: Klaus Barbie

By September 1942, Hall knew that she had been compromised. With Barbie still hot on her trail, she wrote to London that "my time is about up," and spent the next two months moving between safe houses to avoid capture. In November, as German troops flooded Vichy France following their defeat in North Africa, Hall decided that it was time to make her escape while she still could. The only way out of France was south into Spain, following the "freedom trail" across the Pyrenees Mountains. Hall and three companions walked fifty miles from Villefrance-de-Conflent in France to San Juan de las Abadesas in Spain. They climbed to an altitude of 7,500 feet, negotiating treacherous mountain passes covered in snow and ice. The journey would have been tough for an able-bodied person; Hall had to do it with a wooden leg. At one point, she radioed to London that Cuthbert was causing her problems. Thinking that she was about to be betrayed, the operator replied, "If Cuthbert gives you trouble, eliminate him." Once in Spain, an exhausted Hall was quickly picked up by the authorities for entering the country illegally. She was jailed for six weeks before the US embassy secured her release. She returned to Britain, her war seemingly over.

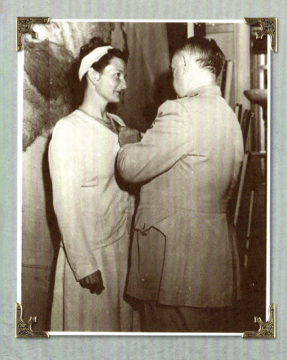

Left: William Donovan presents Virginia Hall with the Distinguished Service Cross in 1945 in a private ceremony.

Above: Hall secretly radioed London from a remote barn. Her radio was powered by a bicycle rigged to turn an electric generator.

RETURN TO FRANCE

When the British considered it too dangerous to send Hall back to France, she signed up with America's OSS instead. She returned to France as part of Operation Fortitude in the months before D-Day, this time disguised as an old peasant woman. To play the part with conviction, she had her pristine American teeth ground down by a dentist. The sabotage team that Hall organized in France was credited with derailing numerous trains, blowing up four bridges, and killing one hundred and fifty German soldiers. At its peak, Hall's network comprised more than one thousand resistance fighters. At the end of the war, Hall was awarded the Distinguished Service Cross—the only woman to be given this honor in World War II. President Truman proposed a public ceremony, but Hall already had her eye on a future career in spying, and declined the offer. She spent fifteen years working for the CIA, and never spoke publicly about her wartime activities. The details of Virginia Hall's extraordinary achievements were only revealed decades after her death in 1982.

— CHAPTER 8 —

THE COLD WAR

At the end of World War II, the alliance between the Soviet Union and the West quickly crumbled. In 1945, reflecting on the age of the nuclear bomb, English author George Orwell coined the term "cold war" for the continual state of tension these terrifying new weapons would bring. The term stuck, and the Cold War between East and West would last for more than 40 years. In 1949, the North Atlantic Treaty Organization (NATO) was formed to create a military alliance in the West. The Soviet Union followed suit, consolidating its power in Eastern Europe with the Warsaw Pact, and engaging the services of its puppet regimes to expand its spy networks in the West.

In the US, the Cold War prompted the formation of the CIA, which organized covert activity around the world aimed at preventing the spread of the Soviets' sphere of influence, overthrowing democratically elected regimes in the process. The Soviets ran a number of successful spy rings in the West, activating long-term moles such as the Cambridge Five. The West relied more on information from defectors disillusioned with the actions of their own side. This was an era of double-agents and triple-agents, during which paranoia became the "new normal."

FORMATION OF THE CIA

Right:
William Donovan

Right:
Roscoe Hillenkoetter

The Central Intelligence Agency (CIA) was formed in 1947 as a response to a growing perceived threat from the Soviet Union. While the agency was forbidden from operating on US soil, it was given a wide remit for its activities abroad, authorized to carry out covert direct action in addition to gathering intelligence. The CIA would play a major role in US foreign policy as the Cold War progressed, including operations whose consequences still echo to this day.

WARTIME INTELLIGENCE

When the United States joined World War II in 1941, responsibility for collecting intelligence was spread across a variety of agencies, including the FBI, the State Department, the Army, and the Navy, with little coordination. Rivalries between the agencies even led them to withhold sensitive information about Japanese intentions from President Roosevelt in the months before the attack on Pearl Harbor. In June 1942, Roosevelt addressed this issue by creating the Office of Strategy Services (OSS), headed up by lawyer and World War I veteran William "Wild Bill" Donovan. Living up to his nickname, Donovan proved an erratic but effective operator, and the OSS was soon conducting operations across Europe, linking up with resistance fighters. In the lead-up to the D-Day landings in Normandy in 1944, the OSS had more than 500 agents working inside occupied France.

THE COLD WAR BEGINS

Despite proving extremely effective, the OSS was disbanded by President Truman at the end of the war, seen as surplus to requirements in peacetime. However, the uneasy wartime alliance between the US and the Soviet Union soon began to unravel as Europe split into the democratic West and communist East, separated by an "Iron Curtain." In 1946, President Truman responded to the new realities of the Cold War by establishing the Central Intelligence Group (CIG), recruiting many former members of the OSS.

In 1947, Congress passed the National Security Act, creating the National Security Council (NSC), headed by the president, and the Central Intelligence Agency (CIA), which would come under the NSC's control. This new structure removed any lingering confusion as to which agency was in charge of intelligence. The former Deputy Director of the CIG, Roscoe Hillenkoetter, was appointed the first Director of the CIA. One third of the new agency's staff were veterans of the OSS, including future directors Allen Dulles, Richard Helms, and William Colby. Unlike its Soviet equivalent, the CIA was forbidden from acting on home soil. However, it was given extensive freedom of action abroad.

FIRST REGIME CHANGE

The CIA's remit was significantly widened in 1949, when President Truman authorized the agency to fund secret missions free from standard government oversight. This marked the start of a long series of covert CIA operations abroad, including support for military coups against democratically elected governments, many of which have

Left: Allen Dulles

"AN INTELLIGENCE SERVICE IS THE IDEAL VEHICLE FOR A CONSPIRACY."

Allen Dulles, Director of the CIA 1953–1961

only been officially acknowledged in the last decade. The first such operation took place in Iran in 1953. The prime minister of Iran, Mohammed Mosaddegh, had nationalized the Anglo-Iranian Oil Company (now known as BP). Concerned for its business interests in the region, the UK secretly approached the US for help in removing Mosaddegh. The resultant coup was jointly engineered by the CIA and Britain's MI6, in operations with codenames "TPAJAX" and "Operation Boot," respectively. Mosaddegh was overthrown, and a new regime established under the increasingly autocratic and authoritarian control of the Shah Mohammad Reza Pahlavi. British and American business interests had been protected at the expense of Iranian democracy, sowing the seeds for the Islamic Revolution that overthrew the Shah in 1979.

Left: Mohammed Mosaddegh spent his final years under house arrest. Many of his supporters had been tortured and executed after the coup, including Hossein Fatemi, the Foreign Minister who proposed nationalizing Iran's oil and gas reserves.

"NO SUCH AGENCY"

The National Security Agency (NSA) was formed in 1952 by a presidential directive from President Truman. Truman stated that its mission was "to provide an effective, unified organization and control of the communications intelligence activities of the United States conducted against foreign governments." Its very existence was initially classified information, leading to its nickname among the intelligence community, "No Such Agency." The NSA was initially responsible for creating and breaking ciphers and protecting government security systems. Over the years, it has grown into a role as the US government's "eavesdropper in chief," collecting data on all forms of electronic transmission. The NSA is forbidden from targeting US citizens, but the leaks from former NSA operator Edward Snowden in 2013 revealed the wide extent to which it has been listening in on Americans. Falling outside congressional scrutiny, the NSA is perhaps the most secretive and least accountable of all US government agencies. Its budget is classified, but is thought to be in excess of $10 billion per year. Its employees are estimated at anything between 35,000 and 55,000, many of them working out of the ultra-secure headquarters in Fort Meade, Maryland.

Below: NSA Headquarters in Fort Meade

THE WEST HITS BACK

By the late 1940s, a "Red Scare" was in full swing within the United States, and many figures lost their livelihoods due to past sympathies with communism. While much of the fear was unfounded, Soviet spies had indeed been recruited from communist sympathizers during World War II, a fact that was revealed due to a rare instance of lax coding discipline within Soviet intelligence. The evidence from decoded communications was matched up with information from Soviet defectors to reveal the spies' identities. While the US failed to establish equivalent spy rings within the Soviet Union, it would continue to receive valuable intelligence from Soviet defectors throughout the Cold War.

Left: A mock-up of the "Fat Man" plutonium bomb

Right: In evidence in his trial, David Greenglass made this sketch to illustrate the information about the "Fat Man" bomb that he passed to Julius Rosenberg.

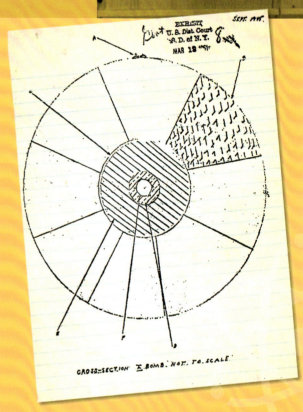

THE VENONA PROJECT

The Venona project was as highly secret decryption project that ran from 1943 to 1980, working out of Arlington, Virginia. During this time, teams of cryptologists painstakingly decrypted more than three thousand messages intercepted from Soviet diplomatic communications during and immediately after World War II. The messages were encrypted using the "one-time pad" system, which normally produces unbreakable codes. However, the demand for new one-time pads skyrocketed during the chaotic early days of Soviet involvement in the war, and duplicate pages were produced in 1942. This mistake created a four-year window during which some messages were not completely secure.

ATOMIC SECRETS

The Soviets' error was spotted at Venona in November 1944 by Lieutenant Richard Hallock, who was working on messages dealing with trade issues. Hallock's colleague Meredith Gardner used this breakthrough to analyze NKVD messages. Progress was slow and hard, and often only parts of messages could be decoded, but in 1946, Gardner managed to break codes that revealed the existence of spies inside Los Alamos National Laboratories, the site of the secret Manhattan Project to develop the atomic bomb.

In 1949, the Soviet Union tested its first atomic bomb, the RDS-1. The device closely resembled the US "Fat Man" bomb that was detonated over Nagasaki in Japan in 1945. The Venona decryptions revealed that this resemblance was no coincidence. Detailed information from Los Alamos had been passed to the Soviets by physicists Klaus Fuchs and Theodore Hall and engineer David Greenglass. In total, the Venona decryptions produced the names of more than

Above: A witness testifies at the trial of Oleg Penkovsky and Greville Wynne. Wynne (left) and Penkovsky (right) listen from the back of the room, sat next to guards.

"I DECIDED TO GIVE ATOMIC SECRETS TO THE RUSSIANS BECAUSE IT SEEMED TO ME THAT IT WAS IMPORTANT THAT THERE SHOULD BE NO MONOPOLY, WHICH COULD TURN ONE NATION INTO A MENACE."

Theodore Hall, speaking in 1998 following his exposure as a Soviet spy

three hundred suspected spies, including one codenamed "Homer," who turned out to be the Cambridge spy Donald Maclean. The results were presented to the FBI, and investigations were launched. However, the project was considered too valuable to risk exposing its existence, so while Fuchs and Greenglass were tried and convicted, Hall was never prosecuted, and his involvement only came to light when the Venona files were declassified in 1995.

SOVIET DEFECTORS

The information from the Venona project was supplemented by documents from Soviet defectors. One of the earliest was Igor Gouzenko, a cipher clerk at the Soviet Embassy in Ottawa, Canada, who defected three days after the end of World War II with more than one hundred documents relating to Soviet spy rings. Later information supplied to the CIA by Polish intelligence officer Michael Goleniewski would expose the Portland Spy Ring in the UK in 1961.

Probably the West's most valuable spy within the Soviet Union was GRU colonel Oleg Penkovsky. In 1961, he provided information to the UK and US detailing the plans for Soviet missile bases in Cuba. Penkovsky was exposed by Soviet spies at the NSA and MI6, and arrested in 1962. He was tried and convicted of espionage alongside British engineer Greville Wynne, who had acted as his courier. Penkovsky was executed a year later, while Wynne was released in 1964 as part of a "spy swap." Another GRU defector, Viktor Suvorov, later wrote of Penkovsky that, "Thanks to his priceless information the Cuban crisis was not transformed into a last World War."

SENT TO THE CHAIR

On June 19, 1953, husband and wife Julius and Ethel Rosenberg were executed by electric chair at Sing Sing prison, New York. Julius had been convicted of passing information to the Soviet Union during World War II, and Ethel of assisting him. Julius Rosenberg had been recruited as a spy in 1942 by Soviet agent Semyon Semyonov. In his role as an electrical engineer for the Army Signal Corps, Rosenberg had passed thousands of classified reports to the Soviets. He had also recruited a number of other spies, including his brother-in-law David Greenglass at Los Alamos. When they were exposed in 1950, Greengrass's evidence was critical in securing the convictions of his sister and brother-in-law, although he later admitted that he had exaggerated Ethel's involvement to save his wife from prosecution. The flimsy-looking case against the Rosenbergs was criticized at the time, and their execution was condemned across the world, coming as it did at the height of Senator Joseph McCarthy's anti-communist witchhunt. Evidence from the Venona files released in 1995 leaves no doubt as to Julius's guilt, and reveals that a group of communists had indeed infiltrated the US military during World War II.

Left: The Rosenbergs leave court after being found guilty of treason in 1951. They were executed two years later.

From left to right:
Guy Burgess,
Donald Maclean,
Kim Philby

THE RISE AND FALL OF THE CAMBRIDGE FIVE

The outbreak of World War II led to a vast and rapid expansion of British government agencies. The KGB's talented and ambitious deep-penetration agents—previously recruited from Cambridge University—wasted no time in working their way into positions of importance.

Donald Maclean and Guy Burgess both entered the diplomatic service, although they also moved to other departments that provided them with oversight to a mass of high-grade intelligence. John Cairncross worked for the Code and Cipher School at Bletchley Park and then MI6, before assignment to the Treasury. Anthony Blunt worked for MI5 throughout the war, providing his Soviet handler with full lists of MI5 agents and details of surveillance techniques. Kim Philby joined MI6 and rose quickly through the ranks. In 1944, he was made head of MI6's counter-intelligence section. The man responsible for catching spies was himself a spy!

FROM CAMBRIDGE TO AMERICA

Although Blunt and Cairncross largely dropped their spying activities after the war, the other three KGB agents carried on. Their focus of attention turned to the United States, now

the Soviet Union's main adversary. Maclean had arrived in the US in 1944 and gained access to US atomic secrets, briefly working alongside fellow Soviet mole Alger Hiss. In 1948, Maclean returned to Britain, where he ran the Foreign Office's American desk. A year later, Philby arrived in Washington, acting as liaison officer between British intelligence and the CIA and FBI—a perfect position from which to identify US intelligence interests. Burgess was transferred to Washington in 1950, living in the Philby household and working in the British embassy.

Philby seemed to revel in his life as a double agent, but Burgess and Maclean began to crack under the strain. Heavy drinking was becoming a problem and their frequent homosexual encounters raised eyebrows in Washington. The FBI had even begun surveillance of both men, fearing that they might be susceptible to blackmail by a foreign power.

COVERS BLOWN

More dangerous still were the results coming forward from the US Venona codebreakers, which by 1951 had identified Maclean as a Soviet spy. Philby, however, had knowledge of this development and realized he had to act swiftly. Unable to directly contact Maclean in London, he engineered a ploy with Burgess: over a weekend, Burgess's drunken antics were

Left: Anthony Blunt

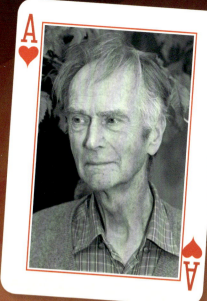

Left: John Cairncross

"HE NEVER REVEALED HIS TRUE SELF. NEITHER THE BRITISH NOR OURSELVES EVER MANAGED TO PIERCE THE ARMOR OF MYSTERY THAT CLAD HIM. HIS GREAT ACHIEVEMENT IN ESPIONAGE WAS HIS LIFE'S WORK, AND IT FULLY OCCUPIED HIM UNTIL THE DAY HE DIED."

KGB handler Yuri Modin on Kim Philby

sufficiently disgraceful to have him sent back to London, thus enabling him to personally warn Maclean and their Soviet handler, Yuri Modin, of the danger.

Aware that the increasingly unstable Maclean would break under interrogation, the KGB engineered his escape to the Soviet Union. Burgess helped in the operation, secretly driving Maclean to a port on England's south coast prior to him sailing to France and then on to Russia. Burgess was supposed to stay in Britain but for whatever reason he too fled with Maclean.

Philby's close association with Burgess made him an object of suspicion. He was recalled from Washington and subjected to repeated interrogations, but held firm in the knowledge that there was no evidence against him to ensure a guilty verdict in a court of law. Philby was, however, dismissed from MI6 in 1955. Through his good contacts, he gained work as a journalist, eventually based in Lebanon. In 1961, new evidence confirmed Philby as a Soviet spy, and in 1963 an MI6 officer was sent to interview him. Philby apparently confessed to his past, but before anything could be taken further, the KGB exfiltrated him to the Soviet Union, where he lived until his death in 1988.

AFTERMATH

The flight of Burgess and Maclean to Moscow caused British intelligence much embarrassment and soured relations with the CIA and FBI. But the consequences of the affair ran deeper, and in both British and US intelligence agencies, fears developed that there were more moles working within their ranks. This diverted resources away from combating Soviet spies to repeated searches within their own organizations. The searches produced little except for ill-feeling among those falsely suspected of wrong doing. Meanwhile, the newspapers had a field day in looking for the "Third Man," who eventually turned out to be Philby. The search continued for the other Cambridge spies, who were eventually tracked down but not prosecuted. The "Fourth Man" (Blunt) was publicly exposed in 1979, and the "Fifth Man" (Cairncross) in 1981.

THE HONEY TRAP

At the height of the Cold War, British high society, and the Conservative government under Prime Minister Harold Macmillan, was severely compromised by a headline-grabbing scandal that questioned Britain's whole security setup. It became known as the Profumo Affair. As it turned out, there was little evidence that security had ever been breached, but sex parties involving peers, government ministers, Soviet diplomats, and girls-about-town provided fodder for tabloid newspapers with an insatiable taste for tarts and treason.

"WE KNEW WE WERE TALKING ABOUT SPIES. I KNEW HE KNEW I KNEW. I WAS DIGGING MY OWN GRAVE."

Christine Keeler

Left: Christine Keeler snapped by the paparazzi. Despite being jailed for nine months for perjury at Stephen Ward's trial, Keeler made the most of her new-found fame.

Above: John Profumo arriving at court

THE PROFUMO AFFAIR

Yevgeny Ivanov was a Soviet attaché in London in the early 1960s. He was popular, handsome, and a frequent guest at parties thrown by Stephen Ward. A society osteopath, Ward was famous for inviting beautiful young women to his gatherings, often held at glamorous locations such as Lord Astor's stately retreat, Cliveden House. Among them was Christine Keeler, a Sixties good-time girl. It was alleged that she became Ivanov's mistress. Unfortunately, Keeler at the time was also briefly the lover of the married British Secretary of State for War, John Profumo.

In 1962, Profumo's affair with Keeler hit the headlines. The tabloids made the most of it, and investigated Ward's parties. Soon other names were in the news, including a friend of Keeler's, Mandy Rice-Davis, who claimed to have had an affair with Lord Astor. The tabloids also soon sniffed out the potential Soviet spy/honey trap story, although there was no solid evidence. Profumo lied about his affair when questioned in the House of Commons and was forced to resign.

FALLOUT

Ward committed suicide after being tried for living on immoral earnings, while the two girls rather reveled in their new-found fame and notoriety. Profumo's wife forgave him, but his ministerial career was over. Prime Minister Harold Macmillan resigned on the grounds of ill-health a month after the publication of the Parliamentary report on the scandal. Ivanov was called back to Moscow, always publicly denying the honey trap angle.

A MARINE ABROAD

In 1987, Clayton Lonetree became the first member of the US Marine Corps to be convicted of espionage. He had been assigned as a guard at the US Embassy in Moscow in 1984, signing a non-fraternization agreement in which he promised not to engage in any friendships with Soviet citizens. In 1985, Lonetree struck up a conversation at a seemingly chance meeting with a young woman named Violetta Seina on a subway train. The meeting led to a long walk, after which they embarked on a clandestine affair. However, their encounter had been anything but accidental, and Seina was in fact a KGB agent. She introduced Lonetree to her "uncle Sasha," in reality Soviet intelligence officer Aleksey Yefimov, who recruited him by threatening to expose their affair. Lonetree agreed to pass documents to Yefimov from the Moscow embassy and later from the embassy in Vienna, Austria, when Lonetree was transferred. Lonetree handed himself in to the CIA in December 1986. At his sentencing, he was supported by a plea for leniency from the Commandant of the Marine Corps, General Alfred Gray, who said of Lonetree's motive that it "was not treason or greed, but rather the lovesick response of a naive, young, immature, and lonely troop in a lonely and hostile environment." Lonetree served nine years of a fifteen-year sentence before his release in 1996, claiming all along that he had not handed over anything of real value.

It was later claimed by the Soviet spy within the CIA, Aldrich Ames, that the KGB had lured Lonetree into spying to divert their attention from Ames's activities.

Right: Official Marine Corps portrait of Clayton Lonetree

THE WARSAW PACT AND ITS SPIES

Signed in 1955, the Warsaw Pact established a common defense treaty between the Soviet Union and seven European countries: East Germany (GDR), Romania, Poland, Hungary, Czechoslovakia, Bulgaria, and Albania. Operating closely to Soviet orders, each member state established intelligence and security agencies to spy on their own populations and to run operations in the West. The largest and most brutal of these agencies were East Germany's Stasi—likened to the Gestapo in its methods and achievements—and Romania's Securitate.

Above: Willy Brandt (left) and Günther Guillaime (right)

Above: Markus Wolf   Above: Erich Mielke

The German Democratic Republic (GDR) established the Ministry for State Security (Stasi) in 1950. Modeled on the KGB, it grew to become one of the most effective—and feared—intelligence agencies in the world. By 1989, the Stasi was operating nearly 300 agents worldwide, half of them based in West Germany. It also concentrated efforts on infiltrating NATO Headquarters in Brussels, obtaining information about Western military capabilities and strategies. Everything was passed on straight to Moscow.

LONG-TERM MOLES

From 1953 to 1986, the Stasi's spy rings in the West were coordinated by the secretive chief Markus Wolf. Wolf's identity was unknown in the West until 1978, leading to the nickname "the Man without a Face." As Chief of Foreign Operations, Wolf directly supervised agent Günther Guillaume, who had emigrated from East to West Germany in the 1950s and rose to become a close aide to FRG Chancellor Willy Brandt. Guillaume was exposed as a spy in 1974, prompting Brandt's resignation. Wolf later stated that it had been a mistake to compromise Brandt, who had been working for improved relations with the Eastern Bloc.

Among the most valuable of the Stasi's long-term moles were a married couple—West German Rainer Rupp and Briton Ann-Christine Bowen. Rupp had been recruited as a student in 1968 and recruited his wife when they married in 1972. By the mid-'70s, they were both working for NATO in Brussels and passing documents to the Stasi. Rupp was periodically on duty at the Situation Center of NATO HQ, from where he provided information about NATO's nuclear first strike policy in the event of a conventional attack from the East.

In addition to learning of NATO's military strengths and tactics, the Stasi's spies provided an insight into the West's knowledge of the Warsaw Pact's capabilities, allowing Moscow to assess how well it was keeping its secrets. East Germany even learned information that the Soviets had withheld from them, such as the exact number of nuclear weapons stationed on GDR soil. The Stasi's spies painted a picture for Moscow of a well-armed enemy prepared to use its nuclear weapons first. This both deterred the more hawkish factions within the Soviet Union and provided an impetus to build its own ability. Ultimately, it contributed to the decision made in the 1980s by Mikhail Gorbachev that the West's military superiority was such that it could not be matched, hastening the end of the Cold War.

"FOR ANYONE TO UNDERSTAND A REGIME LIKE THE GDR, THE STORIES OF ORDINARY PEOPLE MUST BE TOLD. NOT JUST THE ACTIVISTS OR THE FAMOUS WRITERS. YOU HAVE TO LOOK AT HOW NORMAL PEOPLE MANAGE WITH SUCH THINGS IN THEIR PASTS."

Anna Funder, author of *Stasiland*

A NATION UNDER SURVEILLANCE

Under the direction of Erich Mielke from 1957 until the fall of the Berlin Wall in 1989, the Stasi ran a hated secret police force at home. It spied on all aspects of the daily lives of East Germans through a vast network of informants numbering hundreds of thousands. By 1989, it was even feared by some within the Stasi that dissident groups contained so many informants that they were being made to appear stronger than they actually were, encouraging more people to join in. In total, the Stasi maintained files on six million people—one third of East Germany's population. The extent to which the Stasi was listening in—literally—to people's affairs was memorably portrayed in the 2006 film *The Lives of Others*.

Mielke was also responsible for preventing people from leaving, and directed the construction of the Berlin Wall in 1961. Prior to the Wall, more than three million East Germans had fled. Under Mielke's orders, anyone attempting to escape was to be shot. In total, 239 people were killed attempting to cross the Wall, while more than 5,000 made it.

Right: Four-year-old Michael Finder is tossed by his father into a net held by residents across the border in West Berlin in a desperate bid to escape the East in 1961.

DISAPPEARING DISSIDENTS

Like the Stasi, Romania's secret police force, the Securitate, relied on an enormous network of informants to squash dissent. Thousands of people were secretly disappeared during the increasingly autocratic rule of Nicolae Ceausescu from 1965 to 1989. However, the death in custody of poet Gheorghe Ursu in 1985 could not be kept hidden, and caused an international scandal that severely weakened the Ceausescu regime. Ursu had been placed under surveillance by the Securitate. He was finally arrested for possession of a journal in which he had recorded his thoughts on the culture of denunciation that pervaded Romanian society. Shortly after his arrest, Ursu was beaten to death by his cellmates on the orders of the Securitate. The head of the Securitate at the time, Tudor Postelnicu, died in 2017 while awaiting trial for the murder of Ursu. As his regime collapsed in 1989, Ceausescu and his wife had been summarily tried and executed for genocide.

Above: The photograph of Gheorghe Ursu in his Securitate file

REGIME CHANGE IN LATIN AMERICA

As the Cold War entered into deep-freeze in the late 1940s, the US embarked on a policy of "containment" in which it would intervene in the name of limiting the influence of the Soviet Union in Latin America. The Monroe Doctrine of 1823 had set out US opposition to further European colonialism in the Americas. In the context of the Cold War, it was repurposed to justify US intervention and "regime change" in anti-Soviet terms. The first of many interventions came in 1954, with a coup that had more to do with bananas than Bolsheviks.

From 1931 to 1944, Guatemala was ruled by the brutal, highly personalized dictatorship of General Jorge Ubico. Ubico pursued a policy of close alignment with the United States, and granted generous concessions to the United Fruit Company, which owned nearly half of Guatemala's farmland, controlled much of its infrastructure, and paid virtually no taxes. Ubico was overthrown in an uprising in 1944, and in 1951, reformist Jacobo Arbenz was elected president, winning 60 percent of the vote. Arbenz initiated a program of agrarian reform, in which uncultivated land would be redistributed among landless agricultural laborers, with compensation paid to the landowners. United Fruit, most of whose land was uncultivated, saw Arbenz's program as a threat to its position and turned to the United States government for help.

PLANTING FALSE RUMORS

United Fruit found sympathetic ears in the US government, including Secretary of State John Foster Dulles, who had previously worked for the company. In the US media, the Arbenz government was painted as a communist regime with connections to the Soviet Union, an allegation that was never substantiated. At the direction of United Fruit's public relations counsel, the renowned publicist Edward Bernays, articles about the threat of Guatemalan communism began to appear in *The New York Times*, and other publications soon followed suit. Meanwhile, from 1952 onward, the CIA had been helping to organize an army of exiles in Honduras and El Salvador under General Carlos Castillo Armas.

ORGANIZING THE EXILES

Documents declassified in 1995 reveal the level of CIA involvement with Armas, which was initially authorized by President Truman and continued under Eisenhower. Initial funds of $225,000 were agreed, and Armas began to train special operative teams with a list of intended assassination targets. However, their cover was blown and the initial operation, codenamed PBFORTUNE, was aborted.

Above: Jacobo Arbenz, pictured in 1950.

In 1953, Operation PBSUCCESS was initiated with the intention to use "sabotage, defection, penetration, and propaganda" to overthrow Arbenz. Eisenhower approved a budget of $2.9 million for "psychological warfare and political action." New assassination lists were drawn up, and Guatemalan leaders were sent death threats as part of a concerted campaign of intimidation. As it turned out, only about two hundred people were killed in a relatively bloodless coup. Exaggerated reports of the size of Armas's invading forces led the Guatemalan army to refuse to back Arbenz, who fled into exile on June 27, 1954. Armas was installed as the new president, and United Fruit returned to its privileged position. Shortly afterward, the country descended into a decades-long civil war.

The US officially denied any involvement in the Guatemala coup. However, while issuing the denial, US Ambassador to the UN, Henry Cabot Lodge, also warned the Soviet Union to "Stay out of this hemisphere," adding to the false impression that Arbenz had Soviet backing. The CIA's first covert operation in Latin America had been a success, and marked the start of a series of interventions aimed ostensibly at halting the spread of communism, but which can also be seen as acting in support of US business interests opposed to democratically elected socialists.

DEATH OF ALLENDE

The CIA undertook a series of covert operations in Chile in the 1960s and early 1970s, including a failed attempt to prevent the election of socialist Salvador Allende in 1970. The extent of CIA involvement in the 1973 coup, which led to the death of Allende and marked the start of General Augusto Pinochet's murderous regime, remains disputed. The agency acknowledges that it funded actions to undermine and discredit the "Marxist-leaning" Allende, spending $8 million on its efforts. It stops short of admitting direct involvement in Allende's death, and to this day, many documents relating to the Nixon administration's prior knowledge of the coup remain classified. However, the CIA has admitted that its operatives were in close contact with the plotters, who at the very least acted with tacit US approval.

Above: Salvador Allende greeting supporters in 1972.

CUBA AND THE USA

At 3 a.m on January 1, 1959, Cuban dictator Fulgencio Batista boarded a plane in Havana bound for the Dominican Republic. He was fleeing, ousted from power following a six-year-long guerrilla campaign against him led by Fidel Castro. The US cautiously welcomed the Cuban Revolution at first, but relations soured and Cuba looked to the Soviet Union, resulting in tensions that brought the world to the brink of war. The tensions remain to this day, with a communist regime less than 100 miles from US territory.

As President Kennedy later admitted, the US bore a great deal of responsibility for the brutality of the Batista dictatorship in the 1950s. Pronouncing Batista an ally in the battle against communism, the US had provided him with military support to suppress the rebels. In return, Batista had allowed US businesses to all but take over the Cuban economy. Batista had also established close relationships with the US mafia, turning Havana into a playground for the rich, complete with casinos, drugs, and brothels. Meanwhile, most Cubans lived in grinding poverty.

While the US initially recognized the new government, relations broke down in 1960 when Cuba nationalized US-owned property. President Eisenhower imposed economic sanctions, while Cuba turned toward the Soviet Union for help. It became increasingly clear that Castro intended to establish a communist regime, and Eisenhower authorized the CIA to begin covert operations to overthrow him. This would result one year later in a bungled invasion that left the agency's credibility in tatters.

Above: Castro (right) and fellow revolutionary Camilo Cienfuegos enter Havana in triumph in 1959.

BAY OF PIGS FIASCO
The invasion was doomed from the start. A band of Cuban exiles living in Florida were recruited and trained in secret in Panama. CIA files reveal that the training went very badly. Few from the CIA could speak Spanish and they treated the recruits with barely concealed contempt, while the operation was far from secret and news of the plan soon reached Cuba. On the day of the invasion on April 17, 1961, 1,511 exiles landed at Playa Girón, a beach in the Bay of Pigs in southern Cuba. The Cuban army was expecting them, the US air support they had been promised failed to materialize, and they were overwhelmed in three days of fighting. Far from inspiring a revolt against Castro as intended, the CIA had handed him a famous victory that solidified his support and pushed him further into the arms of the Soviet Union. The Cold War was heating up.

CUBAN MISSILE CRISIS
On October 16, 1962, President Kennedy was shown a photograph taken by a U2 spy plane two days earlier. The image appeared to show a Soviet base in Cuba with nuclear-capable ballistic missiles. The CIA had been aware of rumors

Above: Cuban dictator Fulgencio Batista alongside US Army Chief of Staff Malin Craig during a visit to Washington, D.C., in 1938.

"THE GREATEST THREAT PRESENTED BY CASTRO'S CUBA IS AS AN EXAMPLE TO OTHER LATIN AMERICAN STATES WHICH ARE BESET BY POVERTY, CORRUPTION, FEUDALISM, AND PLUTOCRATIC EXPLOITATION."

American reporter Walter Lippmann, writing in 1964

Left: Cuban troops move in on the Bay of Pigs invaders.

that Soviet premier Nikita Khrushchev intended to create a nuclear base on Cuba, but this was the first definitive proof. In response, Kennedy quarantined Soviet military ships on their way to Cuba and demanded the removal of all missile bases.

Over the thirteen days that followed, the world inched toward conflict. In a television broadcast on October 22, Kennedy informed Americans of the situation, explaining that the US was blockading the island and would use force to remove the bases if necessary. There followed several days of tense standoff during which the CIA provided more images of Soviet bases.

On October 27, an American spy plane was shot down over Cuba and the US assembled an invasion force in Florida. The whole world feared a nuclear war, and US Secretary of Defense Robert McNamara later said that he thought it was "the last Saturday I would ever see." However, on October 26, Khrushchev had contacted Kennedy with an offer to remove the bases in return for a US promise not to invade Cuba. Kennedy agreed and the crisis was averted. Kennedy also secretly agreed to remove US missiles from Turkey. He later thanked CIA Director John McCrone for the accuracy of their intelligence. After the Bay of Pigs fiasco, the agency's success had been much needed.

Above: President Kennedy signs the Proclamation for Interdiction of the Delivery of Offensive Weapons to Cuba at the Oval Office on October 23, 1962.

GET CASTRO

Fidel Castro died of natural causes in 2016 at the age of 90. He had survived as many as six hundred conspiracies to assassinate him, some directed by the CIA, others by Cuban exiles or the Mob. In 1960, the CIA offered mobsters $150,000 to kill Castro. Months later, they laced a box of Castro's favorite cigars with a deadly botulinum toxin, but they never made it into Castro's mouth. Other plans seemingly straight from a Bond movie included blowing Castro up while he was scuba diving, putting poisonous fungus in his diving suit, and injecting him with a needle disguised as a pen. A separate approach sought not to kill Castro but to undermine his authority, including an idea to dust his boots with a powder that would make his beard fall out. In 1993, Marita Lorenz, a former lover of Castro, claimed that she had been recruited by the CIA in 1959 and given poisoned pills to drop into his drink.

According to Lorenz, Castro had rumbled her plan. Instead of having her arrested, she says that he had handed her a loaded gun and said, "You can't kill me. Nobody can kill me." Whatever the truth to Lorenz's tale, the CIA never could kill Fidel Castro.

Above: Fidel Castro on a visit to the United States in 1959.

THE IMPOSSIBLE SPY: ELI COHEN

Above: By 1964, it was all going too well for Cohen. However, his comfortable lifestyle lulled him into complacent carelessness. His downfall would be rapid.

OPERATION SUSANNAH

One of Israeli military intelligence's first major operations was codenamed Susannah. It was designed in 1954 to gather intelligence, bomb foreign interests, and distribute disinformation to support the British presence in the Suez Canal zone in Egypt. Operation Susannah deployed a ring of resident Egyptian Jews. It proved a top-class failure: most of its operatives were identified, tortured, and imprisoned, and its two leaders were hanged. One of the ring's few survivors was Eli Cohen, born in Egypt in 1924. It is not clear what his role was in Susannah, but he was in Israel by the early 1960s, and recruited and re-trained in intelligence techniques. A false nationality and identity was developed for him as a Syrian Arab from Argentina.

One of the most important intelligence successes by the young state of Israel was the infiltration in 1962 of a secret agent into the upper ranks of its hostile neighbor, the Arab state of Syria. The agent's name was Eli Cohen. In an elaborate sting, this Egyptian-born Jew was provided with a convincing cover story that eventually gave him almost unlimited access to Syria's strategic secrets. The intelligence he passed on proved critical to Israel's defense—but at a fatal cost.

CHARM OFFENSIVE

After spending some time in South America, playing the part of a charismatic, well-heeled Syrian ex-pat businessman, Cohen was invited to Syria, where he charmed his way to the highest levels of government. In Syria, Cohen developed a lifestyle which suited him. He threw lavish parties (all funded by Israeli intelligence) providing sex and alcohol to his guests. He acquired a reputation as an international fixer, capable of raising and investing funds, and came to be a trusted Syrian governmental consultant. He was even, it has been claimed, considered for a senior position in the Syrian defense ministry.

CAUGHT RED-HANDED

Ensconced in Syria, Cohen's primary means of communication with his masters in Israel was by coded messages sent by a short-wave radio transmitter hidden in his apartment, although secret letters and even covert meetings with Mossad agents were also used (Mossad controlled him from 1964). Cohen's very success in Syria contributed in part his downfall. With increasing US support for Israel during the Cold War of the 1960s, Soviet intelligence was keen to find a way of disrupting the relationship, and offered their security services to several Arab nations, including Syria. They smelled a rat in Damascus and, using transmission detection equipment, they quickly identified Cohen's apartment as a source of numerous transmissions of coded information. In January 1965 the flat was raided, the transmission equipment found in a kitchen cabinet, and Cohen was arrested. He was summarily tried and sentenced to death. Despite pleas for clemency from Israel, Eli Cohen was hanged in public in Marjeh Square in Damascus on May 18, 1965.

Above: Eli Cohen's execution by hanging was performed in public and televised.

THE GOLAN HEIGHTS

Cohen scored two major successes concerning the still-disputed Golan Heights territory, occupied by Israel since the Six-Day War in 1967. In an early attempt at economic sabotage, Syria planned to divert the streams supplying the river Jordan that flow from the Golan Heights, which would starve Israel of its primary water supply. Cohen feigned investment interest in the project, and supplied Israel with details which allowed them to bomb the seemingly innocent hydraulic construction sites north of the Heights. At the same time, Syria was constructing three lines of concealed defenses, bunkers, and mortar batteries on the Heights themselves. Cohen failed to gain access to these, but cheerfully suggested that planting fast-growing eucalyptus trees around the fortifications might conceal them from Israeli observers. The newly planted trees provided targets for Israeli gunners and air crews during the Six-Day War.

Above: Map showing Israeli Army advances during the Six-Day War of 1967.

"I AM WRITING TO YOU THESE LAST WORDS, A FEW MINUTES BEFORE MY END, AND I WOULD LIKE TO BEG YOU TO BE IN A GOOD RELATIONSHIP FOREVER."

Eli Cohen's last letter to his wife

Below: Israeli troops after their capture of the Golan Heights.

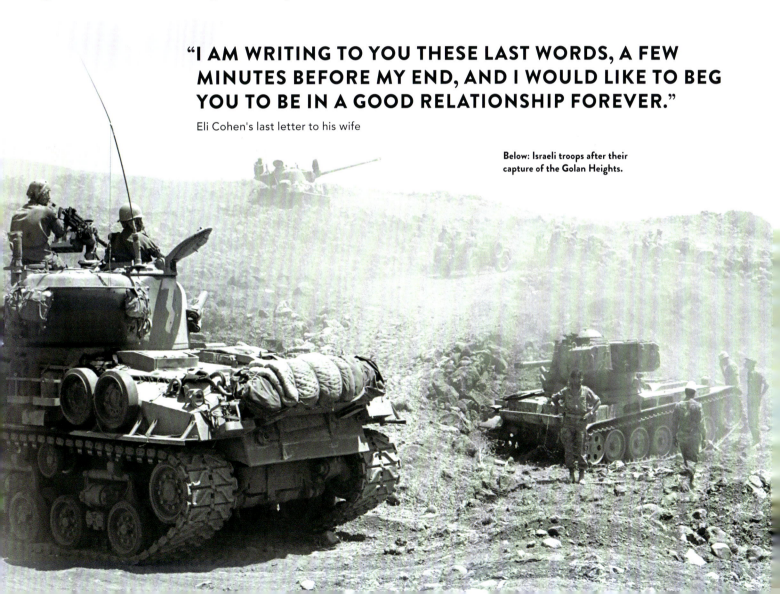

WALKER FAMILY

The spy ring created by US naval officer John Walker Jr. was very much a family affair. Motivated purely by financial gain, Walker started spying for the Soviets in 1967. By the time he was caught in 1985, he had recruited his best friend, Jerry Whitworth, his older brother Arthur, and his son Michael. However, family ties had also led to his downfall.

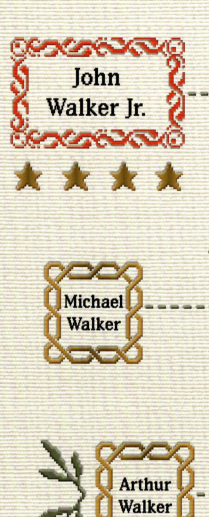

John Walker joined the Navy from school in 1955 as a radio serviceman. In 1967, he was assigned as a communications watch officer, running the communication center for the submarine force. In this role, he oversaw the communications in and out of the subs, including the codes and ciphers used to decode the messages.

SECRETS FOR CASH

In 1967, Walker walked into the Soviet embassy in Washington, D.C., with an audacious but simple proposition: buy my secrets for money. The Russians were skeptical of the offer at first. For starters, the front door of the embassy in was most certainly surveilled by the CIA. Who was this foolish man? Walker had a cipher card with him as an example of the kind of intelligence he could offer. After some analysis, the Russians realized Walker did have valuable information. He was interviewed at length inside the Soviet agency to ensure he wasn't a CIA plant. He was strictly interested in an exchange of money for information, and they came to an agreement.

During the course of the relationship, Walker provided sensitive submarine cipher data, communications repair manuals, blueprints of naval vessels, operational orders, war plans, technical plans, images of weapons, and other secret documents. From his information, the Soviets were able to decipher US submarine communications. They also learned that the US Navy was able to identify and track Russian subs based on the cavitation (the sonic output of tiny bubbles) created by their subs' propellers. It is thought that Walker's information inspired the Soviets to aid North Korea's 1968 capture of the surveillance ship USS *Pueblo*, which enabled them to get their hands on the communications hardware directly.

In 1973, Walker recruited his best friend Jerry Whitworth, a Navy communications specialist.

Left: The USS *Nimitz*, on which Michael Walker served.

Jerry Whitworth

Whitworth gave Walker cipher and communications information. At first, Walker lied to Whitworth, telling him the information was going to US ally Israel. After he came clean and told Whitworth the information was going to the Soviets, they continued their arrangement. Whitworth continued collecting information for Walker until 1983, when he retired from the Navy.

Walker retired from the Navy in 1976, concerned that he might be investigated. To keep the information flowing, he recruited his older brother Arthur, a military contractor who shared ship design and weapons system information. Walker also recruited his son Michael, who was stationed on the USS *Nimitz*. He tried to recruit his daughter, Laura, who was in the Army, but she refused.

A DRUNKEN DENUNCIATION

Walker's downfall was finally brought about by another family member. In 1968, a year into Walker's spying activities, his wife Barbara had found a cache of classified information in their home, and he had admitted he was spying for the Soviets. They divorced in 1976, and Barbara became increasingly concerned by his attempts to recruit their children to his scheme. She phoned the Boston FBI on several occasions when drunk, but was not taken seriously. In 1984, following another drunken denunciation, Norfolk FBI looked at the file and decided to start their own investigation. They interviewed Laura Walker, who confirmed that her father was indeed a Soviet spy. Meanwhile, Whitworth wanted out of the espionage business. In May 1984, he contacted the San Francisco FBI and confessed, offering to cooperate if given immunity. However, he appears to have changed his mind and promptly disappeared.

The FBI began monitoring John Walker's communications, and learned about a planned dead drop in May 1985. They followed him to a rural area in Montgomery Count, Maryland, where they watched him drop a package. When the FBI retrieved the package, they found classified information from the USS *Nimitz*, the aircraft carrier of Walker's son, Michael. The package also included some code, which turned out to be the names of the others in his spy ring. John Walker was arrested the following day. Michael Walker was arrested aboard the *Nimitz*, and Arthur was also taken in. They tracked down Whitworth on June 3, 1985.

Above: A spy satellite in orbit.

FALCON AND THE SNOWMAN

In the 1970s, two boyhood friends teamed up for a criminal adventure involving espionage, drug smuggling, and bank robbery. Christopher Boyce (nicknamed "The Falcon" for his love of falconry) worked at the National Reconnaissance Office (NRO), handling satellite communications. He stole classified documents about spy satellites and communication ciphers, which he handed to his friend Andrew Lee (aka "The Snowman"—a cocaine and heroin dealer). Lee delivered the documents to the Soviet embassy in Mexico City, using the trips to buy and smuggle drugs back into the US.

Lee was caught quite by chance. In January 1977, he was arrested for littering in front of the embassy. He was carrying filmstrips of satellite plans at the time. Under interrogation by the Mexican police, Lee admitted that he was a spy and implicated Boyce. Lee was returned to the US, where he was sentenced to life in prison. Boyce was sentenced to forty years. However, Boyce escaped in 1980, and went on a spree of bank robberies as he planned his escape to the Soviet Union. He spent nearly two years on the run before he was given up by an accomplice. Boyce and Lee have since been released.

THE DECLINE AND FALL OF THE SOVIET UNION

In the early 1980s, paranoia grew within the leadership of the KGB as intelligence revealed the apparent possibility of a nuclear first strike by the US. This combined with domestic economic worries to force the Soviet Union to change its policies in the course of the decade. The changes, initiated by General Secretary Mikhail Gorbachev, would lead to the break up of the Soviet Union, and an end to the Cold War. This marked the end of the KGB, but not of Russian intelligence. Its successor, the GRU, continues to perform many of the same functions.

ON THE BRINK

Between 1981 and 1983, under the direction of President Ronald Reagan, the US military made ostentatious displays of its prowess and confidence, moving ships close to sensitive Soviet bases and flying aircraft directly at Soviet airspace only to peel away at the last moment. Meanwhile, the US's nuclear arsenal grew significantly, and Reagan announced ambitious new plans for the Strategic Defense Initiative, popularly dubbed "Star Wars." The increased tensions threatened to spill over into nuclear conflict in November 1983 when NATO organized its annual "Able Archer" exercise, in which it simulated a period of high alert. New elements were added to the 1983 exercise to add realism, including the involvement of heads of state and periods of radio silence. Suspecting that the exercise might be a ruse to hide preparations for a real nuclear strike, the Soviet Union readied its own nuclear capability and placed units in Eastern Europe on high alert. Tensions only eased when the five-day exercise was ended.

While its military insecurity mounted, the Soviet Union was also experiencing economic problems. The disaster at the Chernobyl nuclear power station in 1986 cost the economy more than 18 billion rubles. Combined with the rocketing costs of maintaining nuclear parity and continuing to compete in the space race, the country was pushed to the verge of bankruptcy.

GLASNOST AND PERESTROIKA

Mikhail Gorbachev became General Secretary of the Communist Party (the de facto president) in 1985. Recognizing that the status quo was unsustainable, he instigated reforms to reinvigorate the Soviet Union under two main banners. "Glasnost" constituted a policy of openness and signaled an increase in government transparency. "Perestroika" involved a political movement for reform that introduced market-like reforms to enable the communist economy to better meet the needs of its citizens. The increased openness led to popular demands for even more freedoms across the countries of the Warsaw Pact. These demands culminated in a series of revolutions in 1989 in Poland, Hungary, East Germany,

**Above:
NATO's planned deployment of the new US intermediate-range Pershing II missile in Western Europe during the Able Archer exercise caused alarm in the Soviet leadership.**

Bulgaria, Czechoslovakia, and Romania. In 1991, the "Iron Curtain" was symbolically toppled with the fall of the Berlin Wall.

FAILED COUP

The KGB had originally supported Gorbachev's reforms, but the fall of the Iron Curtain had not been part of its plans, and in August of 1991, eight high-ranking KGB officers decided to take matters into their own hands. The eight leaders, including the chairman Vladimir Kryuchkov, formed the "State Committee on the State of the Emergency" and attempted to overthrow the government on August 19, 1991.

Above: Vladimir Kryuchkov

While the coup collapsed two days later, it precipitated the demise of the Soviet Union, which formally ended on December 25, 1991, when Gorbachev resigned, closed his office, and handed over his powers to incoming Russian president Boris Yeltsin. It was the conclusion of five months of dissolution, during which republics in the USSR seceded from the union, creating eleven new countries. The KGB of the Soviet Union became the SVR (Foreign Intelligence Service) of the Russian Federation. The SVR would become the FSB, and finally today's GRU.

Below: Mikhail Gorbachev and Ronald Reagan sign the Intermediate-Range Nuclear Forces Treaty in 1987, part of a series of agreements that would end the Cold War.

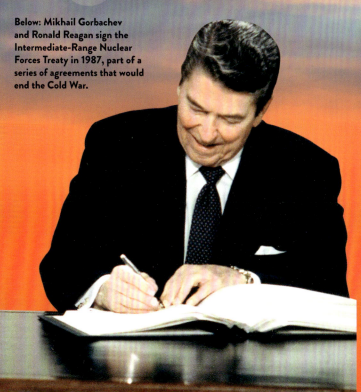

A SPY'S ESCAPE

In 1985, Oleg Gordievsky, the head of the Soviet Embassy in London, received an emergency cable to return to Moscow. An MI6 agent since 1974, Gordievsky's cover had been blown by Soviet double agent Aldrich Ames in the CIA. MI6 did not suspect anything amiss, so Gordievsky planned his return. However, he took with him a secret escape plan written in invisible ink in a volume of Shakespeare's sonnets.

When he arrived in Moscow, the KGB interrogated Gordievsky for five hours, but he was then released. It was now that he activated his escape plan, which required him to send a covert signal to MI6. Once the signal was confirmed, he took a train then bus to Vyborg, a town close to the Finnish border. Here, he waited for hours in an unmarked spot on the road. Finally at 2 a.m., two cars arrived and picked him up. There followed a tense moment at the border checkpoint when the cars were surrounded by the KGB. But they were waved through with Gordievsky hidden in the trunk. He knew he was finally safe when the driver of his vehicle played Sibelius's *Finlandia*.

Left: Oleg Gordievsky meets President Reagan at the Oval Office in 1987.

"A GROUP OF FSB OPERATIVES, DISPATCHED UNDER COVER TO WORK IN THE GOVERNMENT OF THE RUSSIAN FEDERATION, IS SUCCESSFULLY FULFILLING ITS TASK."

Vladimir Putin joking at an address to ex-colleagues at the Federal Security Service (FSB)

CHAPTER 9

TOOLS OF THE TRADE

New technologies have long been applied to national security problems to improve the quantity and quality of intelligence data. This includes cameras that could capture important data in an instant, from the popular subminiature Minox to disguised cameras in clothing, ties, buttonholes, or jewelry. Aerial cameras took to the skies first as pigeon cams, and later as sophisticated stealth aircraft with multiple sensors for gathering data across enemy lines.

This information had to be shared with the home base. Messages could be hidden in plain sight via tiny microdots, which could send a page of information in the size of a period, while compact suitcase radios enabled covert communications. A fountain pen might really be a single-shot miniature firearm, and a lighter could hide a camera. Some countries developed poisons that were near-impossible to detect, and sometimes even the local wildlife had secret uses.

STEGANOGRAPHY

Steganography is the practice of concealing information within something else, and it has a storied tradition in spycraft. While cryptography conceals the contents of the message, steganography hides the fact that there is a message at all—for example, a letter written in invisible ink, hidden between the lines of a conventional letter.

Right: Greek historian Herodotus recorded some of the earliest known uses of steganography.

The Ancient Greeks were the first to use steganography. Writing in the fifth century BCE, the Greek historian Herodotus tells how Histiaeus, the ruler of Miletus, a Greek city in modern-day Turkey, delivered a message tattooed on the shaven head of a trusted servant. Once the hair had grown in to cover it, the messenger was sent on his way. The Spartan king Demeratus I, meanwhile, warned his countrymen of an imminent Persian invasion by sending a blank beeswax tablet—normally a message would be written in the beeswax, but in this case, it was written on the wooden frame covered by the wax.

The fascination with steganography techniques continued through the ages. In 1499, German Benedictine abbot Johannes Trithemius wrote a three-volume work on the subject called *Steganographia*. The first two volumes focused on the details of the various methods, including a number of codes. The third volume, however, was seemingly concerned with the occult, and outlined various methods to communicate with spirits over long distances.

In 1676, German scholar Wolfgang Ernst Heidel claimed to have uncovered coded secrets in the third volume of *Steganographia*, but he kept the secret by writing about it in code. In 1996, a Dutch journal published a paper on the third volume by Dr. Thomas Ernst. Finally, in 2010, a mathematician at AT&T Labs named Jim Reeds, building on Heidel's notes and Ernst's paper, declared the matter of Trithemius's volume on demonology to be solved. The writing was steganographic code, concealing even more writing on steganography.

CODED QUILTS

Hidden messages were not always sent using words. In the American South of the 1800s, the locations of safehouses along the Underground Railroad — a secret network for escaped slaves— were communicated to illiterate slaves via codes sewn into quilts. According to author-historians Jacqueline Tobin and Raymond Dobard, quilt patterns were used to send secret messages to people on their journey to freedom. The "Drunkard's Path" was a warning to walk irregularly to evade slave catchers and their dogs. The patterns "Flying Geese" and "Bear Paw" indicated an instruction to follow the direction (geese fly north in springtime) or the footsteps (in the case of the bears) of the animals.

Above: This Underground Railroad quilt shows arrows pointing toward a central square, indicating that a safe haven is nearby.

INVISIBLE INK

During the American Revolutionary War, both the British and American armies used invisible ink to write secret messages between the lines of a cover letter. They used a variety of ingredients for the task, including ferrous sulfate, milk, vinegar, fruit juice, and urine. To reveal the hidden message, the reader would hold the letter over a warm light, such as a candle or a hearth fire. Today, messages can be hidden by writing in ultraviolet-sensitive ink—invisible under normal light but brightly glowing when exposed to UV.

Left: These intercepted microdots from German spies during World War II were found taped to the inside of an envelope.

SHRINKING THE MESSAGE

Sending coded messages requires the recipient to understand the code. Other methods to avoid detection involve making the message as small as possible. The microdot was probably the most important development in steganography in the twentieth century, and is still used today. It was based on a photographic shrinking method developed in the nineteenth century by French photographer René Dagron to send messages via carrier pigeon. In the 1920s, new methods were devised in Germany using a special camera and microscope to shrink a whole page of readable text as small as 0.001 square millimeters—pages of text in an area no larger than the period at the end of this sentence.

Right: Mark IV microdot camera

THE MORSE CODE CAPTIVE

Some steganographic messages can be found in amazingly plain sight—if you know what to look for. US Navy pilot Jeremiah Denton was caught by the Vietcong after ejecting from his damaged A-6 Intruder over North Vietnam in 1965. Held as a prisoner of war for almost eight years, he was made to participate in a number of propaganda press conferences. During one interview, under the bright camera lights, Denton realized he could communicate a secret message while playing along with the interview. Using Morse code, all the while nodding and agreeing that he was being well treated, he blinked out a word that US authorities could understand: T-O-R-T-U-R-E.

CAMERAS

A century ago, cameras were large devices that required specialized expertise to operate. Over ensuing decades, they became smaller and simpler to use. Cameras came into their own as spy devices with the development of the subminiature device. This tiny piece of intelligence-gathering equipment could be hidden in a pocket or disguised as a pocket watch, cigarette lighter, and even as a gun. Cameras were also hidden in clothing and jewelry to take photos in plain sight.

Echo 8

THE ORIGINAL SPY CAMERA

The Minox is the archetypal spy camera model—so popular that it got screentime in James Bond films. The brainchild of Baltic German inventor Walter Zapp, it was the first successful subminiature camera. Zapp started working on the idea in 1932, creating wooden models to explore the possibilities of miniaturization. The first working prototype was ready in 1936, and the Minox Riga model went into production in 1938. It was smaller than a cigar and weighed less than a cigarette lighter. It was simple to develop the negatives using the companion daylight-developing tank. While Zapp's goal was to make a user-friendly camera accessible to non-experts, the Minox quickly became a popular tool for espionage, easily hidden in a pocket or closed fist. Zapp took out a total of sixty-six patents for his innovations, but he sold the rights for a lump sum in 1950. This proved an unwise business decision as more than a million Minox cameras were eventually sold.

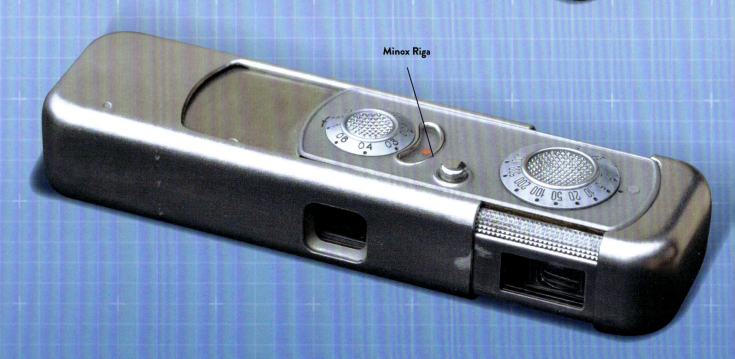

Minox Riga

In the 1950s, subminiature camera technology spread and new models were made specifically with spying in mind. In 1951, the Suzuki Optical Company of Japan produced the Echo 8, which was also a fully operational cigarette lighter. To take a picture, the user simply held the lighter up as if to light a cigarette, pointed the hidden lens in the direction of the image, and snapped. It could take twenty photos before being reloaded.

SOVIET COPIES

Soviet manufacturers soon followed suit in the manufacture of subminiatures. The Kiev 30, introduced in 1974, was small and had a short focusing range, which made it useful for document photography. It was made at the Arsenal factory in Kiev, where the Soviets copied a number of Western camera designs. The KGB also used the Tochka 58, a subminiature camera based on the Minox with a clockwork wind-up mechanism.

Today, modern digital technology, with no need to accommodate bulky film, has taken miniaturization to a new level. You can buy tiny spy cameras that record video and sound for under $50. They can be disguised as a pen, fitted into eyeglasses, speakers, smoke alarms, or light bulbs.

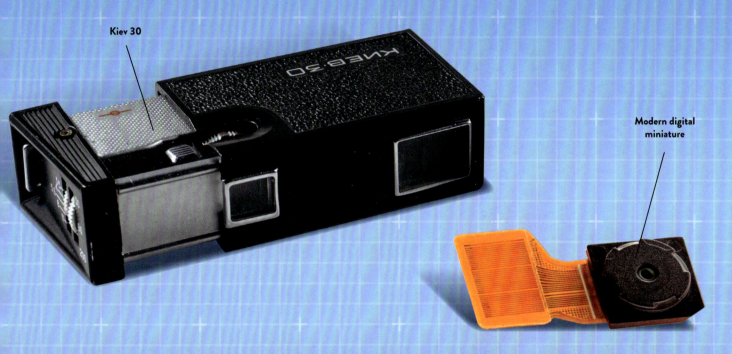

Kiev 30

Modern digital miniature

WALTER ZAPP

Born in Livonia (now Latvia) in 1904, Walter Zapp trained as an engineer, working on his ideas for miniature cameras in his spare time. Production of his Minox Riga camera started in Riga in 1938, but was interrupted by World War II. Zapp fled to Germany in 1941 with the Soviet Union about to enter the war, taking his new invention with him. For the rest of the war, Zapp worked with the company AEG on the development of electron microscopy. He founded Minox GmbH in 1945, and later partnered with Rinn & Cloos, a cigar manufacturer, to whom he sold his patent for the Minox for a lump sum and annuity. Zapp left Minox in 1950, but returned to work there in his 80s when the company was in trouble. In 2001, he was awarded an honorary doctorate from the Latvian Academy of Sciences. Zapp died in 2003, at the age of ninety-seven.

SOE COVERT COMMUNICATIONS

The invention of wireless telegraphy in the first two decades of the twentieth century transformed communication and, by the outbreak of World War II, the technology had become a critical tool for rapidly conveying information and instructions to and from command headquarters and the battlefront. It also allowed covert information-gathering to occur on an unprecedented scale. The equipment required in the field needed to be compact, portable, and easily disposed of.

THE SOE NETWORK

Britain's Special Operations Executive (SOE), along with SIS, and Naval Intelligence, were foremost among the Allied agencies running agents within enemy territory in Europe during World War II. Between them, they developed a range of wireless devices and accessories which could be easily carried and concealed, but which were essential to the flow of information. Messages were usually sent in Morse format using the "Silk" code or "one-time pads" for encryption and decryption. This system was practically infallible (unless the one-time pad was used repeatedly). The main flaw was the potential detection of transmission frequencies (although these were varied), which could provide security forces with not only evidence of telegraphic activity, but the opportunity for interception, and the ability to find the location of the transmitter.

Right: Morse transmission key

Right: A Type A Mk III suitcase radio used by SOE operatives. It comprised a sender-receiver, a Morse key, headphones, and a spares box.

COMMUNICATING ACROSS A CONTINENT

The orbit of SOE's operations in Europe, from Norway to Greece, demanded not only a variety of linguistic skills when dealing with radio communications (even in code), but wide-ranging levels of security. Not all SOE operatives were trained in wireless telegraphy, and few were entrusted with the one-time pad codes. It was simply too dangerous. In the early years of the war, local language-speaking wireless operators were dropped in. They operated as crucial links between several networks of SOE operatives or resistance groups. One such was Georges Bégué, who was active in central France in summer 1941, before having to escape via Spain. Bégué later helped to develop *messages personnels*, a system of sending disguised messages embedded in BBC overseas broadcasts.

The SOE "Jedburgh" units were developed around the D-Day and Anvil/Dragoon landings in France in 1944 to make contact with resistance groups behind enemy lines. Each group comprised one UK or US officer, one representative of the local resistance group, and one wireless operator. They acted as nuclei, coordinating sabotage operations.

THE SWEETHEART RECEIVER

The most compact of SOE's receivers was developed by a Norwegian refugee, Willy Simonsen. Never adopted officially by the War Office, some five thousand units were built commercially and dropped over occupied Europe. The crystal earphones were susceptible to altitude damage and were delivered in hermetically sealed tobacco tins.

Left: The Type 31/1 Receiver, known as "Sweetheart," comprised a body-wearable receiver, a replaceable two-battery unit, and earphones.

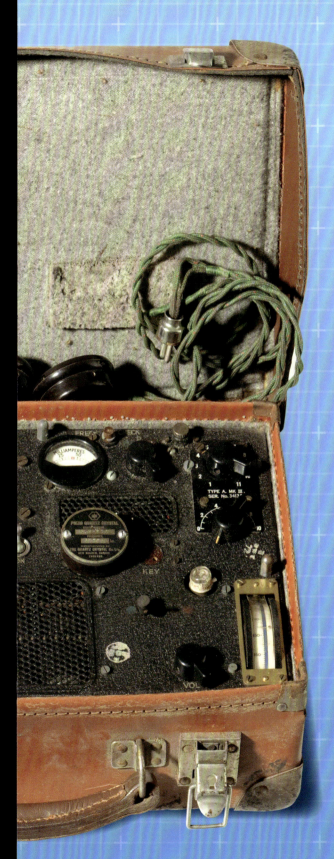

PORTABLE POWER

Most SOE receivers and transceivers were powered by flashlight or hearing aid batteries. However, these batteries had a limited lifetime and were not always easy to obtain. The Alcon steam generator became standard issue in the later years of the war, especially for the Jedburgh units, providing just enough power to generate or receive a signal using a simple heat source such as a cigarette lighter or matches.

Right: The Alco steam generator. Alco was a US company specializing in steam railroad engines. The device was a miracle of miniaturization.

ACOUSTIC KITTY

Humans have used animals in warfare ever since we trained horses and domesticated dogs—and that includes spying on enemy forces. Back in the 1960s, the CIA was desperate to find any and every edge over the Soviets. They faced an age-old problem—surveilling a target without being noticed. Just one of many off-the-wall ideas from the era culminated in a project combining animals and espionage: Acoustic Kitty.

MICROPHONE IN EAR CANAL

WOW!

ANTENNA WIRE ALONG SPINE

TRANSMITTER AND POWER SUPPLY

Begun in 1961, the idea involved not planting bugs in rooms, but surgically implanting bugging equipment in animals such as cats. The animals would then be deployed near Soviet embassies and other sensitive locations, and eavesdrop on conversations as the cats wandered by windows and perched on park benches near their targets.

It took audio engineers at the CIA more than five years to come up with electronics small enough to use. Finally, in 1966 after years of experimentation on various cats, they tested the proof of concept with a gray-and-white tabby. The cat was implanted with a microphone inside the ear canal, hooked up to a tiny battery and transmitter under the skin, and equipped with an antenna running along its spine to its tail. The cat was still a cat, though, and they had to overcome the fact that the cat could be distracted, chiefly by hunger. The cat's brain was also wired with electrodes in order to suppress the cat's appetite (along with sexual arousal!).

Conflicting reports indicate that the cat either could not be counted on to do its job—since, unlike dogs, cats are hard to train and more independent—or worse, that it was simply run over by a taxi within moments of its first field test outside the Soviet embassy in Washington, D.C. Project Acoustic Kitty was ultimately unsuccessful, and was ended in 1967 after more than $20 million had been spent on its development.

WOAAAH!

OTHER ANIMAL ESPIONAGE AND INTERFERENCE

The Cold War saw tests of various bird species—including a raven named Do Da—equipped with spy cameras to fly over Soviet installations, but this was far from the only era humans had employed animals in military and intelligence work. During World War II, many animals were considered as delivery methods for explosives and incendiaries. For example, the British forces came up with the idea of hiding rat carcasses stuffed with explosives among German supplies. All these ideas were either eventually discarded, or failed—sometimes with spectacular results.

The Russian army tested dogs trained to run under enemy tanks carrying explosives … until the test dogs ran under friendly tanks instead. Meanwhile, in the United States, a flock of bats had tiny incendiary bombs attached to them, with the intention to release them over enemy territory, where they would set fire to buildings. That project was called off after the entire flock flew into a hangar on an Air Force base, which burned to the ground when the incendiaries went off.

Farther back in history, Renaissance-era art from the 1500s shows off the concept of weaponized animals. As with modern war efforts, the idea was to send cats and birds carrying burning incendiaries into enemy territory. Before then, a third-century BCE Sanskrit text, along with seventh-century CE Chinese military manuals, tenth-century Russian tales, eleventh-century Viking accounts, and an early modern history of Genghis Khan, all mention or depict the use of birds and cats bearing flammable devices.

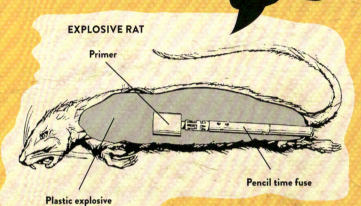

EXPLOSIVE RAT

Primer

Pencil time fuse

Plastic explosive

PIGEON CAMERA

In 1907, a wayward homing pigeon became the inspiration for the pigeon camera. German apothecary and amateur pigeon fancier Julius Neubronner used homing pigeons to send medications to the local sanatorium and receive shipments from his distributor. One pigeon failed to return, showing up four weeks later, seemingly fat and happy. Neubronner wondered what it had been up to, and came upon the idea of strapping a camera to the bird. The pigeon was fitted with a harness to hold the camera, which was set to take photos at regular intervals. While pigeons were used to carry messages during both world wars, it is unclear to what extent Neubronner's idea caught on and they were used for reconnaissance. In the 1970s, the CIA developed a still-classified pigeon camera—but we don't know when or how it was ever deployed.

SPIES IN THE SKIES

At the beginning of the Cold War, the United States wanted to monitor ongoing activities in the USSR, especially to assess its nuclear capabilities. They needed a spy plane that could penetrate Soviet airspace undetected. In theory, if a plane could fly at 70,000 feet (21,300 m), neither then-current missiles nor fighter pilots could reach it, even if it was detected. This was the beginning of the U-2 spy plane, which remains in use today.

Left: U-2 on an early flight

The U-2 was developed at Lockheed by aeronautical engineer Clarence "Kelly" Johnson, who worked in a separate division of the company known as the "Skunk Works." Johnson based his design for the U-2 on the Lockheed Starfighter supersonic interceptor prototype, with long wings and a short fuselage. He removed landing gear from the wings, leaving a "bicycle" configuration under the fuselage, thus reducing weight but requiring very skilled pilots to land the plane safely.

The plane was developed in total secrecy in just nine months. The first test flight was flown in August 1955, and the aircraft became fully operational by 1956, fitted with cameras and sensors to collect intelligence data.

HARD TO HANDLE

The U-2 flies so high that the pilot must wear a pressure suit similar to that of astronauts. It was found to be so difficult to pilot that it quickly earned the nickname "Dragon Lady." It was essentially a jet-powered glider, and needed a ground chase car driven by another U-2 pilot to assist landing. Pilots would fly the plane as close to the ground as possible— within a foot or two—then stall the engine.

Early missions on the U-2 were flown with three cameras. One took a continuous horizon-to-horizon photograph. Another took panorama pictures of the Earth's surface at high resolution. The third was a "trimetrogon," which consisted of three lenses, the center one pointing straight down, with the other two angled 60 degrees on either side.

THE U-2 INCIDENT:
EXCHANGE AT THE BRIDGE OF SPIES

The US believed that the U-2 could not be shot down. However, on May 1, 1960, pilot Gary Powers discovered to his cost that this was not the case. His fateful flight occurred just a few weeks before a summit between US President Eisenhower and First Secretary of the Soviet Union Khrushchev.

Powers' approved flightpath was the first complete flyover of the USSR. He was to take off from a secret CIA base in Pakistan and fly across the Soviet Union to Norway. Soviet intelligence was aware of the flight, and detected it as soon as Powers entered Soviet airspace. Near the city of Sverdlovsk (modern-day Yekaterinburg) in the Ural Mountains, surface-to-air missiles damaged the U-2. As the aircraft spun out of control, Powers bailed out before he was able to pull the plane's self-destruct levers. He parachuted right into the arms of the KGB.

Knowing only that it had disappeared, the US claimed that the U-2 was a NASA weather research aircraft and Powers was a private citizen doing weather research for NASA. However, the KGB had recovered the U-2, including its flight plan and sensors. As the truth continued to be withheld, Khrushchev called off the summit.

Powers was put on trial, convicted of espionage, and sentenced to ten years in a prison. Less than two years into his sentence, he was swapped for Soviet spy and KGB Colonel William Fisher. The swap took place at the famous "Bridge of Spies" in Berlin, Germany. Powers returned to the United States, but not to a hero's welcome—some felt he had failed his country by not pulling the self-destruct lever or ingesting the cyanide pill that was part of his kit.

Above: Powers in a pressure suit

The U-2 also carried various sensors in the nose and collected weather data. While the focus was to gather data about Soviet capabilities, the U-2 was also deployed in the Caribbean during the Cuban Missile Crisis. In 1962, a U-2 captured photos of Soviet missile installations in western Cuba (see pages 156–157).

USE TODAY

The U-2 continues to be used for civilian, private sector, and military data collection equipped with sophisticated sensors that track weather, environmental, and non-intelligence military data. Most of its reconnaissance duties have been taken over by satellites.

Above: Today, NASA collects data using the ER-2, a modified U-2.

COLD WAR WET WORK WEAPONS

The extermination of spies, dissidents, and political adversaries reached industrial proportions during the regimes of Hitler and Stalin. During the Cold War, such expedient measures continued, but on a smaller, covert scale. Most frequently, the problem confronting an assassin (or "wet worker") was how to carry out the "hit" discreetly, and get away with it. A number of ingenious solutions were developed by both East and West.

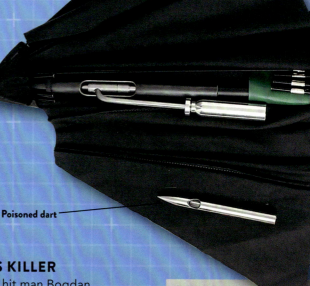

Poisoned dart

ELIMINATING ENEMIES

For centuries, poison was the preferred *modus operandi* for dealing with prominent targets, be they emperors or political rivals. It was easily administered, effective, and, until forensic science developed, virtually untraceable. In the 19th century, anarchists keen to grab headlines turned to the bomb and the gun. In the 20th century, especially during the Cold War, more brutal and barefaced assassinations occurred, although many were successfully covered up. Some, such as the shooting of US President John Kennedy, remain open to speculation. It seems, for covert "wet workers," however, poison has returned as the weapon of choice.

Left: The assassination of Leon Trotsky (1879–1940) in Mexico, by order of his former comrade-in-arms Joseph Stalin, was particularly brutal. Trotsky was killed with an ice axe by Spanish Soviet agent Ramón Mercader.

GAS KILLER

KGB hit man Bogdan Stashinsky used a cyanide gas weapon to assassinate Ukrainian dissidents Lev Rebet in 1957, and Stefan Bandera in 1959, in Munich. He would roll the weapon in a newspaper. As the target approached, Stashinsky pulled the pin at the rear of the weapon, discharging cyanide gas into the victim's face. This caused almost instant death, the "hit" appearing to have died from a heart attack.

In 1961, Stashinsky defected to West Germany, where he confessed to the murders. He was sentenced to eight years in prison, but only served four years before he was released. He is thought to have been handed over to the CIA, who gave him and his wife new identities to allow them to disappear.

Above: Lev Rebet was a survivor of the Auschwitz concentration camp, where this photograph was taken.

THE CASE OF THE POISONED UMBRELLA

One of the most notorious covert assassinations occurred on the streets of London in 1978. The target was Georgi Markov, a celebrated Bulgarian writer. On September 7, as he was waiting for a bus on Waterloo Bridge on his way to work at the BBC, he was stabbed in the calf with an umbrella. The man holding it apologized in a heavy accent. Later, Markov developed a fever, and he died in the hospital three days later. An autopsy revealed he had been poisoned with ricin, for which there is no known antidote. The assassin is believed to have been a Dane of Italian descent, coerced into working for the Bulgarian secret police. He is still at large.

Below: The poison umbrella was the perfectly disguised weapon for the streets of London.

Above: Police officers in protective suits search the grounds of Salisbury Cathedral for evidence.

Trigger

It was also a functional umbrella.

THE SALISBURY POISONING

In 2018, a former spy and his daughter were found foaming at the mouth in a park in Salisbury, England. Sergei Skripal was a former double agent for the CIA now living in the UK. Skripal's daughter Yulia had just arrived from Moscow. They had been poisoned with Novichok, a deadly nerve agent developed in the 1980s. Secret agents had sprayed Novichok on Skripal's door handle. The nerve agent was kept in a perfume bottle that had then been thrown away, but was found by a local man. He gave it to his girlfriend, who later died. Sergei and Yulia eventually recovered.

Three GRU officers are believed to be responsible. While Russia never accepted responsibility, President Putin's comments about the 2010 spy swap that had freed Skripal may hold the answer: "Traitors always come to a bad end."

CONCEALED DANGERS

Many different ingenious methods were invented to conceal weapons and other equipment, including hiding them in clothes.

During World War II, the US developed the Sedgley OSS glove pistol as a covert assassination weapon. The single-shot gun was fired by pressing it against the victim and making a fist. In the 1960s, the KGB invented the ultimate kiss of death for a female assassin—a single-shot pistol disguised as a tube of lipstick.

Other equipment created for the well-dressed Cold War spy included a camera that could be attached to a tie pin, and a tracking device concealed inside a shoe.

Left to right: Lipstick pistol, tie pin camera, glove pistol

CHAPTER 10

SPIES IN FICTION

Spy fiction as a distinct genre began to emerge at the end of the nineteenth century, a hybrid that owed much to the classic adventure story and detective novel. By the early 1900s, spy fiction was proving hugely popular with the reading public, fascinated by tales of intrigue and violence in which the secret agent hero battled against the evil machinations of villainous foreign spies.

From its popular origins, the spy novel developed to become more nuanced, although from the start literary authors such as Rudyard Kipling and Joseph Conrad had written fiction with an espionage element. The Cold War was a golden period, allowing the escapist James Bond stories of Ian Fleming to co-exist alongside the complex fiction of Graham Greene and John le Carré.

While espionage novels sold in their millions, they were eventually eclipsed in popularity by the spy on the screen. Alfred Hitchcock's 1935 adaptation of John Buchan's *The Thirty-Nine Steps* proved an immediate hit, and set the pattern of filmmakers turning to the printed word for source material. This was never more the case than with the transfer of James Bond to film, guaranteeing the suave secret agent a genuinely global reach.

ORIGINS

The spy novel emerged as a distinct literary genre during the international tensions leading up to the outbreak of World War I. The rivalries between Europe's great powers fueled a rising tide of jingoistic nationalism that was highly receptive to fiction embodying intrigue and espionage. In Britain, spy novels of all kinds found a mass audience.

THE RIDDLE OF THE SANDS

Set in the early 1900s, Erskine Childers' novel *The Riddle of the Sands* involves two Englishmen—Davies and Carruthers—on a sailing holiday among the Frisian Islands off Germany's North Sea coast. Childers was himself a keen sailor, and the book authentically charts the two friends' voyage around the sandbanks of this part of the German coast. Davies explains to Carruthers his suspicions about sinister German naval activity. The two men then become embroiled in dubious activity with nefarious individuals. Along the way, they uncover a German plan to construct a port capable of holding a fleet of tugs and barges to transport a German invasion army to England. Davies and Carruthers eventually manage to escape back to Britain and warn the authorities of their discovery. *The Riddle of the Sands* was an enormous commercial success, and influenced the development of espionage fiction for decades after its publication.

The Anglo-German naval race and fears of British military decline formed the back drop to William Le Queux's *The Great War in England* in 1897 (published 1893), a best-selling novel about a foreign invasion thwarted by the intervention of a British spy. This was the first of a series of similar themed books by Le Queux and his rival E. Phillips Oppenheim. While the works were of indifferent literary merit, their mass popularity was so great that they even helped influence the British government to strengthen the Royal Navy and create a dedicated intelligence service (later MI5 and MI6).

Above: Rudyard Kipling

INFLUENTIAL WORKS

Distinct from these journeymen exercises was Anglo-Irish writer Erskine Childers' *The Riddle of the Sands* (1903), a well-written suspense tale that became a model for spy fiction (see left). Another classic was Nobel-winner Rudyard

Above: Joseph Conrad

Kipling's *Kim* (1901), a spy adventure set against a backdrop of Anglo-Russian rivalry in Afghanistan during the late nineteenth century. A second literary giant, Joseph Conrad, wrote two novels with strong espionage elements, *The Secret Agent* (1907) and *Under Western Eyes* (1911), although their complex structure and morally ambiguous content would have made them heavy going for most of the thriller-reading public of the day.

John Buchan's *The Thirty-Nine Steps* (1915) saw the arrival of secret-agent Richard Hannay, who went on to feature in a series of adventures that pitted the stiff-upper-lipped hero against a host of (mainly) German scoundrels. World War I provided the setting for several other espionage novels, among the best being *Ashenden* (1928) by W. Somerset Maugham, a selection of short stories that drew upon his experiences of working for British intelligence during the war.

DEPRESSION-ERA WRITERS

The emergence of the Soviet Union as an enemy of the West, the Great Depression and other economic problems, and the rise of fascism in the 1930s set the background for a new generation of British writers that included Eric Ambler and the young Graham Greene. Whereas the vast majority of spy writers had adopted a right-wing perspective, their heroes being conventionally patriotic types, both Ambler and Greene displayed left-wing sympathies. This was especially the case with Ambler, whose protagonists found themselves pitted against the intrigues of capitalist or fascist villains. *The Mask of Dimitrios* (1939) was Ambler's best-known book before the outbreak of World War II.

While Ambler's heroes often displayed a naive belief in the essential goodness of the Soviet Union, even including the NKVD, Greene's approach was more subtle, with nuanced considerations of guilt, loyalty, and treason. Although he would write his best espionage fiction after World War II, he established his credentials with early works such as *Stamboul Train* (1932) and *The Confidential Agent* (1939).

"HOW MUCH TREACHERY IS ALWAYS NOURISHED IN LITTLE OVERWORKED CENTERS OF SOMEBODY ELSE'S IDEALISM."

The Confidential Agent, Graham Greene

SPY NOVELS: THE COLD WAR AND BEYOND

The Iron Curtain that divided postwar Europe into East and West provided fertile ground for espionage fiction. Spies from both sides fought each other in desperate, covert encounters for material and moral supremacy.

INTRODUCING BOND

Ian Fleming's hero James Bond made his first appearance in *Casino Royale* (1953). In a further ten novels, including *From Russia with Love* (1957) and *Goldfinger* (1959), he established himself as the world's most famous fictional spy. Although Fleming had direct intelligence experience from World War II, his novels had little to do with Cold War spying in any realistic sense, as Bond merely acted the role of a playboy assassin. But the books' clever plotting, glamorous locations, and adroit combination of sex, snobbery, and sadism appealed to an international audience.

By the time of Fleming's death in 1964, his Bond novels had sold over forty million copies, but such was the demand for more material that others continued the series, with efforts by such luminaries as Jeffrey Deaver, Sebastian Faulks, and William Boyd. Bond also attracted a small army of imitators that included a communist rival, Andrei Gulyashki's Avakum Zakhov, who finally beats 007 in a hand-to-hand fight (although for copyright reasons Gulyashki's Bond is reduced to "07"). James Bond's influence continues into the present through the extraordinarily successful film franchise.

INTRODUCING MORAL AMBIGUITY

Far distant from Ian Fleming's world were the novels of former British intelligence officer John le Carré, who established himself as a force in espionage fiction with *The Spy Who Came In from The Cold* (1963). Le Carré's major protagonist, George Smiley, reflected the mundane realities of the Cold War: a middle-aged anti-hero who grapples with the moral ambiguities of his profession, in which success comes not from the use of physical force but through the application of superior intelligence and cunning. Other significant le Carré novels from the Cold War period numbered *Tinker Tailor Soldier Spy* (1974), *Smiley's People* (1980), and the semi-autobiographical *The Perfect Spy* (1986).

Graham Greene, who had served in intelligence during World War II, became an established literary figure in the postwar world. He continued to produce left-leaning spy-based novels that, like le Carré's works, examined the dubious morality of spying, among them *The Heart of the Matter* (1948), the darkly comic *Our Man in Havana* (1959), and *The Human Factor* (1978). Len Deighton shared the

THE SPY WHO CAME IN FROM THE COLD

Published in 1963, John le Carré's third novel was an immediate critical and commercial success that permanently changed the nature of espionage fiction. Veteran British agent Alec Leamas is sent on a final mission before being allowed to "come in from the cold." He pretends to defect to communist East Germany in order to protect a vital asset working for Britain. What seems to be a fairly straightforward double-bluff mission is transformed into a deadly triple-bluff in which Leamas becomes the unwitting tool for British intelligence. The brains behind the mission—the polite, soft-spoken spymaster George Smiley—turns out to be as ruthless as his opposite numbers behind the Iron Curtain. The quality of the writing, the intricacy of the plot, and the moral complexity of its central message raised this spy thriller into a work of literature.

Above: John Le Carré

Above: US author Tom Clancy introduced all-action CIA analyst Jack Ryan to the world in 1984 with *The Hunt for Red October*. New authors have been commissioned to continue the Jack Ryan series since Clancy's death in 2013.

cynicism of the period with *The Ipcress File* (1962) and *Funeral in Berlin* (1964), his anonymous working-class protagonist at war with his own establishment superiors as well as the enemy.

TECHNO-THRILLERS

Frederick Forsyth's *The Day of the Jackal* (1971) revolved around an attempted assassination of President de Gaulle, announcing a move away from the Cold War template in a finely constructed adventure tale, backed by exciting technical detail. This was a forerunner of the techno-thriller exemplified in the work of US author Tom Clancy. His first book, *The Hunt for Red October* (1984), introduced CIA agent Jack Ryan, who would feature in many further bestsellers. Clancy had little interest in the moral nuances of the spy world: his heroes were the good guys, fighting a ruthless enemy who got what they deserved. Another highly successful American espionage writer was Robert Ludlum, whose *The Bourne Identity* (1980) was the first of a trilogy that would achieve even greater success when transferred to the big screen (starring Matt Damon as Jason Bourne).

The collapse of the Soviet empire in the 1990s brought the Cold War thriller to a temporary end. Spy fiction moved into other areas such as corporate malfeasance, drug smuggling, and human trafficking, before the events of 9/11 and the War on Terror provided a new focus of interest for spy writers. Alex Berenson's *The Faithful Spy* (2006) placed CIA agent John Wells undercover inside al Qaeda, while Olen Steinhauer's *The Tourist* (2009) was the first in a series of books featuring reluctant CIA agent Milo Weaver.

The rise of Putin's Russia has marked the first step in a return for the Cold War espionage novel, albeit modified by a diminished ideological element, with Soviet communism replaced by Russian kleptocracy. Whatever changes occur to the world order, the agents of spy fiction will closely follow.

SPIES ON FILM

Spy stories have provided fertile ground for blockbuster movies, in which suave spies overcome dangerous situations to land in the arms of gorgeous women. The international success of the Bond movie franchise overshadowed Ian Fleming's original books. The Bond effect was also seen on television with the two US series from the 1960s: *The Man from U.N.C.L.E.*, and *I Spy*. The archetype of the spy film came to Hollywood from the Master of Suspense himself, Alfred Hitchcock.

Above: Alfred Hitchcock

Left: The stars of *North by Northwest* relax on set in front of Mount Rushmore, scene of a thrilling chase in the film. From the left, James Mason, Eva Marie Saint, and Cary Grant.

PIONEERING SPY FILMS

Director Alfred Hitchcock made his name in Britain in the 1930s, filming an adaptation of John Buchan's spy novel *The Thirty-Nine Steps* in 1935. In the 1940s, he moved to Hollywood, where he set the blueprint for the modern spy film with *North by Northwest* (1959), a story about a man who is mistaken for a mysterious government agent. *North by Northwest* has all the vital components of a spy film: a daring leading man, a beautiful woman, a charismatic villain, a mysterious government agency, a plot to take secrets out of the country, secrecy, deception, and danger. This film sets the stage to introduce James Bond to the silver screen—in fact, the helicopter chase in the Bond film *From Russia with Love* was inspired by the crop duster scene in *North by Northwest*.

BOND MOVIES

One of the most enduring series ever, the James Bond films have spanned the globe with twenty-five films' worth of spy action, starting with *Dr. No* in 1962, and most recently 2020's *No Time to Die*. The role of James Bond, dashing playboy agent, has been shared by some of the most handsome actors in the world, and there's always a new beautiful woman at his side—or, in some cases, facing off against him. The stories all follow a similar arc: a sinister but charming villain is out to destroy the world, and it's up to Agent 007 to stop him. The threat might be stolen nukes, faked war stories, or a ghost from the past. Between the opening barrel-of-a-gun motif and the witty last lines, there are certain to be car chases, close calls, gorgeous women, and unique gadgets. Bond—James Bond—always saves the day ... and always in impeccable style.

Above: Actor Sean Connery discusses his character with its creator Ian Fleming on the set of *Dr. No.*

TINKER, TAILOR, SOLDIER, SPY

John le Carré's 1974 novel *Tinker, Tailor, Soldier, Spy* tells the story of the unmasking of a KGB agent at the top of British Intelligence. It was turned into a miniseries in 1979 and a film in 2011. Le Carré introduced a number of new terms that have since entered into everyday usage, including "honey trap" for a blackmail operation involving sex, and "mole" for an agent who works their way up an organization in order to access secret information.

ENTER THE DRAGON

Kung-fu action meets with intrigue in *Enter the Dragon* (1973), in which Bruce Lee plays a Shaolin martial artist monk who is invited to participate in a tournament on a suspected crime lord's private island. By day, martial arts tournaments are held, but by night, secret passages lead to underground drug-manufacturing operations, culminating in one of the best fight scenes ever filmed, taking place in a maze of mirrors.

MODERN SPY GENRES

The first spy films built upon well-loved characteristics and have since evolved into action, comedy, and anime genres. With the *Mission: Impossible* and *Bourne* series, our leading man became physically powerful but had a mysterious past; in the case of Jason Bourne, he might not even know his own history. The twenty-first century saw the introduction of serious, original multipart TV thrillers that included the US series *Alias*, *Homeland*, *The Americans*, and *24*, plus the German-produced *Deutschland 83*.

WOMEN GET INTO THE GAME

The 2005 sci-fi film *Aeon Flux*, based on a 1990s animated series, features the eponymous assassin living in a future world reminiscent of Eastern Europe. Sneaking into the walled city-state Bregna to steal information or destroy targets, she is sometimes considered a terrorist. However, her unusual relationship with Bregna autocrat and lover-nemesis, Trevor Goodchild, makes them both a strange kind of double agent. *Aeon Flux* is one of the earliest works to depict bio-medical espionage methods—such as sharing secret messages via ingested pills that cause the recipient to know the information directly.

French director Luc Besson's *La Femme Nikita* (1990) portrays a criminal given a second chance after her death is faked in jail, with an opportunity to be trained as an assassin. She takes the opportunity, and the film follows her missions and mishaps. This concept was so successful it was remade as *Point of No Return* in Hollywood and *Black Cat* in Hong Kong, and was also continued for eight seasons across two distinct TV series.

The 2017 film *Atomic Blonde* depicts a female spy who is tough as nails: Charlize Theron plays Lorraine Broughton, a member of MI6 sent to East Germany to track down a double agent days before the fall of the Berlin Wall. Like the Bond series, *Atomic Blonde* is full of intrigue, action, and gorgeous women, as well as a leading lady whose fights and injuries (and those of the men she dispatches along the way) are realistically depicted, from bruises to broken bones.

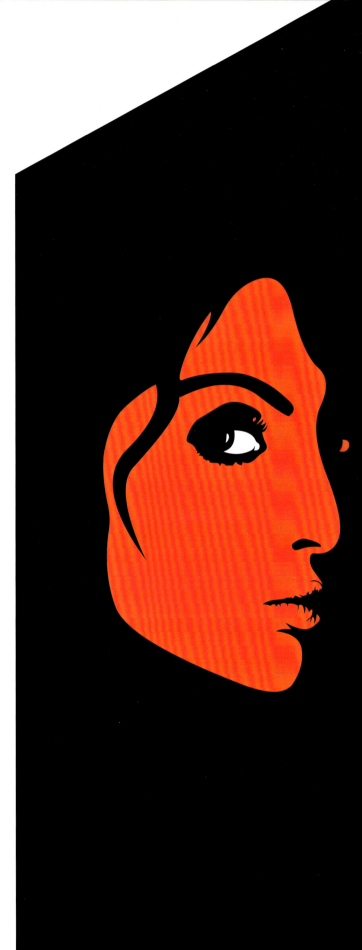

TWISTS ON THE GENRE

Wim Wenders' *Until the End of the World* (1991) is mainly known as a globe-trotting road trip, but it includes much traditional spy tradecraft: cover identities, financial tracking, and a mysterious piece of new technology: a camera that can be used to take images to be shown to a blind person. The chase continues across Europe, Asia, and into the Australian outback.

Everyday people bored with their lives sometimes dream of the life of a double agent. In the Coen brothers' *Burn After Reading* (2008), the memoir of a disgruntled retired CIA agent is found by two bumbling idiots at the local gym, who mistakenly believe they've stumbled upon classified information and come up with a scheme to sell it to the Russians. The resulting escapades go awry in ways not even the most Machiavellian puppet master could have planned, involving a blackmailing wife, a US Marshall, and the real CIA.

Austin Powers: International Man of Mystery (1997) is a groovy Swinging-Sixties spoof on the suave James Bond. Many of the characters are parodies of those in the James Bond series. Doctor Evil, the bumbling and uncool supervillain foil to the hip Austin Powers, is based on Bond's nemesis Ernst Blofeld, who had Persian cats and wore a distinctive tunic with a mandarin collar; Bond girl Pussy Galore is parodied by Alotta Fagina. The two sequels in the trilogy continue the spoofing action: *The Spy Who Shagged Me* is derived from *The Spy Who Loved Me*, while the titular villain of *Goldmember* is a riff on *Goldfinger*.

STRANGER THAN FICTION

The 2012 film *Argo* is based on a real CIA mission to rescue consulate personnel in Tehran after the Iranian Revolution of 1979. As the CIA was exploring ideas to get them out, an unusual solution was proposed: a Hollywood production company scouting locations for an upcoming film. Stereotypical moviemaking people would notoriously be self-absorbed and clueless about the political situation in a country, and it was plausible enough that the CIA went for it. With a little help from the film industry itself, the agency created a cover story, complete with a new script based on a defunct production, concept drawings, and press in *Variety* and *The Hollywood Reporter*. Cover story in place, they went to Iran to make the rescue. The operation was tense, with the extracted personnel flying out in plain sight as a production crew on an international flight. Each crew member had to wear a disguise, play their cover perfectly, memorize key points about the script, and hold it together through airport security.

— CHAPTER 11 —

CORPORATE ESPIONAGE

Espionage is not limited to foreign powers spying on each other. Companies looking for an edge use the same techniques to gather information about their competitors. Information gathering can range from legal activities for "competitive intelligence" or poaching employees from a competitor to illicit activities such as stealing intellectual property (IP) through an internal or external source. While it is legal for companies to research their competitors, and even hire key personnel from them, sometimes the new employee brings more than just talent. And companies can use the stolen information to gain a competitive edge in the marketplace.

In 1996, the United States Congress passed the Economic Espionage Act, allowing the prosecution of companies and individuals in the case of stolen trade secrets or attempted stealing of trade secrets to benefit a foreign power. Individuals can be fined up to $250,000, and organizations can be fined up to $5 million. Nonetheless, IP theft can and does still happen, and with modern digital storage, it is easier than ever to walk away with terabytes' worth of valuable data in the palm of your hand.

THE COST OF COMPETITION

Many corporate espionage tales begin with a disgruntled employee. As with intergovernmental spying, inserting a deep-cover agent is a long and perilous investment. It is a much simpler task to find someone already on the inside for whom money speaks more loudly than loyalty.

In the early 1980s, IBM still dominated the world of business and personal computing, but Japanese businesses were working on building compatible technology at a lower cost. Each time IBM released a new product, competitors had to buy the new devices along with everyone else, then spend months reverse-engineering any new technology before they could develop their own compatible components. This gave IBM an effective six-month to one-year window of market exclusivity.

Between 1981 and 1983, two Japanese companies—Hitachi and the National Semiconductor Corporation—joined forces to gather information about the new upcoming IBM product line, code-named Adirondack. The goal was to learn enough that they could develop and release their own compatible technology as soon as IBM released their new system, thus breaking IBM's exclusive monopoly and getting a jump on any other competitors.

IT ONLY TAKES ONE

The IBM leak started with an IBM research scientist named Raymond J. Cadet, who left his job with copies of ten out of a total of twenty-seven top-secret binders on project Adirondack, publicly known as the 308X series. This was a new line of mainframe computers. Cadet took a new position at National Advanced Systems (NAS), a Silicon Valley subsidiary of National Semiconductor, which marketed Hitachi's computers in the US Cadet's boss at NAS, Barry Saffaie, learned about the binders and allegedly made several photocopies of them. In the summer of 1981, Saffaie flew to Japan, where, according to the US Justice Department, he delivered one set to Hitachi, where they ended up in the hands of senior engineer Kenji Hayashi.

Another IBM employee, Maxwell Paley, had recently left the company to work for a technology consulting firm. Paley offered Hiyashi, who was his regular contact at Hitachi, a legitimate study of the 308X project. Hiyashi replied that he didn't need the study as he already had a number of binders on the Adirondack series. But if Paley had the missing binders, he would be very interested. Paley suspected that something was wrong, and alerted his connections at IBM.

GOING UNDERCOVER

Alarmed by the detail involved, IBM contacted the FBI, who initiated a seven-month-long sting operation. Undercover FBI agents posed as IBM consultants who had access to the desired information and were willing to sell it on the black market. Two Hitachi employees paid $648,000 for the documents, while Japanese firm Mitsubishi was also caught buying secrets for $26,000.

When the sting operation was complete, the FBI arrested six Japanese businessmen living in the US and issued a warrant for a dozen others based in Japan. Two Hitachi employees pleaded guilty to criminal charges and were fined $14,000. IBM sued Hitachi and National Semiconductor Corp for $2.5 billion. Hitachi settled out of court for $300 million, but things were trickier with National Semiconductor, which refused to settle. In 1983, IBM brought a new suit for $2.5 billion in damages, but it was settled for $3 million.

A REFRESHING GLASS OF ESPIONAGE

In 2006, Coca-Cola executive assistant Joya Williams was feeling unappreciated in her job. A friend introduced Williams to Ibrahim Dimson, a white-collar criminal recently released from jail, and together they came up with a scam based on her access to information on new products. Dimson sent a letter to Pepsi on official Coca-Cola stationery, offering trade secrets in return for money. He thought the plan had gone off without a hitch when he successfully exchanged a duffel bag of documents (and a small vial of a "secret" product under development) for a Girl Scout cookie box stuffed with $30,000 in rolled-up bills.

Unknown to Dimson and Williams, they had actually made a deal with FBI Agent Gerald Reichard. When Pepsi had received Dimson's letter, they had turned it over to Coca-Cola, who then brought in the FBI to find their internal leaker. Williams and Dimson were arrested and given eight- and five-year sentences respectively.

DRIVING AMBITIONS: THE FORMULA ONE SPY

The Formula One race series is known for high emotions, high stakes, and adrenaline rushes both on and off the track. In this environment, it's easy to get caught up in something bigger than yourself. The year was 2007 and McLaren was giving Ferrari, the most successful Formula One team in the world, a run for its money. Back at the garage, Ferrari was going through some management changes. One change in particular had upset Ferrari's mechanic of fifteen years, Nigel Stepney, who felt passed over for the promotion he felt he deserved.

In any highly competitive arena, competitors want to know what their adversaries are up to, and which innovations they have implemented, not necessarily to copy them, but to help them compete. In Formula One, car design and engineering are critical to success. McLaren was the top ranked team at the time. Seeking revenge for being passed over, Stepney approached his friend Mike Coughlan, who was the chief designer at McLaren, with information that could jeopardize Ferrari's season.

FOILED BY A FAN

Stepney was concerned that Ferrari's new technical designs were breaking the rules of the FIA (Fédération Internationale de l'Automobile, the governing body for F1). He shared his concerns with Coughlan, along with almost 800 pages of confidential Ferrari technical documentation. This exchange between colleagues might have stayed a secret if it hadn't been for an F1 fan at a British shop. Coughlan's wife took the documents to a local copy shop in Woking, England, just down the road from McLaren headquarters. The clerk was asked to scan the 800 pages onto a pair of CDs that would be picked up the next day.

But this clerk was a Ferrari fan, and page after page of the job had "Ferrari Confidential" marked all over it. The clerk looked up Coughlan's name and discovered that her husband worked at McLaren. That's when the clerk took matters into his own hands. He contacted Ferrari via email to tell them about the confidential documents in the hands of McLaren's chief designer.

Above: McLaren's Lewis Hamilton leads Ferrari's Kimi Raikkonen in the 2007 Malaysian Grand Prix. The teams were closely matched, with Raikkonen winning the driver's championship from Hamilton by a single point.

When McLaren management found out about the documents, they weren't interested. They told Coughlan to break ties with Stepney and get rid of the files. But Ferrari had already taken action and raided Coughlan's home, discovering the CDs. At this same time, Stepney was discovered in the Ferrari garage sabotaging a car by pouring powder into its gas tank. He was fired on the spot.

When the scandal hit the press, McLaren was under scrutiny and the FIA got involved in the investigation. The investigation found that only Coughlan had seen the stolen information. Ferrari was furious and appealed the result.

Left: Nigel Stepney celebrates Michael Schumacher's win at the 2000 Japanese Grand Prix during happier times as Ferrari's chief mechanic.

"THEFT IS NOT INNOVATION."

David Anderson, United States Attorney

A later investigation revealed that some of the stolen information had been shared via SMS with McLaren drivers and engineers, and they had used this information to their benefit.

PENALIZING MCLAREN

McLaren was fined $100 million and all the team's constructor points for the 2007 season were taken away. In addition, the team had to agree that all 2008 McLaren vehicles would be inspected to ensure no Ferrari knowledge had been used in their engineering. Separately, the FIA addressed Stepney's concerns about the potential illegality of Ferrari's designs, concluding that certain devices were indeed illegal. However, the FIA chose not to penalize Ferrari, who won the constructor's championship for 2007.

Coughlan was banned from working in Formula One for two years, and eventually returned as part of the Williams F1 team. Stepney was sentenced to twenty months in jail after a plea bargain and a 600-euro fine. He never worked in F1 again, and died in 2014 when he was hit by a truck while standing on the M2 motorway in England.

SELF-DRIVING SUBTERFUGE

Above: The driverless Google Waymo navigates using LiDAR mounted on its roof.

Self-driving cars depend on LiDAR (Light Detection and Ranging) technology to "see" the world around them. The race to perfect self-driving vehicles has made this technological eyesight a prime target for IP theft.

This story worthy of a spy novel began when Anthony Levandowski, an engineer working on Google's self-driving car project Waymo, left the project in 2016 after almost a decade at Google. When he left, Google claimed Levandowski stole 14,000 files, including LiDAR trade secrets.

After leaving Google and with the stolen LiDAR details, Levandowski started his own company, Otto, which was acquired by Uber in August 2016 for $680 million, barely eight months after he had left Google. Uber also put him in charge of their self-driving projects. A few months later, in February 2017, Waymo sued Uber and Otto for Levandowski's downloaded LiDAR trade secrets. Some in Silicon Valley thought this was unusual because Google already had a stake in Uber for $258 million. Why would Google sue a company they had invested heavily in?

In the subsequent lawsuit discovery and investigation, Levandowski refused to cooperate, and Uber fired him. This was a very difficult time in the news for Uber as they had several other high-profile scandals to defuse at the same time, so in February 2018, Uber settled with Waymo for $245 million worth of stock shares. The two companies had made things right.

But that's not the end of the story. There was still the Levandowski loose end. Because Levandowski refused to cooperate, in September 2019 the United States Attorney General's Office and the FBI charged him with theft in a criminal case. He was tried, and ordered to pay $179 million to Google. Levandowski is now seeking bankruptcy protection.

THE SWISS BANK BATTLE

The normally decorous world of Swiss banking was shaken by revelations of a bitter conflict between Credit Suisse and rival UBS in 2019. Former Credit Suisse banker Iqbal Khan and his family were subjected to surveillance and tailed by private eyes from Credit Suisse, fearful that Khan might be poaching clients for UBS.

Since his appointment in 2015, the CEO of Credit Suisse, Tidjane Thiam, had successfully turned the company around, refocusing the firm on wealth management from its previous focus on investment banking. Iqbal Khan was head of Credit Suisse's wealth management team, and was being groomed for the top spot. Thiam and Khan were good friends and all seemed fine, but below the surface, a rivalry was brewing: Khan had his eyes on Thiam's position.

Above: The Gold Coast on the northeast shore of Lake Zurich is famed for its evening sun and high property prices.

DOMESTIC SQUABBLE

A couple of years earlier, Khan had purchased the home next to Thiam's in the exclusive "Gold Coast" area on Lake Zurich. Instead of moving in, Khan had the home demolished and rebuilt, resulting in several years of construction that certainly added to Thiam's annoyance. At Thiam's annual cocktail party at a posh hotel overlooking Lake Lucerne, Khan got into a heated argument with Thiam's partner about the location of trees that Khan apparently had planted on Thiam's property. The argument continued when Thiam joined them. Khan's fast track to the top was faltering.

Khan went to the Credit Suisse board to complain about the incident, which increased the animosity and halted Khan's rise to the top. He negotiated his exit from Credit Suisse. Normally Khan's move would have involved an extended period of "garden leave"—time in which he was still paid by Credit Suisse but not expected to do any work, usually due

to a non-compete clause or concern about the employee's knowledge about sensitive information. Due to the argument with Thiam, Khan was able to negotiate a relatively short, three-month garden leave from Credit Suisse.

TAILING KHAN

Two months later, Credit Suisse competitor UBS announced that Khan would be joining as their co-president. This news certainly concerned Credit Suisse—one of their top people was going to a competitor leading the same type of division as he had at Credit Suisse. Khan was in a unique position to influence existing Credit Suisse wealth management customers to follow him to UBS. Credit Suisse security hired a private detective firm to follow Khan and note the identities of the clients he was meeting.

Aware that he was being tailed, Khan confronted the surveillance team, leading to a fracas in the heart of Zurich. There are conflicting stories of what happened next. Khan went to the police and stated that the private detective had chased him and his wife. When Khan started photographing the detective's car, Khan claimed the detective started a physical altercation with him.

As a result of this complaint, Credit Suisse opened an internal investigation about the surveillance operation. During the investigation, a contractor at the detective agency shot himself, presumed a suicide. At the same time, the internal investigation showed that one other executive had been followed. Both the head of security and the chief operations officer, Pierre-Olivier Bouée, were fired. Thiam was cleared of any wrongdoing, but resigned in early 2020.

THE TAX EVASION WHISTLEBLOWER

When the Tax Relief and Health Care Act of 2006 was passed in the US, it introduced a system by which whistleblowers could be paid up to 30 percent of any tax revenue recouped by the IRS as a result of their information. Bradley Birkenfeld was working at UBS at the time and aware of US individuals with secret Swiss bank accounts who were potentially evading taxes. In 2007, Birkenfeld released the Birkenfeld Disclosures to the US Department of Justice (DOJ). This resulted in the discovery of widescale tax evasion, and produced a $780 million fine for UBS from the DOJ. Birkenfeld was himself arrested, due to the advice he had given to California real estate investor Igor Olenicoff to evade $200 million in US taxes. Olenicoff was convicted of tax evasion and paid a $52 million fine, while Birkenfeld was convicted of conspiracy to defraud the US government, fined $30,000, and sentenced to forty months in prison. However, upon his release, Birkenfeld received a cool check for $104 million from the IRS—his percentage of the $400 million in taxes recovered as a result of his whistleblowing.

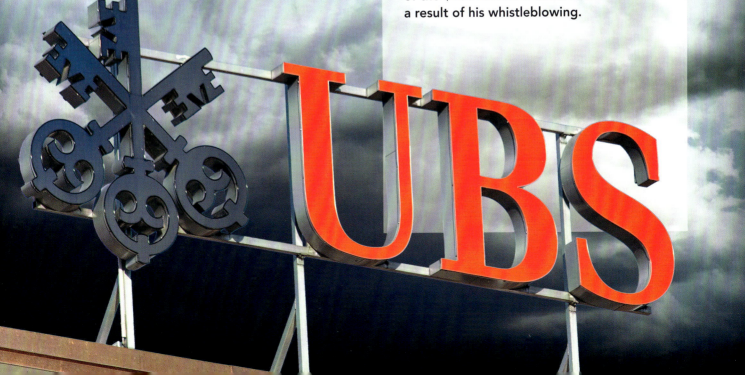

ECONOMIC ESPIONAGE: STEAL TO INNOVATE

China has stated its goal to become the global science and technology leader by 2050. Its current role as a factory to the world already has value not just in its production output, but also in its braintrust and production knowhow. While there are many documented stories of China stealing IP, the stolen IP is a small step toward its bigger ambitions.

INDUSTRIAL AGE ESPIONAGE: THE US VERSUS GREAT BRITAIN

In the early years of its industrialization, the United States was heavily engaged in economic espionage, in much the same way as China is now. One of the Founding Fathers of the United States, Alexander Hamilton, is said to have offered rewards to individuals who acquired "secrets of extraordinary value." It was rumored that the US funded smugglers who imported industrial machinery from Britain—the birthplace of the industrial textile industry. The UK criminalized the export of textile machinery and knowhow. However, that did not stop American industrial spies from touring British factories. During a two-year stay in Britain from 1810–12, US businessman Francis Cabot Lowell visited many mills and memorized the plans to the Cartwright power loom. On returning to the US, Lowell built his own version, improving on the original design, which made him a highly successful industrialist and helped to drive US manufacturing forward.

Right: Alexander Hamilton

STEALING TO INNOVATE

China won't become the global leader merely by stealing from companies in the United States and elsewhere; the Chinese must become innovators themselves. With this goal in mind, it makes sense for China to gather as much information as it can about what is being built today in order to focus on developing these ideas to solve problems at the scale of Chinese manufacturing.

SCALING UP

In the past decade, China has constructed more buildings, homes, and apartments than any other country, as well as innovating prefabrication and construction components. The astounding feat of constructing the Huoshenshan Hospital in Wuhan in just ten days to combat the 2020 COVID-19 pandemic demonstrated the organizational

CROWDFUNDING IP THEFT

Crowdfunding sites enable creators to share new ideas directly with the public and raise money to produce them. These platforms have inspired an explosion of new ideas, but since many of the products or components would be made in China, savvy manufacturers can steal the ideas before they are even funded.

Those seeking crowdfunding must sell their unique and novel feature to their prospective backers and may share detailed images and descriptions that can be used by a copycat. Patenting provides legal protection for ideas, but it takes time and money to take out patents, and many self-funded creators do not have such resources. Crowdfunded ideas such as the Pressy button for Android, the TikTok Lunatik watch kit, and the Stikbox Selfie Stick inspired knockoffs at prices well below the originals, in some cases before the crowdfunding campaigns had ended.

Above: China is now the world's leading manufacturer of electric cars, including high-end sports cars such as the Qiantu K50.

abilities of Chinese industry. To achieve this, construction continued twenty-four hours a day with a workforce of 7,000 people. This is an illustration of the way in which China has not only borrowed IP techniques from other nations, but also scaled them up in a way no other nation can match.

To date, China has benefited from borrowed IP. In one model of development, this can be seen as a natural stage. In this model, everyone borrows from everyone else at first. Then, as industries mature, they begin to value protection over open exchange. It is inevitable that China will itself become a target of economic espionage. For instance, not only does China produce more electric cars than any other country, it is also the world leader in battery technology. There will come a time—sooner rather than later—when China will be more interested in protecting IP than stealing it.

Left: Huoshenshan Hospital was built in just ten days to respond to COVID-19.

A DOUBLE-EDGED SWORD: IP AND INNOVATION

The United States and China have a long and complicated history when it comes to secret-sharing, manufacturing, and intellectual property. Depending on the administration in Washington, China may be seen as the US's greatest business partner, its biggest threat, the land of the future, or perhaps some combination of all three.

China is a major trading partner with the United States, and navigating this complex relationship can be tricky for US companies. Today, China is the factory to the world, and it works closely with US businesses to manufacture a wide range of products. Partnering with China may be a profitable business arrangement, but it creates the risk that competitors will obtain commercially valuable information, through both legal and illegal methods. There has been an uptick in reports on economic espionage cases involving China, but the public only hears about a fraction of the cases, as many incidents deal with classified information.

Restricted

PHISHING FOR SECRETS

Modern economic espionage does not require breaking into a physical location. Today, it is easier than ever to use modern hacking techniques such as phishing (sending fraudulent emails to install malware) to gain access to sensitive corporate information. You can remain halfway around the world in the safety of your own country, sat behind a computer. There are legitimate reasons why a company may need to make its documents accessible, especially with a global workforce, but all it takes is one weak point in the network security for company secrets to be stolen.

OK

Access

USER:

PASSWORD:

Copying

57.6 MB of 203.5 MB

New mail

THE THOUSAND TALENTS PLAN

The Thousand Talents Plan is a state-backed program in China, created to place Chinese nationals at prestigious academic institutions and in other research positions where they have direct access to new innovations that can be brought back to China. This program also uses external assets, such as foreign professors. One example is Dr. Charles Lieber, who was the chair of Harvard's Chemistry Department, which received more than $15 million in funding from the Department of Defense and the National Institutes of Health. Simultaneously, Lieber had a three-year contract with the Thousand Talents program, which is alleged to have paid him $50,000 a month plus living expenses between 2012 and 2017, plus $1.5 million for a Wuhan research lab—information he failed to disclose. In January 2020, Lieber was arrested and charged by the US government.

ABOVE: CHARLES LIEBER

STATE CYBER-ESPIONAGE

In 2014, the US brought charges of state-directed economic espionage against five Chinese hackers based outside the US, who were part of China's exclusive Unit 61398. The hackers broke into at least six companies from 2006 to 2014 to steal trade secrets and other strategic information. The hackers targeted nuclear and solar energy companies. Numerous executives were hacked to install malware on their company's computers and collect information.

Yes   No

CIA SPIES SELLING STATE SECRETS

Intelligence agents themselves often make the most tempting targets for espionage. One such person was Kevin Mallory. Deep in debt in 2017 after years of unsteady private-sector work, this former CIA official received a LinkedIn message from a supposed headhunter, who turned out to be a Chinese spy. In just two months, Mallory was paid $25,000 for classified US secrets, including information that possibly led to the deaths of twelve informants, before the FBI caught up with him. He was sentenced to twenty years in prison.

THE CASE OF THE STOLEN PIGMENT

The company DuPont is known for creating the whitest white for use in paint and other manufacturing. It is a market-leader due to a sophisticated chemical process that extracts titanium dioxide for the pigment. A Chinese manufacturer wanted to use this technique in the early 1990s, but didn't want to pay the $75 million licensing fee. Instead, they enlisted the help of electrical engineer Walter Liew, who founded a company and recruited DuPont scientists to duplicate the process at a fraction of the cost. When Liew was found out and arrested in 2011, his co-defendant committed suicide. Liew was convicted of economic espionage in 2014, and sentenced to a $28 million fine and 15 years in prison.

— CHAPTER 12 —
TERRORISM

Terrorism is method of asymmetric conflict used to force a political response by killing innocent people at random to spread fear in a population. One side of the conflict may see terrorism as a means of liberation or a protest against the lack of liberation. Terrorism is justified as a last resort of the weak against the strong.

In the 1930s–1940s, Jewish terror groups deliberately targeted Arabs before the formation of the Israeli state. Terrorist attacks were carried out by both Catholic Republicans and Protestant Loyalists during the Troubles in Northern Ireland from the 1960s to the 1990s. September 11, 2001, was the date terrorism really came to the US, paving the way for the "War on Terror." The CIA led an international hunt for those involved reminiscent of the Mossad assassinations in response to the PLO terrorist attack at the 1972 Munich Olympics. Terror suspects have been incarcerated and interrogated, leading to ethical concerns over Abu Ghraib prison and Guantánamo Bay.

It seems there are few ethics when it comes to terrorism—whether acting it out, responding to it, or working to stop it. Players often become locked into a cycle of violence, which can become far removed from the initial political problem that sparked the conflict.

ISRAELI INTELLIGENCE

The Talmud states: "If someone comes to kill you, rise up and kill him first." Israel's elite intelligence agency, Mossad, follows this guiding principle to the letter. Since its formation in 1949, Mossad has developed a fearsome reputation, carrying out daring covert operations across the world, and specializing in high-profile assassinations and kidnappings.

CATCHING EICHMANN

Adolf Eichmann was one of the principal organizers of the Holocaust. He managed the logistics for the deportation of Jews to concentration camps. At the end of the war, Eichmann evaded capture in Europe and escaped to Argentina in 1950.

The first breakthrough in the hunt for Eichmann came in 1953, when noted Nazi hunter Simon Wiesenthal learned that he was in Buenos Aires. Wiesenthal passed on the information to the Israeli consulate in Vienna. Mossad finally tracked Eichmann down in 1960. Argentina was unlikely to deport Eichmann, so the head of Mossad at the time, Isser Harel, approved a plan to kidnap him and bring him to Israel for trial.

Mossad agents observed Eichmann for several weeks before abducting him. He was kept in a safehouse for over a week and interrogated to confirm his identity. Mossad agents tried to extract information about the whereabouts of Josef Mengele, the notorious doctor at Auschwitz, who was also suspected to be living in Buenos Aires. Unsuccessful at tracing Mengele, they took Eichmann to Israel. His trial lasted fifty-six days, and was one of the first of its kind to be televised. Eichmann was executed for crimes against humanity on May 31, 1962.

Above: Adolf Eichmann

Left: Director of Mossad from 1952–1963, Isser Harel established its reputation as a far-reaching and ruthless organization.

In the 1930s and 1940s, Jewish settlers in the British-administered Mandate of Palestine came into conflict with Arab and British forces. Zionist terrorist groups targeted Arabs, intending to destroy their settlements and drive them from the land that would become the Jewish state.

DEFENDING THE JEWISH STATE

With the formation of Israel in 1948, roles were reversed, and state institutions were created to defend primarily against Arab terrorist groups. The main intelligence service, Mossad, was formed in 1949. Since its formation, Mossad has grown to become the second-largest intelligence agency in the world behind the CIA. It has acquired a reputation for ruthlessness, with considerable freedom to operate on its own terms.

Israel has many enemies across the Arab world, and Israelis and Jews have been the targets of numerous terrorist attacks. Mossad's responses to these attacks include assassinations—at least 2,700 to date—providing a promise to hunt down anybody involved in terrorist activities against Israel.

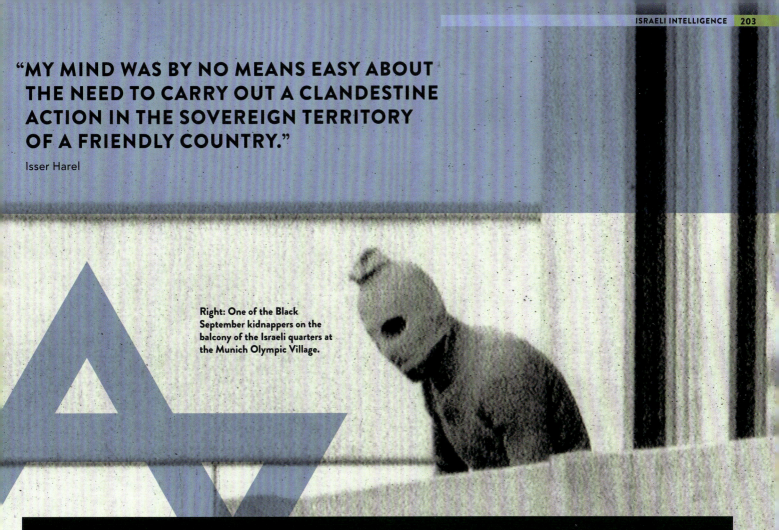

"MY MIND WAS BY NO MEANS EASY ABOUT THE NEED TO CARRY OUT A CLANDESTINE ACTION IN THE SOVEREIGN TERRITORY OF A FRIENDLY COUNTRY."

Isser Harel

Right: One of the Black September kidnappers on the balcony of the Israeli quarters at the Munich Olympic Village.

OPERATION WRATH OF GOD

During the 1972 Olympics in Munich, eleven members of the Israeli Olympic Team were killed by the Palestinian Black September terrorist group. Just before dawn on September 5, members of Black September sneaked into the Olympic Village and used stolen keys to break into the apartments of the Israeli team. The athletes were still sleeping. They resisted the attackers, enabling several to escape, but two were killed and nine were taken hostage. Subsequent negotiations to free the hostages broke down, and a botched ambush and rescue operation led to the massacre of all nine hostages aboard a helicopter on the tarmac of a NATO airbase in Fürstenfeldbruck, Germany.

To deter future terrorist attacks, Israeli Prime Minister Golda Meir approved an assassination campaign that targeted both Black September and the Palestine Liberation Organization (PLO). Mossad executed the plan as Operation Wrath of God, vowing to hunt down and kill anyone associated with the Munich massacre. Israel also retaliated by bombing Syrian and Lebanese PLO bases, and engaged in a campaign of letter bombs sent to PLO officials.

Mossad conducted assassinations in France, Italy, Cyprus, Greece, Switzerland, Britain, and the Netherlands, among those that are known. They assassinated targets via bombs inside their homes, hotel rooms, and cars. Many targets were shot point-blank in the street. Not every operation went smoothly, however. For example, in Lillehammer, Norway, Mossad agents misidentified and murdered an innocent man (see page 117). The success of Operation Wrath of God terrified the Arab world. Mossad had demonstrated that it could strike at Israel's enemies anywhere in the world.

TERROR TACTICS

The 1970s was a decade in which terrorist groups carried out attacks around the world. Many of these groups, such as Germany's Red Army Faction and Italy's Red Brigades—as their names suggest—worked for Marxist revolution. Others were separatist movements based on nationalist ideologies, including the Provisional IRA, who fought to end British rule in Northern Ireland, the Basque separatists ETA, and French-Canadian separatists in Quebec. Globally, the most prominent group of all was the Palestine Liberation Organization (PLO). All these groups used terror as a tactic to further their political aims, including bombing, targeted assassination, kidnapping, and hijacking.

Left: Israeli soldiers evacuate injured students in Ma'alot.

SICARII: THE ORIGINAL TERRORISTS?

The *sicarii* (meaning "dagger men") were a sect of Jewish zealots who operated around 70 BCE, with the aim of ending the Roman occupation of Judea. They commonly attacked their targets in a crowded public market, hiding their daggers under their cloaks. Rumor has it that they did not flee after an assassination, but made a point of standing their ground to watch their victim die.

Founded in 1964, the PLO targeted its terrorist attacks against Israel and Israelis. The PLO was the richest of the new terror organizations, with an estimated $8 billion to $10 billion in assets. In the 1970s, it was responsible for many high-profile terror attacks that made the front pages across the world. These included the 1972 Munich massacre (see pages 202–203). In the Ma'alot massacre in 1974, three PLO terrorists entered northern Israel and took more than one hundred people hostage at an elementary school. Twenty-five hostages, most of them schoolchildren, were killed. In 1985, four PLO gunmen hijacked the Italian cruise ship *Achille Lauro*, killing an elderly Jewish passenger.

"THE RED ARMY FACTION'S URBAN GUERRILLA CONCEPT IS NOT BASED ON AN OPTIMISTIC VIEW OF THE PREVAILING CIRCUMSTANCES IN THE FEDERAL REPUBLIC AND WEST BERLIN."

Ulrike Meinhof, co-founder of the RAF

FOMENTING REVOLUTION

Across the developed world, small but violent terror groups sprang up with the aim of sparking a communist revolution. In Germany, the Red Army Faction (RAF), also known as the Baader-Meinhof gang, focused on assassinations, kidnappings, and bombings, killing thirty-four people in total across three decades of operations. The Italian Red Brigades conducted sabotage operations, kidnapping, and bank robberies to further their revolutionary aims, while the Japanese Red Army declared war on Japan in 1971 in order to start a world revolution. None of these groups organized on the same scale as the PLO, but their actions spread fear among their respective populations, and in Italy, this period of violence has become known as the "Years of Lead."

Above: RAF insignia

Right: In 1978, the Red Brigades kidnapped former Italian prime minister Aldo Moro. He was killed after nearly two months of detention.

Below: Red Brigades insignia

Above: Rescued Air France passengers wave to the waiting crowd while leaving the belly of the Hercules plane at Ben-Gurion Airport.

RESCUING THE ENTEBBE HOSTAGES

On June 27, 1976, an Air France flight from Tel Aviv to Paris was hijacked by four PLO terrorists. The plane was sent to Entebbe, Uganda, where the Ugandan dictator, Idi Amin, welcomed the hijackers. Once they had landed, the terrorists freed the non-Israeli hostages. The Israeli passengers and Air France crew were only to be released in return for the release of fifty-three Palestinian militants and five million dollars.

Facing resistance not only from the terrorists but also from Ugandan soldiers, Mossad organized an elaborate rescue plan. Four transport aircraft secretly flew to Entebbe Airport. Inside the first plane was a Mercedes built to resemble Idi Amin's presidential car, with accompanying Land Rovers to deceive security. The Mercedes was stopped at the checkpoint, but eventually went through, while agents in the Land Rovers shot the security guards. Israeli soldiers entered the airport terminal and killed the hijackers, and began moving the hostages to the aircraft. One hundred and two hostages were rescued, and three killed.

THE TROUBLES: THE INTELLIGENCE WAR IN NORTHERN IRELAND

The conflict in Northern Ireland—known locally as the Troubles—lasted for nearly three decades. For many people at the time, it seemed that the fighting would go on forever, but due in no small part to good intelligence work, it was eventually brought to a peaceful conclusion.

The Troubles began in 1968 when Catholic Nationalist civil rights marches were attacked by Protestant Unionist gangs in collusion with police from the Royal Ulster Constabulary (RUC). Violence escalated and took on a political aspect. The paramilitary Irish Republican Army (IRA) took over leadership of the Nationalist cause, demanding the incorporation of the British province of Northern Ireland into a single united Irish Republic. They were bitterly opposed by Unionists who insisted that Northern Ireland remain in the United Kingdom.

INTELLIGENCE-LED WARFARE

The intensity of the fighting between the two sides was such that the British government sent the Army into Northern Ireland to restore order. Violence lessened for a while, but it soon escalated, reshaped into a conflict between the security forces and the IRA. (Protestant Loyalist paramilitaries contented themselves with murdering Catholics, largely at random.) Throughout the 1970s, a stalemate developed. This began to change when the British security forces moved away from a military strategy into an intelligence-led war.

This new strategy involved multiple agencies: MI5, the RUC, Special Branch, military intelligence and, for field operations, the UK's special forces. Their joint aims were to identify terrorists who could be arrested or eliminated; to provide a flow of accurate intelligence about the plans, attitudes, and organization of terrorist groups; and to influence the political agenda through propaganda or "psyops"—psychological operations.

In the international sphere, MI6 devoted resources to tracing IRA links with foreign terrorist organizations, monitoring contacts behind the Iron Curtain, and tracking down the IRA's sources of finance and arms.

By the early 1980s, this approach was beginning to yield results. Computer analysis of a mass of information from everyday surveillance—random vehicle checks, for example—provided good leads. Arms shipments were regularly intercepted.

Right: Thousands of murals were painted by both sides during the Troubles, often commemorating historic events held to be important to each community's sense of identity.

BRIGHTON BOMBING

As part of their campaign to extend the conflict to mainland Britain, the IRA selected several high-value targets. Their most audacious operation was an attempt to assassinate the British prime minister Margaret Thatcher during the Conservative Party conference in Brighton, England, in 1984. Three weeks before the conference, IRA man Patrick Magee planted a bomb in the Grand Hotel in Brighton, where senior Conservatives would be staying. The bomb remained undiscovered until it exploded in the early hours of October 12. Thatcher narrowly escaped, but five people were killed and thirty-four were injured. In the aftermath, the IRA claimed a propaganda victory, but Thatcher's measured response increased public support for her in Britain.

Left: The Grand Hotel in Brighton, the morning after the bombing.

"TODAY WE WERE UNLUCKY, BUT REMEMBER WE ONLY HAVE TO BE LUCKY ONCE."

IRA communique after the Brighton bombing

INFILTRATING THE IRA

In mainland Britain, MI5 had a good record in identifying IRA active service units, while cooperation with other security services led to the apprehension of bombers attacking targets in Europe. But the single most important element of this strategy was the security services' infiltration of terrorist organizations. The IRA was riddled with informers, so much so that many intended operations became known to the security services and could be dealt with accordingly. By the late 1980s, the IRA suffered repeated military setbacks as a result of superior British intelligence. In one instance in 1987, an IRA active service unit was ambushed by the SAS when trying to attack a police station in the village of Loughgall in Northern Ireland. All eight IRA men were killed.

Although the conflict continued into the 1990s, the Nationalist leadership under Martin McGuinness and Jerry Adams readjusted their strategy. They would abandon military action and, instead, advance their aims solely through the political process. This led to a first ceasefire in 1994—a first faltering step in a peace process that culminated in the Good Friday Agreement of 1998, which restored self-government to Northern Ireland and ensured a power-sharing arrangement between the Unionist Protestant community and Nationalist Catholic community.

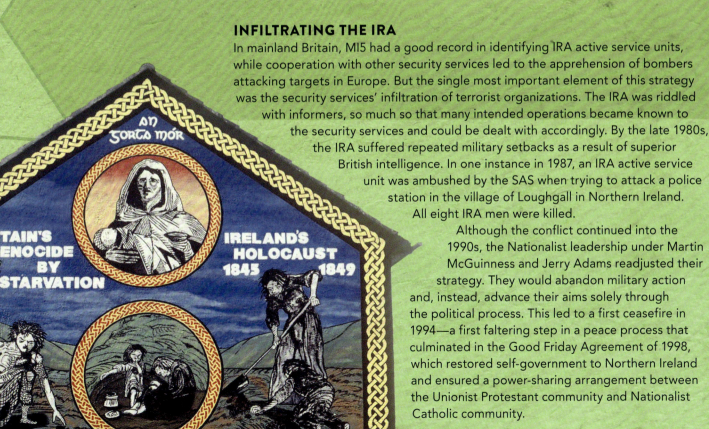

9/11: A FAILURE OF EVALUATION

On the morning of September 11, 2001, coordinated attacks were conducted by nineteen members of the terrorist organization al Qaeda. The terrorists hijacked four different passenger airliners to use as weapons; two of them were flown into the Twin Towers of the World Trade Center in New York City, both of which collapsed to rubble within hours. A third plane crashed into the Pentagon's west side, which partially collapsed; a fourth airliner bound for Washington, D.C., crashed in a field in Pennsylvania after passengers fought with the hijackers. All told, the incidents of 9/11 resulted in 2,977 deaths and more than 25,000 injuries, triggering a "Global War On Terror."

Prior to 9/11, few terror incidents had been attempted on United States soil. The World Trade Center had previously been attacked in 1993, when al Qaeda agents placed a bomb in an underground parking garage, killing six. An attack on Los Angeles International Airport in 1999 was thwarted when its planner Ahmed Ressan was arrested on arrival in Port Angeles. These relatively minor events led people to consider terror attempts on American soil to be bumbling, failed efforts. The events of 2001 changed all that. However, the four attacks could not have succeeded without such a presumption of incompetence, combined with a failure of imagination and information sharing in the intelligence community.

FAILURE TO SHARE

When the USS *Cole* was bombed in Yemen in 2000, the FBI and Naval Criminal Investigative Service (NCIS) worked together to track down the al Qaeda perpetrators, including Fahd al Quso, who videotaped the bombing. Fahd confessed and provided information on the movements of Khallad bin Attash, one of the trusted lieutenants of al Qaeda leader Osama bin Laden. When the FBI and NCIS contacted the CIA, the agency denied having any knowledge of Khallad; in truth, many al Qaeda members had been under surveillance for some time by the CIA's "Alec Station" group. Khallad sent a number of al Qaeda operatives to the US. They were tracked for years by the CIA, but it failed to notify the FBI or other intelligence or law enforcement agencies. In fact, when FBI agents temporarily assigned to Alec Station prepared to notify the FBI that al Qaeda members were entering the country in 2000, CIA managers ordered them not to do so—Alec Station agents were forbidden from sharing any information outside the group.

Above: Firefighters on the streets of New York City shortly after the collapse of the Twin Towers. In total, 343 firefighters were killed when the towers collapsed.

Below: The 9/11 attacks played out live on TV around the world. The towers burned for nearly two hours before collapsing.

Follow-up investigations after 9/11 determined that the CIA had failed to disclose multiple pieces of evidence of al Qaeda's movements to the FBI, INS, and State Department. If they had done so properly, the events of September 11, 2001 might never have happened.

THE SECRET OF AL QAEDA'S SUCCESS

Osama bin Laden and al Qaeda intended to strike at the United States and the West in general in order to provoke them, but they were more successful than even they had anticipated. Those who joined al Qaeda were often untrained, but willing to die for their cause—a fact used to great effect in the four airliner attacks. After 9/11, the US government began to attribute more terror attempts and attacks to al Qaeda, even without direct proof, making them appear even more dangerous. Once the US *causus belli* had shifted to Iraq and Saddam Hussein was blamed, then deposed, Sunni Muslims in Iraq flocked to al Qaeda, which already had a strong pro-Sunni, anti-Shia stance. (In reality, al Qaeda's primary targets were chosen on the basis of this sectarianism, and many more Shia than Americans were killed by al Qaeda attacks.) Rising anti-American sentiment across the Middle East in the wake of 9/11 and the invasion of Iraq meant that al Qaeda had succeeded past their own expectations. They had intended to destabilize the Middle Eastern status quo; instead, they had virtually destroyed it.

Right: Osama bin Laden was killed by American troops in 2011. In the intervening ten years, support for al Qaeda had been strengthened in many Muslim countries.

CONFIRMATION BIAS AND 9/11

When informing oneself on a topic, it is tempting not to pay attention to information that challenges your point of view. This tendency is called confirmation bias, and it may have played its part in hampering intelligence work before 9/11. Previous attacks on the US had been so minor that evidence of more ambitious plans was disbelieved. Confirmation bias also played a part in the invasion of Iraq in 2003. There was no evidence of a connection between Iraq and al Qaeda, but the impression among many Americans that Iraqi leader Saddam Hussein had been one of the masterminds behind 9/11 was not corrected by those in government who wanted to invade Iraq.

AMERICA'S WAR ON TERROR

The 9/11 attacks proved to be a catalyst for a wide set of military interventions by the United States, justified by the imperative to hunt down terrorists. However, the methods used by US forces have themselves helped to create a situation in which even more radical groups have replaced those that came before, and countries including Afghanistan, Iraq, and Syria have endured prolonged periods of violence and war.

After 9/11, the United States targeted the Taliban regime in Afghanistan. The Taliban—Pashto for "students"—emerged from the Islamist Mujahideen, allies of the US in the 1980s during their fight against the Soviet occupation of Afghanistan. By the late 1990s, the Taliban controlled much of Afghanistan. They followed a fundamentalist Sunni ideology, introducing strict forms of Islamic Sharia law, while indulging in the trafficking of women, and violence toward aid workers, civilians, and non-Muslims.

Shortly before 9/11, Ahmad Shah Massoud, one of Afghanistan's most outspoken opponents of al Qaeda and the Taliban, was assassinated—likely in response to a speech before the United Nations in which he warned against an impending major attack from one or both groups. When his

prediction came true, it spurred the US to take direct action in coalition with other nations, and on October 7, several Taliban and al Qaeda camps in Afghanistan were bombed. Soon afterward, coalition forces joined with the United Front, a group of Afghanistani soldiers led by Abdul Rashid Dostum, an ally of Massoud who had been forced into exile. The Taliban were routed from the major cities in short order, with minimal coalition casualties.

Below: US president George W. Bush (center) received support for the invasion of Iraq from several leaders, including British prime minister Tony Blair (far left), Spain's prime minister José María Aznar (left) and Portugal's prime minister Jose Manuel Durao Barosso (right), despite mass protests in their own countries.

Above: US Secretary of Defense Donald Rumsfeld was strongly in favor of expanding US military action after 9/11.

FROM AFGHANISTAN TO IRAQ

Along with targeted killings of high-ranking Taliban and al Qaeda members, the *causus belli* was next shifted to Iraq. The Bush administration claimed that Saddam Hussein's Ba'athist regime had backed the terrorist organizations, and was developing nuclear weapons to boot. These accusations were flimsy at best, but provided an excuse to invade in 2003 and topple Saddam.

The CIA continued to hunt for anyone involved in the 9/11 attacks even after Iraq and Afghanistan were invaded. Suspects were apprehended and imprisoned either in Abu Ghraib prison near Baghdad or in Guantánamo Bay in Cuba. In their torture-filled interrogations, the prisoners were often treated abominably—forced to stand naked or in humiliating positions, threatened with electrocution or other harm, harassed by soldiers with dogs, and force-fed when they attempted a hunger strike.

RETURN OF THE TALIBAN

The Taliban gradually regrouped after the invasions. By 2006, they had resurged enough that their attacks began to escalate further as conflict in Afghanistan dragged on. In 2020, the Taliban signed a peace agreement with the United States government, wherein US forces would withdraw from the region and the Taliban would not sanction terrorist activity on Afghani soil.

The loss in Iraq of Saddam Hussein's totalitarian Ba'ath Party created and encouraged other fundamentalist terror organizations, and neighboring Syria descended into civil war. One group that arose in this period was the Islamic State (IS), a Shia Islam organization that made al Qaeda look like moderates. Also called ISIS, ISIL, or simply "Daesh" (roughly, Arabic for "bigots"), IS split from al Qaeda in a power struggle between high-ranking members.

The events of 9/11 had far-reaching effects. The decade that followed it saw hundreds of thousands of deaths in the Middle East, hundreds of billions lost to or spent on the so-called "Global War on Terror," multiple nations destabilized, and terrorism and violence further on the rise.

FUTILE TORTURE

CIA and military officials subjected the captives held at Abu Ghraib and Guantánamo Bay (and possibly at sites elsewhere) to "enhanced interrogation"—in other words, torture. Mostly they were told only what they wanted to hear. Pain and stress both short the brain's ability to recall details, and memories induced by leading questions can lead a subject to "remember" events that never happened. In addition, stress, along with the physical effects of the torture, can lead to brain damage, resulting in memory loss, PTSD, and more. Quite aside from its morality, torture is not a good way of finding answers.

Left: In 2004, images were leaked from Abu Ghraib prison showing US soldiers torturing prisoners.

THE RISE AND FALL OF DAESH

Founded in 2004 by Abu Musab al Zarqawi, the Islamic State was mostly ignored until around 2011, when it took advantage of instability in the region. By 2014, now led by Abu Bakr al Baghdadi, IS had taken control of the Iraqi cities of Mosul and Tikrit, and declared a caliphate from Diyala, Iraq, to Aleppo, Syria. Its control expanded farther across Iraq and Syria, and by 2015, IS had affiliates in eight other countries. It was influencing attacks around the world, from Syria to Florida. Offensives continued against IS, however, and by the end of 2017, the caliphate had lost almost all of its territory, including Mosul and its capital, the city of Raqqa in Syria. Most IS jihadists surrendered in 2019; al Baghdadi killed himself with an explosive vest.

— CHAPTER 13 —

SPYING IN THE MODERN WORLD

Today's technology enables spying and espionage in more ways than ever. However, the internet has also created a new territory for attacks, along with new tools and platforms for engaging in cyberwarfare. Spying has also been taken to the skies with drones and satellites. On the ground, critical infrastructure systems such as power grids are attacked via malware worms. Data itself has been weaponized, and citizens' beliefs are attacked with propaganda to feed false narratives that benefit a foreign adversary.

Hackers can stay safely in their home countries and hide behind pseudonyms, such as Fancy Bear or Ugly Gorilla, which make it nearly impossible to prosecute them even once they have been identified. No country is without its secret operations, and whistleblowers have put their careers on the line to share information that they felt the public should know. While cyberwarfare might not directly kill thousands of people, one malware worm can cost billions in economic losses or spell the end of a country's nuclear enrichment plan.

OPERATION SNOW WHITE

Founded by science-fiction writer L. Ron Hubbard in 1954, the Church of Scientology has taken an unlikely path toward power and influence. To push it along that path, Hubbard initiated a complex plan for domestic espionage, in which scientologists infiltrated multiple government agencies, stole files, bugged meeting rooms, and lied to FBI agents for the Church's benefit.

The Church of Scientology was granted US tax-exempt status as a religious organization in 1957, but this status was revoked in 1967 after the Internal Revenue Service claimed that Church profits were directly benefiting Hubbard and his family. This kicked off Operation Snow White, an elaborate plot originating from the Church's Office of Special Affairs, then known as the Guardian Office. L. Ron Hubbard penned Guardian Order 732 in 1973, with the objective to remove and correct "erroneous" files about the church by infiltrating government agencies, including the IRS, DEA, Coast Guard, and Department of Justice.

SECRET RECORDINGS

At the core of the operation were two Scientology agents, Gerald Wolfe and Michael Meisner. In 1974, Wolfe took a job at the IRS as a clerk-typist, following Church orders to gather

information and pass it on to top-level Scientologists. Wolfe made a false identification card for Meisner, allowing the pair of them to pass unchallenged through the IRS and collect documents. These cards were to prove invaluable.

Wolfe discovered that the IRS had scheduled a meeting about Scientology. He was instructed to bug the conference room where the meeting was to take place. A radio device was installed in the conference room, and Wolfe and Meisner recorded the meeting from the parking lot.

BREAKING & ENTERING

Meanwhile, the Church of Scientology had initiated a Freedom of Information Act lawsuit. Once they found the attorney representing the government, Wolfe and Meisner broke into their office to collect information on the attorney's strategy. They returned later to copy the documents the legal team had collected.

The next target was the office of Assistant United States Attorney Nathan Dodell, who was working on litigation concerning the Church. A scientologist employed in the Department of Justice stole Dodell's office keys, then copied and returned them. Wolfe and Meisner scouted the office and came up with a plan to "do research" in the library near Dodell's office. On their first attempt, they checked in near the end of the day, and after a brief stop in the library, entered Dodell's office and copied the target documents.

Above: L. Ron Hubbard in 1950

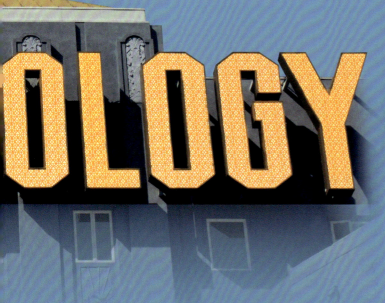

In August of 1978, eleven Church members, including L. Ron Hubbard's wife Mary Sue, were indicted on twenty-eight charges. They later agreed to a plea bargain, pleaded guilty, and were convicted in federal court. In the case *United States v. Mary Sue Hubbard et al* in 1979, Mary Sue was jailed for five years, while three others were fined $10,000. L. Ron Hubbard was named as an unindicted co-conspirator and went into hiding.

The Church succeeded in reinstating its tax-exempt status in 1993. It was a quiet affair, and though the IRS was questioned by media outlets about the details of the arrangement, very little information has ever become public. In the end, the Church of Scientology had pulled off one of the most complex and detailed domestic espionage programs in history.

Wolfe and Meisner returned to Dodell's office after hours two more times. On the second occasion, they encountered the night librarian, who told security about the two late visitors, and was advised to contact the FBI if they returned. Soon after, Wolfe and Meisner returned with a forged letter. The night librarian summoned two FBI agents, who confronted them. However, on seeing their I.D. cards, the agents simply took their details and let them go.

COVER BLOWN

Meisner contacted the Guardian Circle and told them what had happened, and they instructed him to return to Los Angeles immediately. A few weeks later, Wolfe was arrested and the FBI opened a Grand Jury investigation. Meisner was put under house arrest by the Church. As the house arrest wore on, Meisner was increasingly willing to surrender to the authorities and turn himself in. He escaped to Las Vegas, but was convinced to return to Los Angeles where his house arrest was guarded. To get them to lower their guard, Meisner convinced his guards to let him go to a bowling alley, where he made a collect call to the FBI to surrender and cooperate with the investigation.

Meisner's cooperation led to an FBI raid on The Church of Scientology in Los Angeles and Washington, D.C., on July 8, 1977. The Los Angeles raid lasted twenty-one hours and a sixteen-ton truck was filled with documents.

MORMON LEAKS

In 2017, former Mormon Ryan McKnight started the Truth and Transparency Foundation, also called Mormon Leaks, to increase transparency and accountability about the Church of Latter Day Saints. Its most notable success has been the public outing of filmmaker and Sundance Film Festival co-founder, Sterling Van Wagenen. In 2019, Wagenen was sentenced to six years to life in prison for sexually molesting two children. The Church of Latter Day Saints had known about the abuse, which took place in the 1990s, and sentenced Van Wagenen inside its church walls, but since the parents didn't want to press charges, the offense was effectively covered up. The truth came out when Mormon Leaks

released audio of Van Wagenen admitting to the abuse, thus enabling a criminal investigation to be started.

Left: Like other Mormon churches, Salt Lake Temple in Salt Lake City, Utah, is closed to the public.

SATELLITE SURVEILLANCE

The first artificial satellite to be launched into space in 1957—the Soviet Union's Sputnik 1—was very quickly followed by satellites equipped with surveillance equipment. From that moment on, both sides in the Cold War initiated highly secret programs to collect information about each other from space. Today, the US has the most spy satellites, followed by China, Russia, Japan, and Israel.

SECRET SATELLITES

The US launched its first spy satellites into space in 1959. They were launched as part of the long-running Corona program, which remained secret until declassification in 1992. These first spy satellites were equipped with film cameras and collected visual information on the Soviet Union, China, and other geographies strategic to the Cold War. The film canister was parachuted out of the satellite and picked up by a plane midair—although a number ended up falling into farmers' fields.

The Soviet Union's first spy satellites were launched in 1961 with the start of the Zenit series. In order to hide their real purpose of reconnaissance spy photography, the Soviet spy satellites were designed to look like their Vostok manned space series. This was an application of Soviet *Maskirovka* theory—to hide one's real intentions. Keeping the existence, and later the capabilities, of spy satellites secret gave you an advantage.

Below: A USAF Flying Boxcar recovers a capsule containing film from a Corona spy satellite in 1960.

Top right: This image of the construction of a Soviet aircraft carrier in a shipyard in the Black Sea was taken by a KH-11 spy satellite in 1984. It was leaked a year later.

Bottom right: The photograph of the Imam Khomeini Spaceport leaked by Trump.

KH-1 CORONA
(1959–1960)

KH-2 CORONA
(1960–1961)

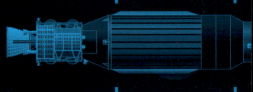

KH-4A CORONA
(1963–1969)

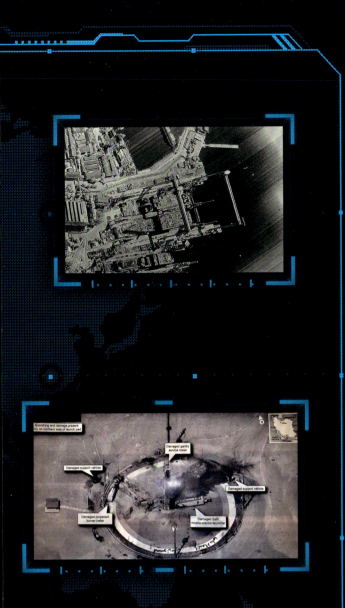

Today, US spy satellites are run out of the National Reconnaissance Organization (NRO), an intelligence agency founded in 1961 to support the analysis of Corona information. Like the Corona project itself, the NRO remained classified until 1992.

IMPROVED RESOLUTION

KH-11 satellites are the current state of the art, and while there isn't much public information about their details, "Misty" is the codename for a variant with stealth technology. Analysts estimate that the visual sharpness of the KH-11 images is 4 inches or less, meaning that it can discern detail on Earth's surface down to anything that is 4 inches (10 cm) wide. For comparison, if the Hubble Telescope were turned towards Earth, its visual sharpness would be 12 inches (30 cm). In 2019, President Trump leaked a suspected image from a KH-11, when he posted an image of the Imam Khomeini Spaceport on social media. Trump had leaked only the second image thought to have come from a KH-11 spy satellite, and the world learned of the previously hidden capabilities of US spy satellites.

Spy satellites do not only watch Earth; they also watch each other. In early 2020, a Russian satellite adjusted its orbit to keep a US spy satellite in visual range at all times. It may have been monitoring the satellite to see what it could capture, or attempting to intercept the satellite's electronic signals sending data back to Earth.

Amateur hobbyists also track spy satellites, based on which rocket put them in space and observations of orbits. Using this information, when Trump shared the classified image of the Imam Khomeini Spaceport, some guessed the leaked image came from USA-224, a KH-11 satellite in orbit since 2011.

CALIBRATION TARGETS

Across the deserts of the Western USA, you may come across a strange sight: slabs of pavement with what look like lines from a piece of modern art on them, or a grid of cross-shaped pieces of pavement. These are calibration targets, and they were critical to the effective working of the first spy satellites. Corona calibration targets were concrete slabs shaped like Maltese Crosses, laid out primarily in a grid structure around Casa Grande, Arizona. On Edwards Air Force Base in the Mojave Desert, there is a series of pavement slabs with white lines on them. These enabled technicians to work out the resolution of images from the spy satellites. While calibration targets are not used today, they are spy history hidden in plain sight—if you know where to look.

A Corona calibration target dating from 1967.

WEAPONIZED DATA

We live in an age of big data, and every time we interact with technology, more data is created. Data is now so cheap to save that there is a vast amount of data on each and every one of us, even if it's not going to be used immediately. Data is collected when we visit web sites, use mobile phone apps, buy something online, go into a store, or use our credit cards. That data is used to create our credit score, and for targeted advertising on social media platforms. We now know, thanks to the revelations of Edward Snowden (see page 224) and others, that governments also collect our data in clandestine ways using sophisticated and intrusive systems.

BIG BROTHER IS WATCHING
Governments keep these systems classified so that adversaries do not learn their true capabilities. Snowden's whistleblowing compromised the security of informants, in many cases causing their death. Government surveillance data collection has goals that are different from those of private-sector data collection. Governments see their use of our data as a means to protect national security.

The Five Eyes is an intelligence alliance between the English-speaking countries of the US, UK, Canada, Australia, and New Zealand, established during World War II in 1941 in order to share intelligence and formulate a plan for a post-war world. Following the end of the war, the five countries agreed to work together to collect and share intelligence data on the Soviet Union, Eastern Europe, and China.

In 1971, a classified global surveillance network, codenamed ECHELON, was created to support Five Eyes' intelligence gathering efforts. ECHELON remained classified until the 1990s. Following 9/11, its surveillance capabilities were expanded, and it was these programs that Edward Snowden revealed in his whistleblowing. The surveillance programs enabled countries to obtain data about their own citizens without spying on them directly, using information gathered by a Five Eyes partner instead.

ENLISTING THE HELP OF CORPORATIONS
Another of the government surveillance programs leaked by Snowden, PRISM began in 2007, under the Protect America Act. Many large technology and telecom companies were involved, including Microsoft, Yahoo, Google, Facebook, YouTube, AOL, Skype, and Apple. Any data that was routed through cables or data centers could be monitored. The Protect America Act (2007) and FISA Amendments Act (2008) immunize private companies from legal action when they cooperate with US government agencies in intelligence collection. Vast amounts of data has been collected by the NSA, with little to no democratic oversight.

SWINGING ELECTIONS

While governments are busy collecting our data, those who wish to be elected into government also use it to win votes. Founded in 2013, Cambridge Analytica was a British political consulting firm that became embroiled in a scandal over the use of improperly collected data from the Facebook app This Is Your Digital Life. It used the data to build profiles with which it could target individuals through Facebook advertising in order to influence the outcomes of elections.

Above: Brexit produced protests from both sides of the debate.

Cambridge Analytica was paid by specific campaigns around the world to identify key voters in specific jurisdictions and influence them to vote a particular way. Among opposition voters, the aim was often to increase apathy and so reduce their likelihood to vote. Among those identified as potential supporters, the aim was to activate apathetic voters, playing on perceived negative attitudes toward highly emotive issues, such as the Black Lives Matter movement or immigration. Notably, the firm used these methods on behalf of the pro-Leave campaign in the UK's 2016 Brexit referendum, and then later that year in Donald Trump's successful presidential campaign.

Above: Christopher Wylie

Following an investigation by the British TV channel Channel 4 News in 2018, which exposed its methods, Cambridge Analytica was closed down. Facebook suffered a sharp fall in its market value when details emerged of the ways in which Cambridge Analytica had mined the website for personal information. The degree to which these activities may have swung the results of two deeply divisive votes remains hotly debated in both the UK and the US.

> **"WW3 IS A GUERRILLA INFORMATION WAR WITH NO DIVISION BETWEEN MILITARY AND CIVILIAN POPULATIONS."**
>
> Philosopher Marshall McLuhan

MASKIROVKA

Maskirovka is an umbrella term in Russian that describes military information operations aimed at distorting the truth to the point of disbelief. Russia first employed the tactics of Maskirovka in its military and domestic operations, but today it has extended them to include attacks on the workings of democratic systems around the world. A key difference between current and past Maskirovka operations lies in its use of the interconnected world of social media. Today, Russia can directly target the citizens of a foreign nation with minimal costs and plenty of plausible deniability.

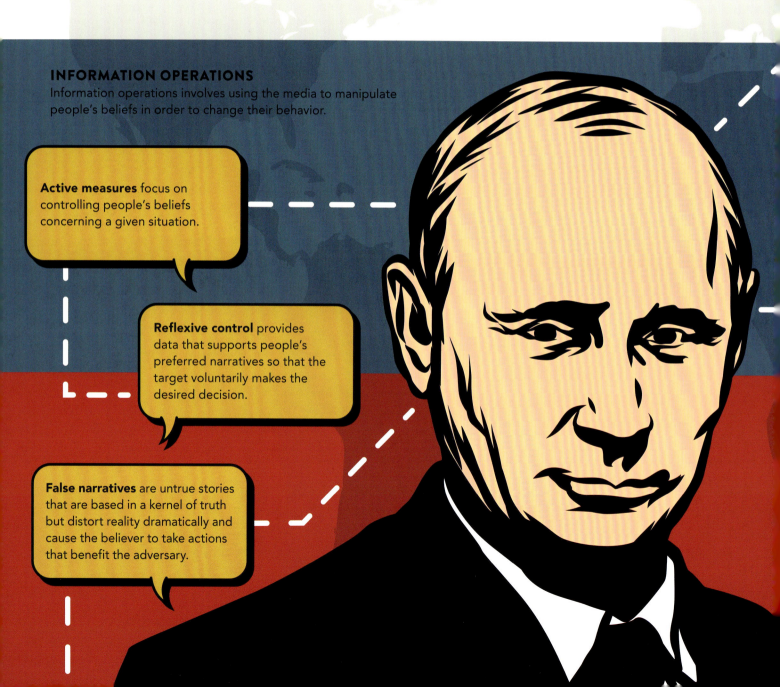

INFORMATION OPERATIONS

Information operations involves using the media to manipulate people's beliefs in order to change their behavior.

Active measures focus on controlling people's beliefs concerning a given situation.

Reflexive control provides data that supports people's preferred narratives so that the target voluntarily makes the desired decision.

False narratives are untrue stories that are based in a kernel of truth but distort reality dramatically and cause the believer to take actions that benefit the adversary.

Information Operations uses the broad availability of information on the internet as a weapon, seeding false and misleading information to cause people to make decisions that benefit a nation state that is not their own. It is a clever technique, and difficult to combat.

In the Soviet Union, information operations tactics were limited to military use, but Russia has extended them beyond this since the 1990s. Russian president Vladimir Putin is a master of Maskirovka. He spent sixteen years in the KGB before becoming the director of the Federal Security Service (the successor of the KGB) in 1995. Since first becoming president in 2000, Putin has put his intelligence nous fully into operation.

Disinformation is false information with the specific intention to deceive, often coming from a nation state.

Misinformation is similar to disinformation in that it is inaccurate information. However usually it is not from a nation state and may hide behind a veil of "entertainment."

Propaganda is state-run media that communicates a specific worldview. This includes RT.com, whose content is heavily controlled by the Russian state.

Bot networks amplify and promote information that supports strategic false narratives.

Deepfakes are synthetic and manipulated media created by deep learning technology, a subset of machine learning. Deepfakes are audio and other media information that have been falsified in order to create "evidence" to support one or multiple false narratives.

Media stories support Maskirovka objectives—many journalists write with a sensational angle to evoke emotion, and generate clicks. Social media algorithms amplify what is popular, irrespective of whether or not it is true.

FALSE NARRATIVES: WHO INTERFERED WITH THE 2016 US ELECTION?

Investigations have uncovered solid evidence that Russia interfered with the 2016 US presidential election. However, there is a false narrative that tells a very different story, in which it was Ukraine that interfered. If people learn about a false narrative such as this from a source that they trust, they are much more likely to believe it, and to cling to that belief even in the face of contradictory evidence. In this instance, those trusted sources included prominent Republican politicians, including President Donald Trump himself.

Above: Fiona Hill, a former security analyst at the White House, testifies before Congress on Russian involvement in the 2016 presidential election.

In 2016, the Department of Homeland Security (DHS) confirmed that an Illinois voter database had been penetrated by Russian hackers. Russia had displayed its ability to infiltrate a database in which it could change data if it wanted to. Seeding a false narrative around who conducted the attacks amplified the message. This played a dual purpose: undermining trust in US democracy; and placing an adversary of Russia—Ukraine—in the hot seat.

CYBERWARFARE

The internet was developed as a decentralized communication system that could survive a nuclear attack. After the end of the Cold War, it became a way of connecting people and geographies. As businesses and countries came to rely on the internet for commerce and communication, it became both a vector for attacks and a target of them. State-funded hacker groups may attack both government and private sector targets.

Cyberattacks can be carried out in a variety of ways. The most widespread involves malware—the unwitting installation of malicious software on a target's computer, introducing spyware, ransomware, viruses, and "worms" that can spread from computer to computer. Malware can also be used to mount "man in the middle" attacks, in which a third party secretly alters communicated information. Phishing involves the use of email and spoof websites to capture the target's authentication credentials, while denial of service (DoS) attacks involve the overloading of a system so that legitimate users cannot access it.

WRITING THE BOOK ON CYBERWAR

As cyberwarfare emerged into the global landscape, a group of experts gathered in Estonia in 2009 to understand how international law applied to cyber conflicts. This resulted in the Tallinn Manual in 2012, and updated to Tallinn 2.0 in 2017. The document, developed by NATO, the Cooperative Cyber Defense Centre of Excellence, the International Committee of the Red Cross, and the United States Cyber Command, focuses on the most disruptive cyber operations to understand what qualifies as an armed attack, which would allow for a state to respond appropriately in self-defense.

RUSSIAN CYBERWARFARE

On December 30, 2015, Russia conducted the first successful power grid attack on Ukraine, hacking into three energy companies' corporate networks via phishing emails and malware. The attack enabled Russia to take control of their supervisory control and data acquisition (SCADA) systems, and remotely turn off electricity substations. At the same time, they conducted a DoS attack on call centers, preventing customers from contacting the companies. Finally, they disabled the companies' IT infrastructure and destroyed key files.

THE WANNACRY INFECTION

The WannaCry ransomware was originally developed by the NSA. In 2017, it was stolen and released by a hacker group called the Shadow Brokers. Infecting more than eighty NHS (National Health Service) systems in the UK, WannaCry wreaked havoc on systems nationwide, demanding payments by bitcoin. It was cleverly disabled by security researcher Marcus Hutchins. When he noticed that WannaCry-infected computers would attempt to access a particular website, Hutchins bought the web address and halted the spread.

NOTPETYA WORM

On June 27, 2017, Russia again targeted Ukraine using a malware worm named NotPetya. The worm was deployed in the auto-update files in tax software used by most of Ukraine's businesses. NotPetya took those Ukrainian systems offline and also found its way onto the internet, where it took down networks worldwide—most notably global shipper Maersk-A.P. Moller, whose entire system was crippled. The attack was attributed to two Russian intelligence services: the FSB (Federal Security Services) and GRU (Main Intelligence Directorate). The White House estimated total damages from the attack at $10 billion, making it the most costly cyberattack in history.

THE SONY HACK

One of the stranger stories of hacking involves a nation state—North Korea—retaliating against Sony Pictures' 2014 film *The Interview*, a comedy about an assassination attempt on North Korean president Kim Jong-Un. The hackers, calling themselves the Guardians of Peace (GOP), threatened terrorist attacks at opening theaters, and eventually released personally identifiable information about Sony personnel, including names, addresses, social security numbers, and salary information—the last of which raised more than a few eyebrows. While North Korea never took responsibility for the hack, the United States Justice Department published a criminal complaint against Park Jin Hyok, a hacker working for North Korea's military intelligence bureau.

Above: When NotPetya infected a computer, this ominous image came up on the screen.

Above: Marcus Hutchins, digital security researcher for Kryptos Logic, who saved the world from a devastating cyberattack in May 2017 from his bedroom.

Above: Nuclear enrichment centrifuges

A DIGITAL NUKE

The computer worm Stuxnet has been called the world's first digital weapon, impeccably designed to hit only its target: the labs at Natanz, the center of Iran's nuclear enrichment program. While no one has ever taken credit for the weapon, experts credit a joint operation between Israel and the United States. Stuxnet was first discovered in 2010, but it is believed it was in development as early as 2005. The worm targeted systems associated with laboratory centrifuges—causing a thousand of them to spin themselves apart, destroying key technology in the enrichment process. The worm was introduced across an "air gap" into a computer network lacking outside physical or wireless connections. To cross the air gap, Stuxnet was introduced physically by an unknown individual via a USB key.

WHISTLEBLOWERS

The disclosure of secret information by individuals for what they believe is in the public interest is nothing new, but the internet age has transformed it, enabling vast amounts of material to be instantly put into the public sphere. Among the most prominent and notorious of recent whistleblowers are Chelsea Manning and Edward Snowden, both of whom revealed classified US documents and whose actions have divided pubic opinion.

Above: Edward Snowden speaking about NSA programs in Moscow in 2013.

Above: Protesters against mass surveillance march on Washington, D.C., following Snowden's revelations.

EDWARD SNOWDEN

In his work as a contractor at the NSA between 2009 and 2013, Edward Snowden saw documents that described covert surveillance among collaborating nations, including the Five Eyes intelligence alliance (comprising the USA, the UK, Canada, Australia, and New Zealand), and telecom and tech companies. Snowden tried to raise his concerns through internal channels but became increasingly disillusioned when they were not addressed. He decided to take matters into his own hands in 2013, leaking highly classified information from the National Security Agency (NSA) that revealed global surveillance programs. Snowden's leaks revealed the extent to which intelligence agencies were spying on people's personal communications, including emails and text messages. Those who were being spied on by the NSA included thirty-five world leaders, most notably the German chancellor Angela Merkel. Snowden also accused the US of engaging in industrial espionage.

Snowden's disclosure resulted in charges on two counts of violation of the Espionage Act from the US Department of Justice, and revocation of his US passport. Snowden was traveling from Hong Kong to Moscow at the time and when he landed in Russia, he could not legally enter the country due to his canceled passport. Russia gave him right of asylum and he has been there ever since. The security services for their part, subsequently stated that improper redaction on some of the leaked files caused exposure of intelligence activity against al Qaeda, which resulted in the death of informants, and increased the difficulty for the NSA to detect global terrorist activities as organizations such as al Qaeda stepped up their security. Snowden's disclosures have initiated a heated debate about privacy and national security and where the line should be drawn between the two.

Above: Chelsea Manning in 2017

THE PANAMA PAPERS

John Doe is an anonymous whistleblower who, in 2016, leaked more than eleven million documents from the Panamanian law firm Mossack Fonseca. The documents dated back to the 1970s, and contained the records of more than 214,000 shell companies that were used by politicians, billionaires, and other influential and well-to-do people for tax evasion, fraud, bribery, and circumventing sanctions.

CHELSEA MANNING

In 2010, Chelsea Manning was a US Army intelligence soldier with access to classified information. She was responsible for a massive leak of data that year via the WikiLeaks organization. The documents included Iraq War logs, diplomatic cables, and Guantanamo Bay files. Among the documents was gunsight footage of an airstrike from an Apache helicopter on Baghdad in 2007, which showed the crew firing on and killing civilians. The footage provoked international debate about the legality of such attacks.

Manning copied the files onto a disguised music CD and a camera SD card. She first contacted *The New York Times* and *The Washington Post* to see if they were interested in the information, but drew a blank. She then sent the files to WikiLeaks, who subsequently started publishing the material in February 2010. Manning was charged with twenty-two offenses, and pleaded guilty to ten of them. Manning served time from 2010 to 2017, when President Obama commuted her sentence.

"LEGITIMATE WHISTLEBLOWERS WHO EXPOSE UNQUESTIONABLE WRONGDOING, WHETHER INSIDERS OR OUTSIDERS, DESERVE IMMUNITY FROM GOVERNMENT RETRIBUTION, FULL STOP. UNTIL GOVERNMENTS CODIFY LEGAL PROTECTIONS FOR WHISTLEBLOWERS INTO LAW, ENFORCEMENT AGENCIES WILL SIMPLY HAVE TO DEPEND ON THEIR OWN RESOURCES OR ONGOING GLOBAL MEDIA COVERAGE FOR DOCUMENTS."

John Doe, Panama Papers whistleblower

THE MITROKHIN ARCHIVE

In 1992, Vasili Mitrokhin, a KGB archivist, walked into the British consulate in Riga, Latvia, and made them an offer they couldn't refuse. Mitrokhin had been head of the archive department at the KGB for thirty years, and when their headquarters was moved, he had to transfer the massive archive from the old location to the new one, a job that took over twelve years. While cataloging the documents, Mitrokhin had made his own copies. Mitrokhin first visited the US embassy in Riga, but CIA officers didn't believe him, so he turned to the British. This resulted in the largest cache of KGB intelligence ever to fall into opposition hands. Some of the operations revealed include the bugging of Henry Kissinger's phone, disinformation campaigns around JFK assassination theories, and operations to discredit Martin Luther King Jr. in order to stir up racial tensions.

DRONES

The US and Israel pioneered the use of drones in the 1970s to prevent losses of aircrew over dangerous environments. Officially called Unmanned Aerial Vehicles (UAVs), drones are robotic aircraft that provide excellent reconnaissance over hostile territory. They are used by the military and by intelligence services such as the CIA.

Drones are made in many sizes, from the light-aircraft-sized Predator to miniature robots as small as insects developed for short-term reconnaissance missions. They are used to collect intelligence data similar to that collected by spy satellites. After 9/11, drones with strike capabilities have been used by the US and others to take out targets remotely.

Above: Engineers study insect flight to produce nimble miniature drones. This one is modeled on a dragonfly.

Right: The huge Predator drone is 27 feet (8 m) long and has a wingspan of nearly 50 feet (15 m).

Detection equipment

DRONE STRIKES

One of the best-known UAVs is the General Atomics Aeronautical Systems RQ-1/MQ-1, also called the Predator. In the 1980s, the CIA and Pentagon began to experiment with drone capabilities. They worked with Abraham Karem, the former chief designer for the Israeli Air Force, to design what would become known as the Predator, for use in both military (USAF) and intelligence missions (CIA). In the 1990s, UAVs began to be deployed in combat missions. The Predator was outfitted with Hellfire ground-to-air missiles (and later succeeded by its larger, heavier-armed cousin, the MQ-9 Reaper), enabling increased accuracy and crew safety. However, drone strikes have also resulted in collateral damage: civilians, including children, have been casualties of UAV strikes in places such as Pakistan and Yemen, turning local populations against the drone-using power.

STEALTH DRONES

In 2007, Lockheed Martin introduced a stealth UAV, the RQ-170 Sentinel. This bat-winged aircraft was fitted with cameras and sensors to collect photos, video recordings, and other data. Sentinels were used in Afghanistan, and one of their first sightings led to the nickname "Beast of Kandahar." In 2011, Iran captured (and later announced they had reverse-engineered) a CIA-operated Sentinel that had been mapping suspected Iranian nuclear sites; the CIA claimed it had been on a mission over Afghanistan and went off course. The Sentinel was also supposedly used in South Korea to gather intelligence about North Korea's nuclear and long-range missiles.

Above: An artist's impression of an RQ-170 Sentinel in flight.

STEALTH SYSTEMS

Stealth technology uses special structures and materials to create a kind of "invisibility cloak" to massively reduce radar, heat, and other signatures emitted by a vessel or vehicle. This involves various techniques, including the use of electronic countermeasures to hide capabilities; thermal- and radar-absorbing paint or materials; or design guidelines that make the aircraft less detectable. To fool the human eye as well as infrared sensors or radar, this can include paint colors and camouflage patterns that enable the vehicle to blend into the sky or local geography.

DAZZLE CAMOUFLAGE

Sometimes camouflage is designed to confuse rather than hide. Dazzle camouflage, also known as razzle dazzle, was a paint technique used during World War I to make ships more difficult to target. It worked in much the same way as a zebra's stripes. As cameras, surveillance, and facial recognition technology have become more pervasive, increasing fears about lack of privacy have seen the dazzle concept applied to makeup and hairstyles. It works by breaking up the expected outlines of an individual's facial features and hair.

Above: The USS *West Mahomet* was first painted with dazzle camouflage in 1908. The stripes made the bow appear greatly distorted, disguising the ship's true shape and direction of travel.

DIGITAL STEGANOGRAPHY

Steganography is a method for concealing information inside something that looks entirely innocent. Digital media files can become secret containers for sensitive information thanks to digital steganography, which uses large files to hide secret information. Image, audio, and video files are large and noisy, which makes it easy to hide text files in their binary code without changing the way the carrier file appears. On the outside, it looks like a normal image, audio, or video file, but using special software on a targeted file, you can share a lot of hidden information. It is nearly impossible to detect which files have been altered in this way, making it a great way for intelligence agents and corporate spies to share information hidden in plain sight.

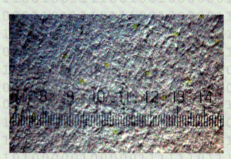

Left: Information has been hidden on this page of printed text in the pattern of tiny yellow dots.

CRIMINAL NETWORKS

Steganography is used by all kinds of people who want to share information without being detected, including criminals, spies, and activists. It may also be used for legal reasons, such as watermarking a Hollywood pre-release film to track how it ended up on Tor. But most of the reasons to use steganography are illicit. Criminals and hackers use it to send stolen data or illegal media such as child pornography.

Embedded in a graphic on a website, unknown to the company itself, an image can hide a crypto miner or credit card skimmer that sends collected data to the criminal. It can be used to conceal malware triggers or activate bot networks—these malware triggers have shown up in images on Twitter. Once downloaded, the images have commands that activate the malware already installed on the machine. There are even methods to transmit secret information in network headers.

TERRORIST PLANS

It has been rumored that gangs and terrorist cells use steganography to share plans and communication. In 2011, while investigating a suspected al Qaeda member, the German Federal Criminal Police (BKA) found a password protected file, with a single pornographic video entitled "Kick Ass." Inside the video they found text files that appeared to document future operations.

Finding files that contain steganography is challenging because the majority of files on the internet are legit, so you need to know where to look. It is a sneaky—and very effective—way to share secret information.

HIDING SECRETS IN A SUNSET

Steganography has been used in economic espionage to exfiltrate trade secrets from monitored networks. In 2018, trade secrets relating to gas and steam turbine technology trade secrets were stolen from General Electric (GE). TKTK Zheng, an employee of GE, moved 40 encrypted files into a temp folder and added them to the binary code of another file, a photograph of a sunset that he sent to his Hotmail account. GE was monitoring the network, and discovered his activities.

Right: Anya Kushchyenko, now a Russian TV host.

Yelena Vavilova

Andrey Bezrukov

THE ILLEGALS PROGRAM

In 2010, the FBI cracked a major Russian spy network, arresting ten deep-cover agents in the US and one in Cyprus. Known as The Illegals Program, the network included Anna Chapman (Anya Kushchyenko), and married couple Donald Heathfield (Andrey Bezrukov) and Tracey Lee Ann Foley (Yelena Vavilova), whose teenage sons were apparently unaware of their parents' spying activities. The network relied on old Cold War methods such as dead drops to communicate with Moscow. The spies used custom steganography software to hide messages inside files, which they would upload sites where their contacts could download them. The investigation uncovered a network of websites from which the spies had downloaded images, which could then be checked to see if additional information had been embedded in the binary code. The ten agents were later returned to Russia as part of a "spy swap."

CHINA VS. THE US

The Chinese Ministry of State Security (MSS), formed in 1983, combines intel gathering abroad with internal security matters, as well as acting as a secret police force. The MSS has been successful in penetrating United States government intelligence agencies. However, it mainly concentrates on economic espionage operations that benefit Chinese businesses.

China is unique in that its intelligence operations focus primarily on gathering non-military information—including technology, trade secrets, and other classified information from US companies, government contractors, and educational institutions. This information can be used by Chinese state-sanctioned businesses to improve their competitiveness in the global economy. Recent operations have been attributed to gathering information to better negotiate the Trans-Pacific Partnership.

DIRECT AND INDIRECT ESPIONAGE

China uses a variety of methods to gather information. Direct espionage involves recruiting ex-CIA employees via LinkedIn or headhunters. Another method involves the exploitation of business and academic relationships—one such example is the Thousand Talents program, which partners with US academic institutions, thereby accessing intellectual property (IP) from groups funded by the National Science Foundation and the Department of Defense.

Hacker groups such as Unit 61398 actively penetrate private sector networks to exfiltrate trade secrets and other strategic information. China also acquires IP by setting up companies in the US. The companies hire key employees away from a targeted rival company or even subcontract to that company directly, and steal secrets. This is how the white pigment formula was stolen from DuPont (see page 199). The FBI estimates that 3,000 businesses in the US are covers for MSS activity. It has also targeted European and Asian companies.

It is challenging to come up with an appropriate government response when information is stolen by a foreign nation for economic advantage, as opposed to secrets stolen for traditional foreign government intelligence. Often a formal response is not appropriate, and this effectively creates a stealthy intel conflict, under the guise of traditional intelligence operations.

TITAN RAIN

Originating from Guangdong, China, and lasting three years, Titan Rain is the name assigned by US federal agencies to a persistent series of hacking attacks against several defense contractor companies. These attacks targeted Lockheed Martin, Sandia National Labs, Redstone Arsenal, and even NASA. It is believed these hacks were the work of Unit 61398.

OPERATION AURORA

In 2012, Google announced that, along with twenty other tech companies, they had been the victims of an attack involving IP theft and targeting of the Gmail accounts of individuals who might oppose Chinese political and corporate interests. Dubbed Operation Aurora by the McAfee cybersecurity corporation, the attackers (once again originating from Chinese locations—including the Elderwood Group in Beijing) exploited a known vulnerability in the Internet Explorer browser to gain access to and modify source code at dozens of high tech, cybersecurity, and defense contractor companies.

THE OPM DATA BREACH

In 2016, this author received a letter notifying them that their data had been leaked—one of 21 million people fallen victim to a breach in the Office of Personnel Management. Hackers broke into the system using stolen contractor credentials, and gathered the government history of current and former personnel as well as information about friends, relatives, and other references listed for security clearances. This pool of data included everyone in the US who has held a security clearance, applied for a security clearance, or was listed as a reference for one, from 2000 onward—a virtual treasure trove of counterintelligence data that could enable the hackers to identify operatives.

WORRIED ABOUT HUAWEI?

Many governments have concerns about the Chinese telecom corporation Huawei. The company has long held ambitions to eclipse Apple and Samsung, while Chinese businesses and government are more tightly intertwined than in other nations. The Chinese government has a history of funded economic espionage operations targeting foreign companies for Chinese government benefit. Collecting this information could be made a whole lot easier if their targets used a native technology platform. Of course, Huawei denies that it has any relationship to the Chinese government, or that it has any backdoors, but based on China's history, it is a hard claim to believe.

— CHAPTER 14 —

THE FUTURE OF SPYING

Innovations have changed the espionage game. However, the objectives of spying and the motivations to spy have changed little. Humans are still humans. Technology is changing espionage in several ways, creating new opportunities while making other avenues obsolete. One example of a dramatic change from the past is the use of cover identities. Before the digital age, it was possible to maintain multiple cover identities in a way that is impossible today, with biometric technologies and jointly operated databases, such as those used at border controls. If you add in the need for a data footprint that includes financial information, it is nearly impossible to develop an effective long-term cover story.

Sometimes the challenges of the changed technological landscape have driven spymasters to return to tried-and-tested analog tradecraft, using dead drops and brush passes. As ever, espionage remains the art of misleading and blending in, although today, spies must blend in digitally as well. And spies still need a deep understanding of the drivers of human behavior, likely motivations, and how to manipulate people at the psychological level to get what they want.

COVER IDENTITIES

In the digital world, it's becoming harder and harder to provide spies with good cover. Spies can no longer move easily through multiple countries without being detected. Even small countries have access to biometric scanners and shared databases. Nation states can also potentially steal biometric data that will identify an undercover agent. This makes it harder to recruit informants, which results in a reduction in the HUMINT available for decision-making.

In the past, it was hard to find out somebody's real identity without a lot of research. Today, a wealth of information is on hand, with public camera data, facial recognition software, open source intelligence, and social media and financial data footprints, including GPS pings from a mobile phone. It is possible to find out exactly who a person is in one afternoon. (It can be even easier if you have access to government databases like those in China, which the government does not need permission to use.) But that doesn't mean you won't be suspected if you don't leave a digital trail—someone without a digital footprint can still raise flags by dint of its absence.

For some operations, fresh recruits are used because they have a digital footprint that isn't yet associated with intelligence work. However, these young agents—known as "cleanskins"—have at most one or two chances for a clean mission before their identity is burned. This doesn't leave much time for them to gain field experience. For some operations, an agency may use an operative's own identity, or "natural cover," hiding them in plain sight. In other operations, there is a policy of "one country, one alias" for operatives because it is now impossible to work under multiple covers in the same country, especially with the advent of facial recognition technology. Some operations use a new agent for a one-time mission, knowing that they can never work undercover again.

Spies commonly used to steal the identities of the dead, but in the future, it could be possible to hack into birth or death registries to create a fake identity that has never been alive (also known as a "shelf baby"). This cover identity becomes plausible when complemented by a basic LinkedIn and Facebook account.

NEW TECHNOLOGIES ADD COMPLICATIONS

Facial recognition is baked into our public world with smart cities, border crossings, and air travel technologies. Facial recognition technology developed in Israel has been broadly deployed in China, which makes it possible to investigate, track, and identify undercover agents and informants. Meanwhile, cell phones provide a comprehensive history of your physical location, in addition to being used for data collection and

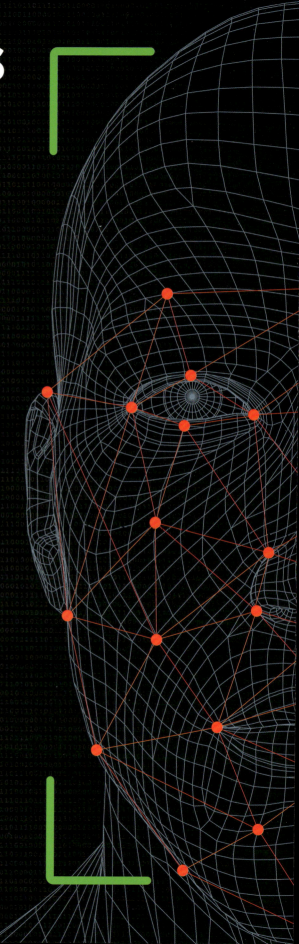

Left: In China, train stations are fitted with gates equipped with facial recognition machines. Passengers are identified by the machines and the fare is automatically deducted from their bank account.

communication. Information can also be compromised if malware is installed on the cell phone. When DNA databases are hacked, this enables the confirmation of someone's identity from a thread of hair or sip from a glass, making it even harder to keep a solid cover.

One way to get around this sophisticated biometric and facial recognition technology is to operate in countries that use less sophisticated systems—but that only works for so long, as the price point of these systems are decreasing and there are agreements between nations. For example, China has developed much of Africa through its "Belt and Road" initiative to create new trade routes connecting Asia, Africa, and Europe, part of which involves the provision of a modern technology infrastructure.

Left: Facial recognition software identifies individuals by measuring the distances between different features. New systems also include an analysis of skin texture.

OPEN SOURCE INTELLIGENCE

Open Source Intelligence is a term that describes the collection of information about a person that they put online themselves or that others put online for them. This could include innocent photos of a wedding you attended on social media, a college yearbook, or an app that encourages data-sharing, such as an exercise tracking app or beer review app that uploads images. These might seem like innocent things to share online, but a smart intelligence researcher can use this information, along with the accompanying metadata, to gain insights about the individual. What might seem like an innocent piece of information could be used against you.

SPIES AND DATA

Thanks to modern tracking technology on the internet and our digital devices, data is collected about us everywhere. Much of the data is collected through private sector companies like Google, Facebook, and other data brokers. And this information is used in situations well beyond advertising. In the case of Cambridge Analytica (see page 219), data was purchased along with public voter data to create detailed behavioral profiles, not unlike the kind of detailed files that case officers may have on a potential informant.

Devices such as computers and cell phones are able to associate our online activity with the device. Information is collected about which website you visit, what posts you read on Twitter and Facebook, what ads were displayed to you, and whether you interacted with them. Messaging internal to a site or application—such as in-game messaging or Facebook Messenger—can also be monitored.

MONITORING EMAILS

Gmail, which had a colossal 1.5 billion users by 2019, is the world's largest email provider. Following the maxim that "If you're not paying for it, then you're the commodity," Google has built its advertising model for Gmail around the concept of a free email address. You get free email, but they get to monitor your email content for keywords that can be used to show you relevant ads. It's even possible for sites to monitor the words you type into these platforms or applications that you end up deleting. There have recently been a number of hacks of customer relationship management (CRM) software that not only release personal information about an individual, but also the names of individuals associated with the person.

The bottom line is that many companies collect vast quantities of data about our online and offline activities. Data brokers do not have to follow rules of disclosure that government agencies must follow, and there are a wide range of potential customers for the information they have to sell. Nation states can potentially buy vast quantities of data from companies. A state could set up a front company to purchase this data, then use it or cross-reference it along with data they collected elsewhere to learn who they may want to target or who is vulnerable. If states can buy this kind of data so easily, is this even espionage?

JAMES BOND AS A DATA SCIENTIST

With all this data critical to the future of espionage, our image of a suave James Bond spy may need to change to that of a data scientist using sophisticated machine learning algorithms to pull insights from these pools of data. While there will always be a place for field operations, many agents can now spy without ever leaving their desk.

METADATA

A piece of data, such as an image, audio, video, or document, has metadata attached to it. This provides the context around the original piece of data. For example, an image file will contain metadata showing the date and time that the photo was taken, file size, author, location, camera, and keywords. Metadata is added to help search and categorize the file, but it can also provide useful information to intelligence. Just knowing the timestamp on tweets gives clues as to what part of the world you are likely to be in. You don't necessarily need to know the content of a conversation if you know the frequency, length, and engagement with someone—whether via email, on a social media site, or through your cell phone. Digital technology stores this information perfectly for years.

CREATING THE RIGHT DIGITAL TRAIL

When you combine authoritarian government technology with data acquired through legal and illegal means, you produce a situation in which it is dangerous to be an informant and difficult to conduct covert operations. It might seem like it's better to have no data footprint and try to clear out any information that has been collected about you. However, you need to look like a normal person who goes about their activities and interests and financial transactions. Even switching off your phone for a period so that it cannot track you may appear suspicious. Leaving an electronic information trail is the norm, so the absence of one is a red flag. This is a serious headache. Data from a very wide variety of sources needs to match the agent's cover story—even seemingly innocent information on a payroll must be consistent in case it is cross-checked.

Left: Nearly every digital device you use will leave an interconnected digital trail. Security organizations can use this data to build a profile and monitor your movements and actions in almost any part of the globe.

TRACKING AND HACKING

Our data lives in the cloud, in secure and less secure databases, on our computers, and on our cell phones. Some data is collected by the government, but much more is collected by private companies. Whoever stores our data is responsible for securing it, but information security is costly and sometimes complex, and not all companies do it well. This makes our data a target for hackers, whether they're bored teenagers, cybercriminals, or state-sanctioned hacking teams.

Many countries can now carry out cyberespionage, not just the usual suspects. There is a low barrier to entry and hacking can be appealing to countries with skilled security professionals but few professional jobs. Hacking is the future of espionage and it's not going away.

CELL PHONE TRACKING

Our cell phones are with us at all times and they hold an enormous amount of information about our lives—they are our digital twins. If someone can gain access to your phone, it is a treasure trove of information. And it's not as hard as you might think. Someone can gain remote access to a mobile phone using malware that can be sent in an SMS, or if you get physical access to the phone, you can install spyware, including a whole category marketed for people to install on the cell phones of their partners, children, or other targets.

A sneakier way to target a large number of people is to create an app to collect the information you want to collect but disguised as something else. Maybe it's an entertainment app, photo editing tool, or a communications add-on. When you download the app, it asks for permission to access a variety of data on your phone. This could include your contacts as well as your real-time geolocation and even SMS metadata (with whom you communicate and how often). Once an app has been accepted in the mobile application store, anyone can download it. While anyone can create an app, it must go through a review process before being posted—but this review process can miss the nefarious intentions if they are well hidden behind legitimate features.

CREATING BACKDOORS

Since cell phones carry so much information about us, there are privacy laws in place to protect us. In many countries, law enforcement agencies must follow the rules if they want access to your data. However, these laws and rules do not apply in authoritarian countries such as China, where you must agree to share your data with the government. There are concerns that "backdoors" in cell phones may allow governments to gather information secretly. There is also concern in security circles that China is developing a global surveillance tool in the form of a backdoor on their global technology products. In China, there is a much stronger connection between commercial companies and the government. This data can be combined with other data collected through open or illicit means.

TRACK AND TRACE

In 2020, "track and trace" apps aimed at controlling the spread of coronavirus raised privacy concerns. While they are designed with the noble goal to find and notify you if you have come into contact with someone who has tested positive, the geolocation data used to achieve this is stored centrally and could potentially be misused. There is also concern that when you rush to apply a controversial technology solution, it isn't fully thought through with a robust security mechanism, making it a hacking target for crime or espionage.

COVERT TECHNOLOGY

Covert activities become trickier with increased digital surveillance. It can be harder to hide data, but there may be more "hidden in plain sight" misdirection, such as using digital steganography to send trade secrets and using deep cover individuals. Authoritarian countries with tracking technology are becoming an increasingly hostile environment both domestically and in adversarial environments. Covert activities may shift to "black ops" with teams parachuting into a country instead of entering through traditional ways. There are also situations where technology plays a central role in covert actions, as with the NotPetya, WannaCry, and Stuxnet cyberattacks (see pages 222–223).

Below: Many countries have produced tracking apps to trace people who might have COVID-19. In South Korea, a cell phone app alerts people if they have been in close contact with a person who later tested positive for the virus. The app keeps a record of everywhere the phone has been to, and every phone it has been close to via Bluetooth. It has been widely adopted, as Koreans accept the loss of privacy in the name of public health.

INSPIRATION FROM COLD WAR TRADECRAFT

How can we combat this new digital world of espionage? Some look to the past for inspiration. There has been a return to Cold War tradecraft, using sleeper agents and dead drops in remote locations where there is no surveillance. In the case of the Russian Illegals, with eleven Russian sleeper agents, even some of their children didn't know their parents were spies (see page 229). These agents used dead drops, numbers stations, and other Cold War tradecraft techniques to conduct their activities. Even in a world of surveillance, a spy might have a hobby as an avid hiker. What would stop them from identifying a dead drop in a remote location? For busier areas, they may choose to return to the old-fashioned brush pass, in which one person hands information to another when they pass one another.

WE ARE ALL SPIES NOW

The websites we use for our everyday life, for work, to connect with friends socially, can be penetrated and used for recruiting. Malware can be sent to everyone's phone, and propaganda is hidden in media articles. Meanwhile, you can buy spy gadgets on Amazon, or download apps onto your mobile phone, and satellite imagery on Google makes it possible for anyone with access to a computer to do investigative research. Encrypted communication makes it possible to share secret information across the world, for instance through a Telegram Chat.

SPY TOOLS FOR EVERYDAY USE

Today we can access sophisticated technology that was previously reserved for spies. We can download apps on our mobile phone to enable secure communications and secret hiding folders. A phone has a photo and video camera, and can act as a listening device. We can cover our tracks with messaging tools that are encrypted or messages that auto-delete after a certain time (such as Wickr, Signal, or WhatsApp). Some apps enable end-to-end encryption to make sure no one can gain access to your messages. You need to be aware, though, that the technology provider may still be monitoring metadata or keywords. We can create any number of multiple identities on various platforms, whether an employment or social media site, and you rarely have to legally prove who you are. You can spoof your location using a Virtual Private Network (VPN) to disguise your internet traffic. And teens have discovered how to use a mobile phone as a remote listening device by leaving their phone in a room and tuning in with Bluetooth earbuds.

CITIZEN INVESTIGATORS

Open access to data can uncover a mystery. In the case of the Salisbury poisonings of MI5/KGB double agent Sergei Skripal and his daughter Yulia (see page 177), it was a mystery how they were poisoned. However, the UK had CCTV footage of the men they thought were the killers.

Left: Three images, one spy: on the right, the passport photo of Anatoliy Chepiga, in the middle the passport photo of Ruslan Boshirov, and on the left, the image of Boshirov released by the UK police.

They cross-checked this image data with border entry data to find the cover identity of the suspected agent: Ruslan Boshirov, a supposed sports nutritionist who was visiting Salisbury for a vacation. Investigators had a start with Boshirov's passport information, but they knew it was false. Still, they could start with the CCTV image and an approximate age.

Citizen intelligence investigators from the Insider—an associate of Bellingcat, an international collective of citizen researchers—used these images to start a hunt for the killers, who were suspected to be Russian. They compared the CCTV footage to images from online search engines, photos in military academy yearbooks, search terms, and leaked Russian residential/telephone databases. It was tough work but there was a payoff. From this information, researchers were able to conclusively identify Colonel Anatoliy Chepiga, an intelligence officer in the GRU.

An investigation of the suspects' financial trail identified a hotel in which they stayed, which was found to have traces of the poisoning agent that had been sprayed on Skripal's apartment door. After Chepiga was identified, they ran the image through other databases and discovered he had been in Bulgaria during the suspicious poisoning of a weapons manufacturer, which is now under investigation.

This case shows that it is possible to use open source information to identify someone, but it takes time and creativity to know where to look and what to look for. It's also an example of using a one-off operative. Chepiga's identity is burned, and it will be difficult for him to carry out another covert operation.

THE CIA AND THE PRIVATE SECTOR

In the Cold War era, many agents worked for the CIA for their entire careers. When they retired, their secrets retired with them. Today, agents leave the agency after a time and take their knowledge with them to their next career. Valerie Plame is a former CIA agent who had her cover blown by the Bush administration, making it impossible for her to continue working. So she wrote a memoir, took it to Hollywood, and ended up working on several spy projects.

Another typical path for ex-CIA agents is to set up their own private consulting business or to work with a private military contractor. There are videos of ex-CIA agents sharing their expertise in reading body language, using disguises, deception, and physical surveillance.

In some cases, the situation is reversed. Private-sector experts may join an operation in order to bring legitimacy to the cover. One example is the case of the Canadian Caper, made into the film *Argo*, in which CIA agent Tony Mendez recruited Hollywood professionals to create a fake production company (see page 187).

Above: Valerie Plame

GLOSSARY

Abwehr A military intelligence agency operating in Germany from 1920 to 1945. Germany was prohibited by the Treaty of Versailles from forming any intelligence offices, but the Abwehr was founded in defiance thereof.

Active Measures Term used by Soviet and Russian security services from the 1920s onward, for "political warfare"—propaganda, assassinations, support of insurgent groups abroad, and more.

AJAX-12 Also known as the F-21, a highly successful spy camera manufactured between 1952 and 1991 for use by KGB agents.

Al Qaeda Arabic for "The Base," an Afghani extremist militant/terror organization founded by Osama bin Laden and others during the Afghan-Soviet war in the 1980s, and responsible for the 9/11 attacks, among other incidents.

Aman Hebrew for "The intelligence section," denoting the Israeli military intelligence directorate, an independent branch of the IDF, founded in 1950. Aman is the largest part of the Israeli intelligence community, along with Mossad and Shin Bet.

Anarchism A political and philosophical movement that rejects hierarchy and pushes for abolition of the state, flourishing from the nineteenth century onward.

Assassin An individual who commits a murder of a specific target. The name derives from the medieval Persian *Hashashiyan*, a sect founded in the late eleventh century CE.

Black Chamber The United States' first peacetime cryptanalysis organization, founded in 1919 and succeeded by the NSA.

Black Dispatches Term used by Union military forces during the American Civil War, describing intelligence on Confederate forces provided by black Americans (often slaves who could operate beneath notice within certain places).

Black Hand Secret military organization founded in 1901 in the Army of the Kingdom of Serbia, and allegedly involved in the assassination of Archduke Franz Ferdinand in Serbia in 1914.

Bletchley Park A country manor and estate in Buckinghamshire, UK, built in 1883 and used as the home for the GC&CS.

Bolsheviks From the Russian *bolshinstvo*, "majority." A radical Marxist faction that took power in Russia in November 1917, ultimately becoming the only ruling party in Russia until the fall of the Soviet Union in 1990.

Brush Pass An espionage maneuver in which the two parties cross paths closely and one hands off material to the other while in close, but brief, contact.

Calibration Target A marker in paint or concrete viewable from high altitude and used as a means to calibrate an aircraft's spy cameras.

Case Officer Intelligence official who manages an espionage network, recruiting, and training agents, and liaising with them in the field.

Charlie Hebdo A French satirical magazine known for its anti-right-wing tone. It was attacked in 2011 and 2015 in an apparent response to anti-Islam cartoons featuring depictions of Muhammad.

Cheka The "All-Russian Extraordinary Commission." The first Soviet secret police organization, from 1917 to 1922, succeeded by the GPU.

Cipher A code used to disguise or reveal the contents of a message, or a mathematical algorithm for encryption or decryption.

Club, The Formerly "The Room," an organization founded in the 1930s by Vincent Astor and others, working for Franklin Delano Roosevelt, monitoring banking and shipping data and British intelligence, and thus potential Japanese and German military movement, prior to the outbreak of World War II.

Code *see* **Cipher**

Competitive Intelligence Legal research and gathering of information by one company to determine a competitor's developments and how they might perform in the marketplace.

CORONA A program in which the US used reconnaissance satellites to produce surveillance photographs of the USSR, China, and other regions between 1959 and 1972.

Cryptography The theory and study of ciphers used for secured communication between two parties. Or, the creation of protocols to keep the public, or other third parties, from reading private information.

Dazzle Also called "Razzle Dazzle" or "Dazzle Painting," a technique for camouflaging ships during WWI and WWII. The combination of colors and patterns prevented an enemy from determining the target's heading, range, and speed, rather than hiding the vessel.

Dead Drop A method of indirect information exchange in espionage, wherein the sender of the message or information places it in an innocuous location, and a recipient later retrieves it.

Deep Fake Also called "deepfake," a portmanteau of "deep learning" and "fake." A computer-generated false likeness of an individual used to replace that of another in audiovisual format, with a high potential for deception.

Deuxième Bureau The "Second Bureau," a French intelligence organization from 1871 to 1940, focused on gathering intel related to enemy troops.

Echo 8 A subminiature camera manufactured by Suzuki Optical Company in Japan from 1951 to 1956. The Echo 8 was disguised as a working cigarette lighter and loaded with 8-millimeter film.

Economic Espionage Theft of trade secrets that benefit a foreign power or rival business.

El Al Hebrew for "To the Skies." Israel's national airline. El Al is the only commercial airline that has equipped its planes with countermeasures against surface-to-air missiles. Its extensive security measures mean that it is considered one of the safest air travel companies.

False/Fictional Narrative The background for a cover identity, developed and detailed to give a spy a realistic personal background as part of their espionage operations.

Farm, The A covert CIA training location at Camp Peary, a United States military facility in Virginia.

Five Eyes An intelligence alliance composed of Australia, Canada, New Zealand, the United Kingdom, and the United States, founded after World War II to jointly monitor Soviet and Eastern Bloc communications. Though controversial, the Five Eyes have been sharing espionage information on each other's citizenry, including internet communication.

FOIA The Freedom of Information Act. A law mandating partial or total disclosure of information or documentation under United States government control. This law is intended for greater transparency with the United States public, and defines which records can be released, mandatory protocol for disclosures, and exemptions to the law.

Frequency Principle The study of the frequency (rate of occurrence) of letters, numbers, or groups thereof in a ciphered text. In classical cryptology, this is used to assist deciphering a message by comparing the frequency with the rate letters and numbers occur in unencrypted text in a given language.

GC&CS The British Government Code and Cipher School, which handled SIGINT duties for the UK government and military from 1919 to 1946, when it was renamed GCHQ.

Gestapo Nazi Germany's "secret state police," acronymic from *Geheime Statzpolizei*. It persecuted Jews, homosexuals, and liberals, among many other "undesirables" and dissidents from 1933 until the fall of the Third Reich in 1945.

Great Game Nickname for the rivalry of political and diplomatic powers between Russia and Britain that lasted for most of the nineteenth century, regarding Afghanistan and neighboring regions.

Great Purge A period of political repression in the Soviet Union, overseen by Stalin between 1936 and 1938, which led to the mass imprisonment and execution of minorities, wealthy peasants, government and party officials, and military leaders.

Guardian Office A department of the Church of Scientology focused on intelligence operations, including infiltrating government offices to access confidential files, and harassment of opponents of Scientology. Formed in 1966, succeeded in 1983 by the Office of Special Affairs.

GPU/OGPU The "State/Joint State Political Directorate," acronymic from *Obyedinyonnoye / Gosudarstvennoye politicheskoye upravlenie*. The Soviet Union's secret police organization that succeeded the Cheka from 1922. The GPU was succeeded by the OGPU from 1923 to 1934. It was succeeded by the NKVD.

Hacker Individual with specialized computer knowledge and experience, who engages in the practice of hacking—gaining unauthorized entry to a given computer system, either to test for security flaws ("White hat"), fulfill criminal or malicious intent ("Black hat"), or simply for amusement ("Gray hat").

Illegals Spies operating without official cover identities; sleeper agents.

Informer Someone who provides confidential information, often in the course of a law-enforcement investigation or espionage operation.

Insider Threat An employee or other person who has access to sensitive data or secure systems.

Intelligence Information gathered, often by espionage, to maintain state security. Intelligence is usually divided into two categories: domestic (information on potential threats within that state's territory), and foreign (information on military, diplomatic, and economic matters outside that state's boundaries).

Japanese Red Army A communist paramilitary group created in 1971, with the intent of overthrowing the Japanese government and monarchy and starting a worldwide revolution.

Jedburgh Teams Small groups of three to four Allied agents dropped into occupied Europe during World War II to work with local resistance fighters on sabotage operations, in particular to support Operation Overlord—the Allied invasion of Europe. The teams were operated jointly by the British and the Americans.

KBG The Soviet Union's Committee for State Security, acronymic from *Komitet Gosudarstvennoy Bezopasnosti*. The security agency and secret police force from 1954 to the end of the Soviet Union in 1991.

Kidon Hebrew for "tip of the spear." A department within Mossad supposedly responsible for the assassination of enemies of the Israeli state.

Kiev-30 A Soviet subminiature camera that used 16-millimeter film, had a focusing wheel, and could be further collapsed to three-quarters of its full size.

Legals Espionage agents operating with legal cover identities, for example as diplomats or journalists.

Lucy Ring A spy organization operating during World War II with headquarters in Switzerland. It was run by German refugee Rudolf Roessler and engaged in anti-Nazi operations.

Malware Software, usually covertly installed, that is intentionally designed to cause harm to a computer or computer network.

Maskirovka Russian for "disguise," a military doctrine with procedures including camouflage and disinformation. Building on ideas from Tsarist Russia, the doctrine was developed by the Soviet Union in the 1920s.

Minox camera A subminiature camera manufactured in Latvia from 1937 to 1943. The Minox was later manufactured in Germany. Popularized as a "spy camera" by intelligence agencies in the United States, Britain, Germany, and Romania because of its size and focusing abilities.

Misinformation False information utilized (as in the case of Maskirovka) to deceive a potential spy or other gatherer or user of that information.

Mobilization The act of gathering and preparing a nation's military forces and supplies in readiness for conflict. Prior to World War I, such actions were generally regarded as an act of war.

Mole A spy recruited for long-term covert operation within a rival organization to pass intelligence from that organization to the mole's supervisors.

Moscow Rules A set of general common-sense guidelines (such as "assume nothing" and "trust your instincts") developed during the Cold War and used by spies and others who worked in Moscow.

Mossad Hebrew for "The Institute"; Israel's national intelligence agency, part of the Israeli Intelligence Community along with Aman and Shin Bet.

MQ-9 Reaper Also called the Predator B, an unmanned combat aerial vehicle (UCAV), or drone, utilized by the United States Air Force and capable of remote-control or self-guided flight. The MQ-9 is a "hunter-killer," designed for long-term, high-altitude surveillance as well as combat operations.

NKVD The Soviet Union's "People's Commissariat for Internal Affairs," acronymic from *Naródnyy Komissariát Vnútrennikh Del*, responsible for monitoring police, prisons, and labor camps, which took part in the Great Purge. Renamed the Ministry of Internal Affairs in 1946, and later succeeded by the KGB and Federal Intelligence Service.

Novichok Russian for "novice," a series of nerve agents developed by Soviet and Russian scientists from 1971 to 1993. It was used in 2018 to poison Sergei Skripal, a former double agent for UK intelligence.

Null Cipher A simple steganography method, also called a "concealment cipher." It is a method of disguising a message by hiding it in plaintext among non-cipher text (such as reading only every third letter in a paragraph).

Numbers Stations Shortwave radio stations that broadcast spoken numbers (sometimes accompanied by music or phrases), believed to be coded messages directed to intelligence agents working in foreign countries.

Official Cover An officially recognized position within a diplomatic agency connected to a given government, under which an intelligence operative works and is thus given diplomatic immunity to protect them from penalties for espionage.

Operation Fortitude The codename for the military deception carried out by the Allies in the lead-up to D-Day in 1944. It fooled the Germans into believing that the Normandy landings would occur elsewhere. The deception involved creating dummy armies and utilized false intelligence.

Pandit Hindi for "scholar" or "teacher," indigenous Indian citizens employed by the British as surveyors and explorers of areas north of British-controlled India in the nineteenth century.

Pen Gun A small-caliber, one-shot firearm disguised as a writing implement. One such example is the Stinger, developed by the Office of Strategic Services (OSS), a precursor to the modern CIA.

Phishing The act of gaining access to passwords, account information, credit card numbers, or other sensitive data by pretending to be a trustworthy individual in electronic communication.

Pinkerton Detective Agency Private security and detective agency in the US founded in 1850 by Allan Pinkerton. His agents were hired as personal security for Abraham Lincoln in the Civil War, as well as engaging in private military contracting and, later in the nineteenth and twentieth centuries, union-busting activities.

Pocket Litter Random small pieces of paper, receipts, coinage, or other minor personal effects carried in a spy's pocket in order to lend credence to their cover identity (such as ID cards or ticket stubs).

Polyalphabetic Substitution A form of encryption that uses multiple substitutions, such as a message whose first letter is exchanged for another based on a key, the second letter based on the first letter's shift, the third based on the second, and so on.

Propaganda Selectively manipulated or outright false information, used to influence the audience and promote a given agenda.

Raven / Sparrow A Soviet spy in the Cold War era, trained specifically in sexual or romantic seduction in order to compromise a given target (often one under surveillance at the time). Male "sexpionage" agents were dubbed Ravens while female agents were called Sparrows.

Red Army Faction: Also known as the Baader-Meinhoff Gang, a radical-left militant group founded in West Germany in 1970 in response to the Vietnam War and perceived state and police brutality, responsible for dozens of deaths up until its believed dissolution in 1998.

Red Banner Institute Russia's Academy of Foreign Intelligence, an espionage academy which served the KGB and later Foreign Intelligence Service; Vladimir Putin was one of its attendees.

Red Orchestra The umbrella name given by the Gestapo to groups of loosely associated anti-Nazi resistance operatives across Germany and occupied Europe, who were assumed to be working for the Soviet Union. In reality, many of these groups operated independently of one another.

Red Terror A period of suppression toward political opponents of the Bolsheviks following the 1917 Russian Revolution, including mass killings conducted from 1918 to 1922.

Reflexive Control Sharing information with a given target in order to make them more inclined toward a course of action that the sharer wishes them to perform.

RQ-170 Sentinel An unmanned aerial vehicle (UAV) manufactured by Lockheed Martin, and utilized by the USAF and CIA as a stealth aircraft for airborne reconnaissance.

Romeo Spy A nickname for male East German male spies who were specially trained in the arts of seduction. They were sent to West Germany to form romantic liaisons with women, often lonely secretaries, who could then be turned into agents.

Room 40 The cryptanalysis department of the British Admiralty, operating during World War I and acting as the precursor to the GC&CS. Notable for intercepting and decoding the Zimmerman Telegram, a German diplomatic communique sent in 1917 to propose a military alliance with Mexico, which was used to draw the United States into the war.

Room, The *see* **The Club**

Shelf Baby A false identity created and developed online, starting with a fake birth and developed for several years in real time, for use as a throw-away identity for criminal or covert activity.

Shin Bet Hebrew, a two-letter abbreviation for "security service," also called Shabak, acronymic from *Sherut ha-Bitahon haKlali*, "general security service." The internal security service for Israel, and part of the Israeli intelligence community along with Aman and Mossad.

Sicarii Latin for "dagger-wielders," Judean dissidents in the first century BCE opposed to Roman occupation. They committed murder in order to strike fear into their occupiers. The sicarii are the earliest recorded terrorist organization.

Sleeper Agent Also called a "deep cover" agent, a spy sent to a target location or organization with a cover identity and left to wait until "activated" for a mission. A sleeper agent may still be considered an active participant in treasonous or seditious acts even if non-active, by agreeing to act in principle.

Special Operations Executive (SOE) An intelligence section set up by Britain in 1940, following the fall of France to the Nazis. Its mission during World War II was to link up with resistance fighters in occupied Europe and to carry out sabotage operations. The United States established a similar organization, the OSS.

Spycraft *see* **Tradecraft**

Sting Operation A police or intelligence operation undertaken to catch the subject in the act of committing a crime, often involving the use of undercover agents.

Tailing The act of covertly following a given target in espionage, undertaken singly or by teams of multiple agents.

Tochka 58 A subminiature camera built in 1958 in the Soviet Union and frequently used during the Cold War by the KGB and security and intelligence organizations across eastern Europe.

Trade Secrets Intellectual property critical to company operation, with no other intrinsic monetary value. Trade secrets are the main targets of industrial espionage operations.

ACRONYMS AT A GLANCE

BKA "Federal Criminal Police", from the German *Bundeskriminalamt*
BUF British Union of Fascists
CCTV Closed-Captioned TV
CEO Chief Executive Officer
Cheka The "All-Russian Extraordinary Commission," from VChK, the abbreviation of the Russian *Vserossíyskaya chrezvycháynaya komíssiya*
CIA Central Intelligence Agency
CIG Central Intelligence Group
Comintern Communist International
COVID-19 Coronavirus Disease 2019
CRM Customer Relationship Management (software)
DHS Department of Homeland Security
DNA Deoxyribonucleic Acid
DNC Democratic National Committee
DOJ Department of Justice
DoS Denial of Service

ECHELON Secret code name for a SIGINT group overseen by the US, and jointly run by the US, UK, Australia, Canada, and New Zealand
FANY First Aid Nursing Yeomanry
FBI Federal Bureau of Investigations
FIA International Automobile Federation
FISA Amendments Act Foreign Intelligence Surveillance Act
FRG Federal Republic of Germany, the old West Germany
FSB Federal Security Service
FSB Soviet security service
FUSAG First United States Army Group
GC&CS The UK's Government Code & Cipher School in WWI, now known as GCHQ
GCHQ Government Communications Head Quarters
GDR German Democratic Republic, the old East Germany

GOP Guardian of Peace (Sony Hack)
GRU Main Intelligence Directive
GULAG From the Russian Glavnoe Upravlenie LAGerei, for "Main Directorate of Camps"
HUMINT Human Intelligence
IBM International Business Machines
IP Intellectual Property
IRA Irish Republican Army
IRS Internal Revenue Service
IS/ISIS Islamic State / Islamic State of Iraq and Syria, also known as "Daesh"
KGB The "Committee for State Security," from the Russian *Komitet Gosudarstvennoy Bezopasnosti*
KH-11 Reconnaissance satellite type launched by the US National Reconnaissance Office in 1976
KL-47 A variant of the KL-7 encryption machine used by the NSA beginning in the 1960s
LDB La Dame Blanche
LiDAR Light Detection and Ranging
MI5 British Security Service

Tradecraft Also called spycraft, techniques and technology used in espionage and intelligence. Examples include dead drops, tailing, encryption techniques, and use of spy equipment such as miniature cameras or radios.

Trust, The A fake organization created by the Cheka. Supposedly an anti-Bolshevik organization that had infiltrated the highest levels of Soviet government and military and was working for the return of the monarchy, it was created to draw out tsarist sympathizers and anti-communists.

U-2 A single-engine high-altitude reconnaissance aircraft manufactured by Lockheed Skunk Works in the 1950s. Deployed in 1955, with one shot down over the USSR in 1960, and another over Cuba in 1962. Still used for reconnaissance in the modern era, although more often for scientific and communications research.

Undercover Agent An intelligence agent who has been given a false identity in order to infiltrate an organization or gain the trust of a given individual in order to acquire confidential information.

Underground Railroad A network of secret routes and safehouses established in the United States to help escaped slaves reach the free states or Canada. It operated from the late eighteenth century until the Civil War. It was given its name in 1831 by a Kentucky slave owner, referring to the escape of Tice Davies.

Unit 61398 A department of the Chinese military (People's Liberation Army) stationed in Pudong, Shanghai, and reputedly responsible for several acts of cyberwarfare and computer hacking attacks against the United States and other nations.

Venona Project A counterintelligence program undertaken by the United States Army from 1943, focused on decryption of Soviet communiques, responsible for the discovery of Soviet espionage of the Manhattan Project.

Zenit Russian for "Zenith," a series of reconnaissance satellites used by the USSR from 1961 to 1994. Publicly denoted as "Kosmos" radio satellites to conceal their true missions, the Zenit series took satellite photos for espionage and cartography, and intercepted NATO radar signals.

MI6 British Foreign Intelligence
MICE Agent Motivations: Money, Ideology, Compromise/Coercion, Ego/Extortion
MSS Chinese Ministry of State Security
NASA National Aeronautics and Space Administration
NATO North Atlantic Treaty Organization
NHS National Health Service
NKVD (then MVD and KGB) The "People's Commissariat for Internal Affairs," from the Russian *Naródnyy Komissariát Vnútrennikh Del*
NOC Non-official cover
NRO National Reconnaissance Organization
NSA National Security Agency
NSC National Security Council
OGPU Joint State Political Directorate (Soviet Union)
OPM Office of Personnel Management
OSS Office of Strategic Services
PLA People's Liberation Army

PLO Palestine Liberation Organization
PRC People's Republic of China
PRISM Protect America Act
RAF Red Army Faction, also called the Baader-Meinhof gang
RFC Royal Flying Corps
RDF Radio detection finding
SCADA Supervisory control and data acquisition
SD (SS intel service) The "Security Service," from the German *Sicherheitsdienst*.
SIGINT Signals Intelligence, the deciphering of intercepted communications.
SMS Short Message Service
SOE Special Operations Executive
Stasi/SS East German Security Services
SVR The "Intelligence Service of the Russian Federation," from the Russian *Sluzhba vneshney razvedki Rossiyskoy Federatsii*
TEDD Time in different environments over distance

UAV Unmanned Aerial Vehicle
UCAV Unmanned Combat Aerial Vehicle
UBS Multinational investment, banking, and financial services company in Switzerland, derived from Union Bank of Switzerland
USAF United States Air Force
USSR Union of Soviet Socialist Republics
WWI World War One
WWII World War Two

INDEX

ACKNOWLEDGMENTS

The publisher would like to thank the following for their kind permission to reproduce their photographs.

Key: c-center; b-bottom; l-left; r-right; t-top

Front cover:
Top row l-r:
ZAM881/Shutterstock.com, public domain (pd), pd, Library of Congress, Deutches Reigh/pd
Middle row l-r:
National Reconnaissance Office, Refat/Shutterstock.com, iunewind/Shutterstock.com, Lt. Col. Leslie Pratt/USAF, Giuseppe De Chiara 1968/Creative Commons
Bottom row l-r:
US Department of Defense, Boonchuay1970/Shutterstock.com, Berka7/Shutterstock.com, Spy Museum Berlin

Back cover:
l-r: FOX 52/Creative Commons, 168b Dnalor 01/Creative Commons, Shutterstock.com

Inside pages:
1 Shutterstock.com, 3t Spy Museum Berlin, 3b Alchemist-hp/Creative Commons, 5cl, 5r Shutterstock.com, 10¬–11, 26–27 The John R. Van Derlip Fund, 12bl Rogers Fund, 1924, 12–13 jorisvo/Shutterstock.com, 13t FrancisOD/Shutterstock.com, 14l TonyV3112/Shutterstock.com, 14t JingAiping/Shutterstock.com, 14br People's Republic of China Printing Office, 16 Shal09/Shutterstock.com, 20t Boyd Dwyer/Creative Commons, 20–21 SpicyTruffel/Shutterstock.com, 21t Kirill Skorobogatko/Shutterstock.com, 22–23 Kaytoo/Shutterstock.com, 23br Lippisches Landesmuseum Detmold, 24–25 Zenodot

Verlagsgesellschaft mbH, 27tl Salviati, 27br JeanLucIchard/Shutterstock.com, 28t Yale Center for British Art, Paul Mellon Collection, 28b Chronicle/Alamy Stock Photo, 29t IanDagnall Computing/Alamy Stock Photo, 29br Twin Design/Shutterstock.com, 30–31, 40–41 Paris Musées, 32–33 Geographicus Rare Antique Maps, 33b Rama, 34tr Matthew Corrigan/Shutterstock.com, 34cr Wellcome Trust, 34br david muscroft/Shutterstock.com, 35t Shutterstock.com, 35cl National Museum of Wales, 35cr Wikimedia Commons, 35b Robert B. Miller/Shutterstock.com, 38l Morphart Creation/Shutterstock.com, 38–39 Everett Collection/Shutterstock.com, 39tl, 39br Library of Congress, 41tl, 41tr Paris Musées/Musée Carnavalet, 42l Paris Musées/Musée Carnavalet, 44–45, 55cr Le Petit Journal, 46tr Morphart Creation/Shutterstock.com, 46b, 47cl Everett Collection/Shutterstock.com, 47br International Institute of Social History, 48l Andrew J. Russell/Library of Congress, 48–49 Shutterstock.com, 49c Gift of Cyrus W. Field, 1892/Metropolitan Museum of Art, 50–51 Benjamin F. Powelson, Auburn, NY, 50bl National Park Service, 50br, 51r Library of Congress, 52–53 Shutterstock.com, 54tl M. Lorusso, 54bl Ilya Repin, 54br 55t Shutterstock.com, 55b Walker T. Dart/Library of Congress, 56 Sergei Lvovich Levitsky, Rafail Sergeevich Levitsky, 57tr Aaron Gerschel, 57cl Henri Meyer, 57b Claus-Peter Enders, 58l Wehrgeschichtliches Ausbildungszentrum der Marineschule Mürwik, 58r Hulton-Deutsch/Hulton-Deutsch Collection/Corbis via Getty

Images, 58–59b Bain News Service/Library of Congress, 59 History and Art Collection/Alamy Stock Photo, 60tl Hermann Clemens Kosel, 61tr Cassoway Colorizations/Creative Commons, 60–61 Europeana/Creative Commons, 62–63, 64, 65tl Everett Collection/Shutterstock.com, 66tr Colin Simpson, 66–67b Naval History and Heritage Command, 68tr Brown & Dawson to National Geographic, 68–69 Benjamin Hirschfeld on behalf of Christoph Herrmann/Creative Commons, 69t Everett Collection/Shutterstock.com, 69br Royal Flying Corps, 70–71 Bill Perry/Shutterstock.com, 71tr Gertrude Bell Archive, 72bl Henri Manuel, 74br, 75 US National Archives and Records Administration, 76tr George Grantham Bain Collection/Library of Congress, 77tr Mo/Creative Commons, 77br Shutterstock.com, 78bl Library of Congress, 78br, 78tr Bain News Service/Library of Congress, 79b Interfoto/Alamy Stock Photo, 80–81, 88 Bettmann/Getty Images, 82l Deutches Reich, 83bl George Grantham Bain Collection (Library of Congress), 89–87 Rare Historical Photos, 87tr, 87cr George Grantham Bain Collection (Library of Congress), 89t NSA, 89b Daderot, 90b Vasilieva Tatiana/Shutterstock.com, 91l Baka Sobaka/Shutterstock.com, 91r Olga Popova/Shutterstock.com, 92tl Bundesarchiv, Bild 146-1979-013-43/CC-BY-SA 3.0, 93tl Bundesarchiv, Bild 146-1969-054-16/Hoffmann, Heinrich/CC-BY-SA, 94–95 Everett Collection/Shutterstock.com, 95 Family von Trott, 96–97 FotoErro/Shutterstock.com, 89–99 Gorodenkoff/Shutterstock.com, 99tl Quang Ho/Shutterstock.com,

100br Boonchuay1970/Shutterstock.com, 101tl. 101tc, 101tr Lyudmila2509/Shutterstock.com, 101c Evikka/Shutterstock.com, 101br ID1974/Shutterstock.com, 101br Africa Studio/Shutterstock.com, 102bl CIA, 103tr gallofoto/Shutterstock.com, 103b Phubes Juwattana/Shutterstock.com, 104bl Daderot, 104br Austin Mills/Creative Commons, 104–05t PJ_Photography/Shutterstock.com, 105bl FBI, 105br Slowking4/Creative Commons, 106br Matteo Galimberti/Shutterstock.com, 106–07 oatawa/Shutterstock.com, 108l US Army, 109tl Ewen Montagu Team, 109tr UK National Archives, 109c Royal Navy, 109br Benutzer:smashing/Creative Commons, 110tr Jordan Kalilich, 110br, 111c US National Archives & Records Administration, 111t Gerald R. Ford Presidential Library and Museum, 111br Etan J. Tal/Creative Commons, 112–13b, 113t Shutterstock.com, 113cl Galyamin Sergej/Shutterstock.com, 113cr Mariluna, 114cr McZusatz/Creative Commons, 114cl Alchemist-hp/Creative Commons, 114bl Anders Beer Wilse, 115t Kenneth Dyer/Alamy Stock Photo, 115br Shutterstock.com, 116l Natasja Weitsz/Getty Images, 116r Plisman/Shutterstock.com, 117cl Tasnim News Agency, 117br Lt. Col. Leslie Pratt/USAF, 118¬–19 Everett Collection/Shutterstock.com, 120tl Library of Congress, 120bl Gordon Parks/US Government/Library of Congress, 120br, 121bl Library of Congress, 121tr Eybl, Plakatmuseum Wien/Wikimedia Commons / CC BY-SA 4.0, 122tr U.S. National Archives and Records Administration, 122cr Askild Antonsen/Creative Commons, 122–23b Imperial

ABOUT THE AUTHORS

HEATHER VESCENT

Heather Vescent is an author and researcher. She owns and operates The Purple Tornado, a foresight and strategic intelligence consultancy. Vescent has delivered research insights to governments and corporations in digital identity, military learning, payments, transactions, and new economic models. She is the writer and producer of fourteen documentaries and short films about future technology. Her clients include the US and UK governments, SWIFT, Disney, IEEE, midsize companies, and startups. Her research has been covered in the *New York Times*, CNN, *American Banker*, CNBC, Fox, and *The Atlantic*. She published and co-authored *The Comprehensive Guide to Self Sovereign Identity* and is an author of the *The Cyber Attack Survival Manual*, published by Weldon Owen. Her work has won multiple awards from the Association of Professional Futurists.

Thank you to Rosie Pongracz and Anthony Stevens, Sarafina Rodrigeuz, Liz Watson and Peter Celli, Gloria Mattioni, Rusty Blazenhoff, Maria Anderson, Kelly Kucharski, Susanna Schick, PJ Manney, and Karen Marcelo for your friendship and inspiration. Thank you to my security colleagues: Bob Blakley, Kim Hamilton Duffy, Darrell O'Donnell, and Anil John. A long belated thank you to the Carlsons, who provided a safehouse when it was needed. Thank you to my Twitter feed, anonymous security sources, ex-CIA agents, and whistleblowers.

Many thanks to co-author Adrian Gilbert, to the staff at Weldon Owen and TallTree: Mariah Bear, Ian Cannon, Jon Richards, Rob Colson, and Jonathan Vipond. Apologies to anyone I have inadvertently left out.

Thank you to my two assistants: Archibald and Shoog, who provided relief when I went too far down the KGB and Mossad rabbit holes. Finally, thank you to the many global intelligence professionals, many of whose stories remain untold today, but will certainly become the inspiration for decades into the future.

ADRIAN GILBERT

Adrian Gilbert is an author who has written extensively on military and intelligence matters. Among his publications are *Waffen-SS: Hitler's Army at War*; the best-selling *Sniper: One-on-One*, and the *Imperial War Museum Book of the Desert War*, the latter volume part of a series that won the Duke of Westminster's Medal for Military Literature. In the intelligence field, he was the author of the four-volume QED *Spy Files* series.

ROB COLSON

Rob Colson is an author and editor with a particular interest in the history of ideas. He was a contributing author to the DK books *Battle* and *History*, and was the lead editor of several titles in DK's best-selling *Big Ideas* series. He has written more than seventy non-fiction books for adults and children on a diverse range of subjects, including natural history, technology, mathematics, and the history of science.